Home and Away

Home and Away

A Professor's Journal

James Duane Bolin

Acclaim Press
MORLEY, MISSOURI

Acclaim Press
— Your Next Great Book —
P.O. Box 238
Morley, MO 63767
(573) 472-9800
www.acclaimpress.com

Editor: Randy Baumgardner
Book Design: Devon Burroughs
Cover Design: M. Frene Melton
Cover Photo: © Robyn Pizzo 2016 (Robyn Pizzo Photography), with help from David Pizzo. Contact: rpizzo@murraystate.edu

ISBN-13: 978-1-938905-81-0
ISBN-10:1-938905-81-4
Library of Congress Control Number: 2014917965

First Printing 2016
Printed in the United States of America
10 9 8 7 6 5 4 3 2 1

This publication was produced using available information.
The publisher regrets it cannot assume responsibility for errors or omissions.

Contents

Foreword 6

Prologue 8

PART ONE: Family 14

PART TWO: Home 34

PART THREE: Away 54

PART FOUR: Teaching 74

PART FIVE: Learning 96

PART SIX: History 116

PART SEVEN: Reading 136

PART EIGHT: Writing 158

PART NINE: Calling 178

PART TEN: Life 200

Epilogue 222

Selected Reading List 224

Acknowledgments 229

About the Author 233

Index 234

Foreword

Alone in his one-room, no-frills writing studio, seated at a small desk and surrounded by books, James Duane Bolin allows his mind to wander...

...back to Dixon, Kentucky, and the warmth, safety and unfettered love that were always found in his mother's kitchen.

...on the road to New Haven, Connecticut, fully aware yet knowingly unprepared for the tectonic shift that was coming.

...into his Murray State University classroom where the excitement of a new semester is tinged with the heavy responsibility of molding young minds.

...to the Bodleian Library's Duke Humphreys room for a hand-to-hand encounter with biblical history.

...inside Poor Richard's Bookshop to inhale the intoxicating aroma of slight literary decay.

...to summers past and his daughter's dawning childhood memories of the sweet scent of summer honeysuckle.

...on the ancient grounds of Holy Trinity Church, Headington Quarry, Oxford, England, and the gravesite of C. S. Lewis.

...across the Pacific to Mindanao Island, Philippines, and inside a sweltering, perspiration-stained gymnasium where the international language of basketball is about to be spoken.

...standing in a trout-laden, spring-fed Trigg County, Ky., stream, fly rod in hand, tying to sync his love for the idea of fly fishing with the challenging reality of Norman Maclean's "art that is performed on a four-count rhythm between ten and two o'clock."

Duane Bolin is a Renaissance Man: a Scholar. Historian. Teacher. Writer. Mentor. Traveler. Christian. All wrapped in a cloak of modesty. He is also my friend. But first and foremost, Duane is a husband and father, and his family—wife Evelyn, son Wesley, and daughter Cammie Jo—form the soul of *Home and Away: A Professor's Journal.* Readers will learn that the Bolins' lives, hopes, dreams, and disappointments are not so much different from their own. The author shares this message by weaving the tapestry of his life and that of his family in a way that reflects every family's life—the one that's real, the one that's imagined, and the one that's hoped for. There is much here.

Essays are one of my favorite literary forms, and in this collection Bolin takes the everyday, the ordinary, the mundane—the thread with which every life is tied—and extracts the nuggets and jewels that add life's sheen and sparkle. They are snippets from a life well led. But he can and does sift life's seismic moments—a birth, a death, a son's departure for college—and distills them into the hilltop pauses for reflection and look-to-the-future moments they should be instead of the stumbling blocks they all too often become.

These essays began life as newspaper columns in a small town publication, where the rigid reportage rules of Journalism 101 are a bit loosened. Most of the pieces have been dressed up a bit for inclusion in this collection, but they remain as they began: comfortable and comforting. At its best, newspaper work is based on trust between the two main participants, the writer and reader. Bolin writes honestly about simple things with a voice as comforting as a summer breeze. Readers can ask for no more.

Gary Garth
Murray, Kentucky

Prologue

Oak Grove Cemetery, Dixon, Kentucky.

A Cemetery Run

Driving back home to Kentucky to visit our children's grandparents (our parents) proved to be a precious but exhausting experience for our family of four: father, mother, son, and daughter. Arriving on a Friday in time for supper, our family would be seated for a royal Kentucky feast: ham, turkey and dressing, creamed potatoes and sweet potato casserole, green beans, lima beans, fresh hot rolls, and pies of several flavors—fare you would associate with a small town, county seat, western Kentucky holiday family gathering.

After the feast, gorged and drowsy, we would visit into the night, reluctant to cut the talk short with mere sleep. Our children would finally drift off, but the older children (Evelyn and me) droned on a little longer before reluctantly retiring for the night.

Several years later, the ritual was repeated, not often enough, but as often as possible, considering the circumstances. The grandfather (my father) was already gone, the victim of a heart attack. Only the memory of his goodness remained.

Our family appeared again on a particular Friday, but it was not the same. On Saturday morning, I went through my usual ritual, arising before Evelyn and the children, my mother (the grandmother) already up, of course, busy with coffee, sausage, and gravy. I got up early to go out on a morning run.

I walked down the steep driveway and broke into a jog at the street, turning right at the next drive, which led to the city lake. I circled the lake before climbing the slanting road to the water tower. At the tower I turned left down the familiar lane that led to the cemetery where my father was now buried.

The cemetery was, to be sure, the perfect picture of a cemetery. Nestled in the hills, it reminded one of an English graveyard. A black wrought-iron fence lined the front entrances of the place, and I had always taken the second entrance. I would follow the lane through the cemetery, moving along in a counter-clockwise direction past my father's grave.

I always circled the cemetery twice before retracing my steps back home. But this morning on a whim I decided to turn into the cemetery's first entrance and wind around the graveyard in a clockwise direction. I passed my father's grave as always, but from the opposite direction.

This run was a revolutionary experience for me. I saw for the first time the flowering bush, now with dead, ruined branches, behind the grave.

But I also saw other graves with gravestones etched with the familiar names of neighbors and family friends, names that I had simply never noticed before. The run changed me, and I have not been the same since.

Many of the gravestone names I saw for the first time: neighbors, friends, members of my father's church, customers of my father's county-seat drugstore. The drugstore stood directly across the street from the 1938 WPA-built courthouse, an art deco monstrosity that served as the landmark of the town.

Now, survivors of the Great Depression whittled and traded knives on benches, conveniently positioned on the corners of the square. I remembered the mark that my father had made on the town, his church congregation, his customers at the store, and even on the grizzled whittlers who meandered across the street to the drugstore to buy medicine of a sort—cigars and Milky Way candy bars.

I have come to the conclusion that my meandering cemetery run was revolutionary because I had approached the cemetery from a different direction, from a different angle, a different point of view. The path had been the same, but the perspective had changed. And that, rather than the completely different path of the poet Robert Frost, had made all the difference.

This book, *Home and Away: A Professor's Journal,* will give this teacher, this professor of history, a chance to tell some of my favorite stories, stories that center on some of my favorite topics and themes: family, Kentucky, travels, teaching, learning, history, reading, writing, calling (or vocation), and life. I hope to approach these topics and themes from different directions, from different angles, from different points of view. Will you join me at "home and away" by reading these essays?

For Evelyn, Wesley, and Cammie Jo
and for
Dr. W. J. Pitman

Home and Away

A Professor's Journal

Part One

Family

"Keeping the link intact between our ancestors and ourselves."

Top Left: James Wesley, Cammie, Duane, and Stephen Bolin, c. 1960. Top Right: Evelyn Seaton and Duane Bolin, wedding day, Dec. 18, 1982. Center: Cammie Mann Bolin, c. 1942. Bottom Left: Wesley Seaton Bolin and Cammie Jo Bolin, first day of school, 2000. Bottom Right: Jossie and Marlin Seaton. Lexi Fortner, Cammie Jo and Wesley Bolin, Jessica Baxter.

Family Things

I'm sure that some families have valuable heirlooms passed down from generation to generation, jewelry perhaps, or maybe even land. There is nothing more pleasing, I would think, than to have acres of land, maybe land grants from the War of 1812 in south-central Kentucky, or in our area, land dating back near the time of Andrew Jackson's and Isaac Shelby's purchase from the Chickasaw Indians in 1818, land passed down through the generations, land that would give a family a lasting and unique sense of place.

In our family there is little land to speak of—the old Bolin family homeplace in Hickman County is in the hands of a distant cousin living in Oklahoma—so we must be content with only a few things that we hold especially dear, things we will one day pass on to our son and daughter, in hopes that they will cherish them too, and then in the way of things, pass them on to yet another generation.

We have, for example, Evelyn's grandmother's—Mama Pet's—Singer sewing machine in a wooden and iron case, refinished by Evelyn's father. We have some of Evelyn's mother's quilts, quilts she stitched lovingly for each of her four daughters. We have an old rope bed, the bed on which my grandfather was born, bought at auction years ago. We have from my parents a kitchen table and cabinet that at one time graced their bustling kitchen, the scene of many Sunday dinners and holiday gatherings. I remember the pregame meals my mother would fix for me there: a small steak, a baked potato, and always hot tea with honey, a concoction designed to simultaneously provide for me energy and calm nerves before high school basketball games. I would sit at that very table in mid-afternoon as my mother fussed over me, pouring more tea, spooning out more honey. When the game began, however, Mom read her Sunday school lesson in the stands, as my father cheered or agonized over every play on the court.

Evelyn has a wonderful collection of deep purple Depression glass from her mother, stored safely now in my mother's kitchen cabinet, a comingling of our families of a sort that we have tried to emulate. We have a gorgeous, if frayed, rug from my parents' sunken living room, now in our front parlor. And as I sit here writing these words, I also notice a chair and two old pharmacy scales—one with a marble top, the other glass—from my father's drugstore. At one time, I guess, my father meticulously measured out powders and medicines on those scales as weary customers—coal miners or farmers or school teachers—rested on that very chair, positioned conveniently close by the prescription counter.

In my study, I have on display antique medicine jars and mortars and pestles that once lined the counter behind the drugstore cash register. Next to my father's drugstore treasures I have an old doubletree and a beautiful antique wooden pulley, given to us by Evelyn's father. He was always giving us things, and we cherish them all. He weaved together simple, but elegant, cane-bottomed chairs—one hangs upside down Shaker style in the study—and he refinished the sturdy, but beautiful, wood-grained desk, a desk originally from my father's drugstore and first refinished by my mother, yet another example of a shared family heritage.

Evelyn's father also gave us a five-volume set of Kerr's *History of Kentucky*, published in 1922 in dark blue leather binding. These collections of books are our most numerous and perhaps our most cherished heirlooms. My father's library has been passed down intact to his bookish son, while my outdoorsy older brother got the hunting rifles and a shotgun, along with an impressive knife collection.

My father's books are all here, whole sets of Bible commentaries, along with books of poetry and inspiration. I use them still, and whenever I pull a volume from a shelf, I try to remember how others, our folks, read them in another time and place. These "heirlooms of home" are our family's most prized possessions, a physical link with our childhood homes, a connection to our past.

A Connecting Link

What, after all, is the use of history? While my students might not ask me this question outright, I know many of them wonder. I sometimes wonder myself. Why do I spend my days teaching history to students? Does it all really matter in the end? Is it important for us to make connections with the past?

The writer John Egerton grew up in Trigg County in western Kentucky, but he chose a couple from the other end of the state as the subjects for his book, *Generations: An American Family*. Egerton's book made a huge impression on me when I first read in 1983. In 2003, the publisher brought out a new twentieth anniversary edition (University

Press of Kentucky.) Now I can read it from a fresh paperback edition instead of my old tattered inked-up copy.

Rusting paper clips marking key passages have marred the dog-eared pages of the old edition. Whenever I open it, loose pages fall from the book's spine. Still, I return to the book again and again, quoting memorized passages to my students, semester after semester. The central premise of the book helps me understand more about what I do for a living and why I do it.

Egerton wanted to write the story of a typical American family, but he also wanted to use that family's experience to "encompass the broader history of the American experience." Egerton chose to center his story on Burnam and Addie Ledford from Harlan County in eastern Kentucky and then Garrard County in central Kentucky. The author talked with the two—Burnam in his early 100s and Addie in her late 90s—in scores of interviews.

After the book was published, Burnam died at 106 and Addie at 102. In one of Egerton's conversations with the old man, Burnam uttered a remarkable statement. I want to quote it to you, and I want you to let the import of his statement sink in. Burnam said, "I went to see my great-grandmother on Cranks Creek in Harlan County in 1881, when I was five years old." And then he said simply, "She was born in 1791, when George Washington was president."

Think of it! Burnam Ledford had talked with someone who had witnessed every generation of American history since George Washington! Neither I nor anyone reading this essay can ever do what Burnam Ledford did. Those days are over, now buried only in an individual's memory or a nation's collective past.

Still, Egerton knew, and we all know, even if we hesitate to admit it, that the past, if used wisely, can help us in the present. The author said it this way in 1983: "There remains a remnant of elderly Americans who have seen and heard every generation of citizens in the history of this nation. They are the last connecting link between our ancestors and ourselves. When their time is gone," and that time is now surely gone, "there will be none who remember the nineteenth century."

F. King Alexander told of meeting Margaret Thatcher during his graduate work at Oxford. The prime minister asked Dr. Alexander's friend what she was reading (or studying) at Oxford. When the friend answered, "I'm reading history." Ms. Thatcher responded, "Oh, what a luxury."

But studying history is not a luxury. It is an absolute necessity. Don't you think there is a crying need to "keep the link intact between our ancestors and ourselves," in order to know where we've come from and in order to know ourselves? Reading and thinking about our history—the history of our families, our state, our nation, and our world—allow us to do what Burnam Ledford did, face to face with his great-grandmother. Keeping the link intact between our ancestors and ourselves. A worthy goal, I think, and a goal that I hope we can pursue in the writing and reading of these essays in *Home and Away: A Professor's Journal.* At "home and away" it is surely important "to keep the link intact between our ancestors and ourselves."

My Father's Hands

This Father's Day I am remembering my father, a pharmacist and a minister, a kind, quiet, humble man who grew up in Henry County, Tennessee, and who, after a five-year sojourn in Fort Worth, Texas, an exploratory trip to Oregon, and a short stay back in his native state of Tennessee, settled down in Webster County, Kentucky to raise a family, to run a family owned drugstore, and to pastor small churches in Dixon and in a neighboring county. A World War II veteran, serving on a troop transport ship in the Pacific, my father died on June 6, 1994, the fiftieth anniversary of D-Day.

My father was a father, to be sure, but he was also a minister, a businessman, a friend, a son, a twin brother, and a husband. He had compassion for other people, and I can still recall his subtle way of calming a child who had scratched a knee in a bicycle accident, or who had been injured in a deeper, more devastating way. "There now," he would say softly. "There now; it will be all right." My favorite poem is Alfred Noyes's "Distant Voices," a poem that encourages the reader to "remember the house of thy father." So today, in this essay, I want to do just that.

When I try to bring back my father in my mind's eye, to see him as he was, I remember the slight tilt of his head as he turned in his armchair, leaning back while watching television, to see if I had gotten the comedian's joke or if I had noticed the ballplayer's move. He just glanced back quickly, almost imperceptibly, to see if I had seen. Just a slight turn. But that was enough.

But more often than that, when I recall my father, I remember his hands. There is a faded photograph that I can no longer find of me standing by my father, holding his strong left hand. We are on vacation in Cherokee, North Carolina, and a Cherokee Indian, in full, feathered regalia is holding my brother in his arms. It is a hot summer day and my father is wearing a short-sleeved white shirt and tie. On vacation and he in a tie! I am only three or four, and, too scared to stand next to the Cherokee chief, I am leaning instead shyly by my father's side, reaching up with both hands to grasp his one left hand. But that was enough.

Or I remember my father's hands as he worked on a sermon outline on the front-porch glider. He sat there with his Bible beside him and maybe a commentary or two. He wrote left-handed in a distinct left-handed way that I can't describe except to say that he wrote in a slanting cursive script, with style. He always preached from an outline. Just a sermon outline. But that was enough.

Or I remember him behind the prescription counter, counting out pills or mixing a liquid medicinal concoction. His richly veined left hand maneuvering the bladed pill counter ever so slightly to count out the proper number, just the right amount, just enough. Or tilting the clear bottle at just the right angle to pour with his right hand just the right mixture, before shaking the bottle vigorously, for a few seconds, just enough.

My father pecked out the prescription label on an old manual Royal typewriter, using only two fingers. That was all he needed to get the job done. Just two index fingers. But it was enough.

After filling the prescription, my father would amble around the counter to the antique cash register where he would ring up the order. Just two turns on the brass crank, but with a flourish. Just two strong turns. But just enough.

My father's hands were hands of character, sculpted much more beautifully than the old painting's "praying hands," I think, and just as reverent, and just as purposeful. I will always remember my father's hands. And for now, for now, that is not quite enough.

My Mother's Hands

I remember my mother, Cammie Mann Bolin, every day, but especially as Mother's Day approaches my memories intensify. My mother, born in 1921 at the beginning of the Roaring Twenties, grew to adulthood in the years of the Great Depression, raised with my father two boys during the Cold War, lost and mourned a husband who died on the fiftieth anniversary of D-Day, and then lived out her days, first alone in the house where she had lived with my father, and then at Murray's Glendale Place, two blocks from our home, before spending time at a nursing home and in the hospital before dying at the age of 85 on August 19, 2006.

My mother worked as a schoolteacher in Atlanta, Georgia, Martin, Tennessee, and Fulton and Dixon, Kentucky. She also worked as an assistant pharmacist at Bolin's Drugstore, as a homemaker, and then as a substitute teacher after my brother and I had grown up to honorable manhood (we hope), and married and had families of our own.

My mother worried constantly—a trait that I inherited—but through her worries she ministered consistently to those around her. Her sweet smile could make your day. She sent cards penned in her elegant hand, remembered others in her daily prayers, which more accurately would be described as her hourly prayers, for she followed the biblical injunction to pray without ceasing, and she made sourdough bread, which she always gave away.

Back in Webster County, Mama Bo's meals were legendary, especially Sunday dinners, which she began to prepare the previous night and early the next morning before Sunday school and church, and then completed after church, somehow before everyone else had changed into more comfortable clothes.

I remember those meals and remember the hands that made them. I remember my mother's smile, but I also remember her hands. Her hands were beautiful to me, not in the usual sense of long, slender fingers, but, ironically, in the fact that her right hand was severely crippled. Most folks thought that my mother suffered from debilitating arthritis, the way the fingers on her right hand were shaped, but she actually experienced a gruesome injury that went a long way in forging her determined character.

As a 14-year-old girl, helping her father in his meat shop in the middle of the Depression, my mother inadvertently caught her hand in a meat grinder. The doctors in that rural 1930s outpost did what they could do, and she went through several operations, but in the meantime, not to get behind in her schoolwork, she immediately learned to write with her left hand. And then, after her right hand had healed as much as it would heal, she relearned to write with her now crippled right hand. She graduated from Martin High School as the valedictorian of her class.

The relearning process took such patience and fortitude that is hard to imagine, but the result was that one of my mother's distinguishing characteristics was her beautiful, flowing penmanship, a characteristic always commented on by those who received her thoughtful letters, notes, and cards. And those notes received by my brother's family and by mine on every imaginable occasion—birthdays, anniversaries, and other special occasions—in her rounded cursive handwriting, with the letters made just so, continue to bless us as we find them in desk drawers and in file cabinets today.

I remember my mother's smile, but I also remember my mother's beautiful hands, hands that nurtured me and loved me right up to the night that she died as I stood by her side holding her hand, her right hand, in mine.

Marlin Seaton's Smile

For this Father's Day, I want to write about Evelyn's father—the father of four daughters: Rebecca, Evelyn, Marilyn, and June—and the husband of Evelyn's mother, Jossie, or Mama Jo. Mr. Seaton was one of nine brothers, the only one of that farming family from Heath with a college degree. He graduated from the University of Kentucky in 1950—having been in Lexington with Adolph Rupp and the Fabulous Five—then served in the military in Panama before coming back home to Kentucky.

I don't suppose I could have had a better father-in-law. Mr. Seaton put up with me with exactly the right amount of patience, forbearance, incredulity, and toleration. Anyone who had the good fortune to know Marlin Seaton knew that he was one of a kind. He could be…exasperating. He could be…baffling. He could be…ornery. Mama Jo would have agreed to all of those descriptions. "Now Marlin," she said more than a million times, shaking her head.

Yet, he could be so thoughtful and kind. We have the cane-bottomed chairs that he meticulously, painstakingly worked by hand; he refinished the antique desk in our study, the round table in our family room. Not a room in our house is without an example of his handiwork. He gave me, a Kentucky history teacher, a five-volume edition of Judge Charles Kerr's *History of Kentucky*, bound in blue leather and published in 1922. The set, although beautiful to look at, is not just to sit on a shelf, but rather to use, and Mr. Seaton would ask me from time to time if I had "gotten any use out of those Kerr books." Indeed I have. I have used them again and again, and I will never forget his thoughtfulness in giving them to me.

Mr. Seaton asked me questions that I could never answer. The fact that many of his questions were biblically based certainly did not help, for he knew the Scriptures from cover to cover. Marlin Seaton never mimicked answers he heard from preachers. Rather, he took seriously that original Baptist theological contribution of the priesthood of the believer; he puzzled things out. I took some degree of solace when I learned that he often asked these sorts of questions in his Sunday school class, but for me there was never any backup. Mr. Seaton would ask the question. I would look at him like a deer caught in a car's headlights and mumble, "I just don't know." Mr. Seaton would look away. Dead silence. I would be no help at all.

Mr. Seaton's jokes were legendary. He told them more than once, but like fine wine, I always thought they got better with age. He never changed a detail. You always knew the punch line. But it was always funny.

And woe unto the boyfriend or son-in-law of one of his daughters who darkened Mr. Seaton's door sporting longish hair, a beard, or even so much as a mustache. "My, my, what in the world," he would say. "What happened to your razor? I've got one in there you can borrow." He pulled out his wallet and said, "Here's some money for a haircut." If living today, Mr. Seaton would hold no truck with the Duck Dynasty clan, because as a student of Scripture he took seriously I Corinthians 11:14. Any long-haired boyfriend or son-in-law learned that soon enough and with each visit to Calvert City heard the admonition reiterated. In the end, it was just not worth it: the razors came out, a trip to the barbershop ensued, and the next visit seemed to go more smoothly.

What I remember more than anything about Marlin Seaton, however, was his love. He loved Jossie Seaton, his four daughters, his grandchildren and great-grandchildren, all unconditionally. You could see it in his smile. I could walk in the front door of his Evergreen Street house and he would turn to greet me with a smile that could light up any room. I always thought his face brightened up just like Roy Rogers, even for a lowly son-in-law. "Well, Hello Duane!" he would say.

With that smile, repeated each time I saw him, I knew he accepted me into the family, and that was enough. I knew he knew that I loved his daughter. He knew that Evelyn and all of his daughters loved him. And I hope he knew that I loved him too…even if I could never answer his questions.

Mama Jo's Laughter

It is a tribute to Jossie Seaton that one can hear her laughter in the laughter of all four of her wonderful daughters. Rebecca, Evelyn (my wife), Marilyn, and June each inherited and learned much more from their mother, but to hear them laugh brings Mama Jo immediately to mind.

Jossie Seaton was one of those strong, unforgettable Kentucky women who made an indelible mark on this world through the people she cared for and the causes she championed. She was never idle; I never remember her without something in her hands, some work to be done, or a book to be read.

More often than not, one could find her at the end of her kitchen, stationed at her sewing machine, bolts of fabric all around, a bit of thread between her teeth, looking up at you as you came in the door, smiling at you inquiringly as if to say, "What can I do for you?" Except when Mama Jo thought it or said it, she really meant it. "What can I do for you?" really meant, "In what way can I help you?" "How can I make life easier for you?"

For it was Jossie Seaton's calling in life to serve others. Whether she worked at the Calvert City Library, or made her one-of-a-kind purses and diaper bags she sold at craft shows for years, or fished and camped with her husband Marlin, or attended her daughters' or grandchildren's and great-grandchildren's band shows, concerts, or ball games, or faithfully attended Sunday school and church—her ulterior motive was always to support and serve. For Mama Jo, faith and family came first. No one questioned that reality.

Jossie Seaton also loved the University of Kentucky Wildcats, although she rarely saw the entirety of a game. During crucial points in every televised contest she, out of nerves and necessity, would have to get up from the couch and pace into the kitchen and busy herself with we never knew what. When the game was safely in hand again, she resumed her place in the living room, at peace with the world.

At Christmastime, Mama Jo was at her best and in her element. No one has experienced Christmas until having done so at the Seaton household on Evergreen Street in Calvert City, Kentucky. There sat Marlin Seaton in a corner shaking his head, but taking it all in. Mama Jo was in the middle of it all. After all, she had prepared for months, wrapping presents and planning for each member of the family.

Jossie Wallace Seaton died on April 2, 2003. Later that year, Evelyn and her sisters found presents that Mama Jo had already put up for Christmas. For me, I hear it still every Christmas, every Easter, every family reunion, every time the family gets together. And I hope I always will. Ringing out over all the commotion, over all the comfort and joy of celebration, the laughter of Jossie Seaton. For me, it was, and for my family it will always remain, the sound of joy and hope and courage and life itself.

My Brother Steve

My brother Steve is perhaps the smartest individual I have ever known. Steve's smarts are not necessarily contained in the category of "book knowledge," although he can master the contents of any book he chooses to read. Of course, his politics are different from mine and he does not root for the proper college basketball team. But my brother's intelligence rises above politics and sports and even the dry pages of any book.

I don't think there is anything Steve cannot do. When we were children growing up in Fort Worth, Texas, our parents wanted us to learn music, so we took violin lessons and played in the Fort Worth children's orchestra. We moved away from the city, and the violin lessons stopped abruptly, but even then it was obvious that it was the elder son who had been blessed with the musical talent.

Sure enough, although I love a variety of music, and indeed, have tried unsuccessfully through the years to learn to play a variety of instruments—violin, piano, trumpet, guitar, cello—Steve is the one who learned to play the guitar, both acoustic and electric bass. Steve was good enough to play in a band. He never took lessons, I don't think; he taught himself.

Such expertise holds true in all areas of life, for Steve can do everything that I am unable to do. He can fix literally anything around a house, rebuild a car engine, fill a prescription, kill and dress a deer, construct a deck, and, as an EMT, deliver a baby or save someone's life.

To me, my brother is a modern day Thomas Jefferson. There is nothing he cannot do, if he really wanted to do it.

James Parton, Thomas Jefferson's biographer, wrote that the sage of Monticello could "calculate an eclipse, survey an estate, tie an artery, plan an edifice, try a cause, break a horse, dance a minuet, and play the violin." Parton's description referred to a young Jefferson, before he ever wrote the Declaration of Independence, became secretary of state or president, or founded the University of Virginia.

Of course, John F. Kennedy gave Jefferson his greatest compliment when JFK hosted a roomful of Nobel Prize winners at the White House in 1962. "I want to tell you how welcome you are to the White House," Kennedy said. "I think this is the most extraordinary collection of talent, of human knowledge, that has ever been gathered together at the White House, with the possible exception of when Thomas Jefferson dined alone."

This is the way I think of my brother, although I have never told him how I feel. Steve and Sharon found each other, and their strong love for each other, for their son Chris and his family, and their grandchildren has brought them great joy. Their faith and their family come first in their lives. So Steve needs to know how much his quiet example has meant to me through all these years.

In his acceptance speech for Best Actor in the 2014 Academy Awards, Matthew McConaughey said that his hero was himself. When he was fifteen, he decided his hero would be himself in ten years. Ten years later, he set it forward another decade. Each decade he does the same. My own heroes have always been other family members.

When our father lay on his deathbed, when he could still hear and understand, I got real close to his face, and I looked into his beautiful, crystalline blue eyes and told him that I loved him, and I told him that he was my hero. I wish I had told him this more often when he was in his strength, not just during his last few days following open heart surgery.

Without hesitation I also claim my brother Steve as my hero. His love for me and for my family is unconditional, as is my love for Steve and his family. I admire my brother's many gifts, and I am grateful for how he has used them in service to others, especially when it meant dropping everything and, without asking any questions, driving down to Tuscaloosa, Alabama, to pick up a dimwitted brother from the Bear

Bryant Inn and hauling said dimwitted brother, along with a broken down MG Midget, back to Webster County with only a few—only a very few—well-chosen words all the way home.

Back to School

Having a son and a daughter, five years apart in age, one seventeen, the other almost twelve, is quite a blessing. Having children in school and especially having them return to school, the first day of school, on a hot, humid August day or on a cold January morning after an all-too-short Christmas break, is a hard, hard thing. Oh, I've heard all of those stories about parents rejoicing that their children are back in school, out from under the noses of privacy-seeking parents. I can't abide such nonsense. I know it's hard for the children, but believe me, it's hard for the father and mother as well.

It's so hard, not wanting summer to end, or not wanting the holidays to end, dreading the routine, the early morning falling out of bed, already exhausted before the day has even begun, a hurried shower, out the door with a piece of toast or a muffin or a half a banana, the columns of math problems, the endless writing assignments, the Spanish translations, the reading of numbing textbook chapters, the geography and science for the sixth-grade daughter, the precalculus and physics for the eleventh-grade son, after-school band practice in the fall semester, after-school academic team practice—practice, practice, practice—hurried lunches, cramming down chicken nuggets or pizza squares or tater tots in a crammed cafeteria lunchroom or in a classroom trying at the same time to cram in bits of Latin (*amo, amas, amats* in between the bites of fries or tots), after school and after whatever practice is on for that day, a hurried supper (hurry, hurry, hurry) before yet another practice, or homework, social life reduced to frantic instant messaging with friends, hurried entries in a Web journal defining a life by tapping it out in nervous paragraphs for all the world to see, then reading, and then prayers before bed (Lord, bless my family and friends and help me get through the day at school tomorrow), and then rolling up into a cocoon of covers for a few hours of fretted sleep, awakened all too soon by a concerned and sympathetic mother, knowing that the roller coaster routine is to begin again, school day after school day in a long school year that in Kentucky will touch on all four seasons, beginning in the middle of summer, continuing through the glorious, unnoticed fall, the dying days of winter, and finally the rebirth of spring when the school routine becomes ever more frantic, but at least with signs of hope for a merciful end, and at last the promise of a new beginning.

Having children is a wonderful thing. Having children in school and especially having them return to school on a hot August day or a cold January morning is a hard, hard thing. Oh, I know it's hard for the children, but believe me, it's hard for the father and mother as well.

School Days

Our children went back to school last week in that annual rite of childhood and teenager-hood, Wesley for his senior year in high school and Cammie Jo, now in the seventh grade. Five years apart, they have never been in the same school together, although they have enjoyed some of the same teachers. For them, school days have combined the exciting and the mundane, hard academic work and socializing, successes and challenges. Their school days have been, as well, a constant process of maturation.

These first days of a new school year involve those things that are new: an adjustment to new hours, represented at least in earlier morning wake-up calls, if not always in earlier bedtimes; new patterns of living and being; and encounters with new subjects and new teachers and new friends. These early days of school also mean a reintroduction to the old: old friends to be sure, but also old worries and concerns—and old parents.

I've heard it said that children keep parents young, but that's not the way I feel. With each new school year, I feel the gap widening between youth and the aged, between matters that occupy the minds and hearts of the young and parental concerns. I feel more and more like an old fogey, a creature belonging to the past, an anachronism.

I try to think back to my own first days of a new school year. I remember wearing new clothes and carrying new school supplies, not in a backpack, but in a book satchel. One year I carried a Roy Rogers lunchbox, in anticipation of the lunchroom shenanigans that always seemed to take place during those few minutes between bites of peanut-butter sandwiches and gulps of milk. I carried new, freshly sharpened Ticonderoga pencils, in anticipation of the themes we would write and notes we might pass. And just as I wore into the classroom new blue jeans with the too-long legs folded up in anticipation of how tall I was sure to grow, each new school year we still anticipate how much we will grow. We anticipate with good intentions all that is before us, all that is before our children and ourselves.

So, here's to the hope that the anticipation of all that will be great and good can override any fear and anxiety. I speak for parents as well as students. I speak for the school administrators, the principals and the counselors. I speak for the teachers, those folks who are in the business of transforming lives. The great southern writer Walker Percy paid tribute to a great teacher in his life when he wrote that the teacher says *"Look!"* and the grateful student says, *"Yes, I see!"* Here's to the hope for a vision of what our students, our children, will see and for what they will become.

So, last week we took part in a family ritual. After a hurried breakfast, we gathered at our front-door stoop to unfurl a colorful back-to-school flag. The banner shows Snoopy from Peanuts fame marching with confidence to his own school. With a baseball cap on backwards, our Snoopy wears sunglasses and totes a yellow backpack. We took our pictures of Cammie Jo and Wesley with the confident Snoopy, and then took off for the high school and middle school in anticipation of all that yet another school year will bring.

Taxi Service

Now we know the secret to parenting. Evelyn and I want the best for our children—we want to be good parents—and now, after more than seventeen years of blessed parenthood, we have learned the secret. Parents must run a safe and efficient taxi service. In a brief while, the demand for the Bolin Taxi Service will lessen somewhat when our son acquires a permanent driver's license. To his chagrin, we have resisted and obstructed and even delayed the process. He will get his license in good time, but we have not minded an extended period when he only held a learner's permit. Soon, soon the time will be upon us when the actual license will be procured. All in good time for us; none too soon for him.

Even after Wesley is out from under our constant scrutiny, when he can take off on a drive of his own, and even after he owns a car of his own—he is holding out for an MG Midget, an exciting if not altogether practical choice—we will continue to run our taxi service for our daughter, still a few years away from the age of driver's accountability.

For years now we have driven our children to and from a dizzying array of activities. The destinations have included, at one stage or another, band practice, saxophone quartet practice, school activities of every sort, church choir and youth activities, friends' houses for parties, restaurants for get-togethers, soccer practice, basketball practice, and shopping trips. Of course, our two children have different interests, and being five years apart in age, their activities range over decidedly different times and venues. Never the same place at the same time.

Please know that Evelyn and I aren't complaining about our very active taxi service, our recent discovery of this secret of parenting. Instead, we dread the days in the not too distant future when our children will be on their own, and not dependent on Mom and Dad for transportation at all. We rue the day. We much prefer our present hectic pace.

During those soon-to-be lonely days, Evelyn and I will be driving along, no one else in the car, no one in the back seat, just the two of us, thinking about those too-many-to-count morning trips to school, beginning in kindergarten and on into the middle school and high school years. As we approached the school, backpack and perhaps a musical instrument case flung in the back seat, we try to anticipate the day ahead, for ourselves and for our children, perhaps remembering a class assignment or planning for the weekend already. We sing our family morning song that we have sung on the way to school for years, we promise to pray for each other throughout the day, we give a customary peck of a kiss goodbye, and then we watch our son or daughter gather up a ridiculous, backbreaking load of indispensable things, push the car door open and closed, nod or wave one more time, and then turn to walk away into the building for yet another school day filled with experiences of growing and learning and becoming.

We watch our children disappear, swallowed up into the school. We drive slowly away, thinking of the hard days to come when our morning ritual will be very different indeed, less hectic perhaps, certainly less frantic, but too quiet and too uneventful as well. In those days to come, we will miss unashamedly these present days when the Bolin Taxi Service is in high gear.

Becoming Real

It is a humbling experience to stand before a class full of students, some of whom are eager to learn and some of whom not so eager.

There is something very inspirational about an earnest search for truth. Students don't want to play charades; they don't want to just go through the motions. They want to learn, most of them, and they want to experience reality in the classroom. An honest search for "the real thing" is what we are after. We, teachers and students alike, are tired of masquerading. We strive for the real, the genuine, not a cheap imitation.

As a teacher, it is a constant struggle for me to shrug off the mask with which I attempt to cover my inadequacies, to reveal my true self to students, colleagues, and even members of my family. Why should this be such a struggle? Why is it a struggle to be Real? Margery Williams centers on the process of becoming Real in *The Velveteen Rabbit,* one of my family's favorite children's stories. As is true of the very best children's stories (C. S. Lewis's *The Chronicles of Narnia* and Kenneth Graham's *The Wind in the Willows* and E. B. White's *Charlotte's Web* come immediately to mind) the mother or father who faithfully reads the stories to the daughter or son is rewarded as richly as the child. In our family, Evelyn has been the real teacher, the one who has been so richly rewarded in that way.

In *The Velveteen Rabbit,* a conversation between the Skin Horse and the Rabbit is really about the moral and theological problem of becoming the person that we are meant to be in the company of those that we love the most:

> The Skin Horse had lived longer in the nursery than any of the others. He was so old that his brown coat was bald in patches and showed the seams underneath, and most of the hairs in his tail had been pulled out to string bead necklaces. He was wise, for he had seen a long succession of mechanical toys arrive to boast and swagger, and by-and-by break their mainstrings and pass away, and he knew that they were only toys, and would never turn into anything else. For nursery magic is very strange and wonderful, and only those playthings that are old and wise and experienced like the Skin Horse understand all about it.
>
> "What is REAL?" asked the Rabbit one day, when they were lying side by side near the nursery fender, before Nana came to tidy the room. "Does it mean having things that buzz inside you and a stick-out handle?"

> "Real isn't how you are made," said the Skin Horse. "It's a thing that happens to you. When a child loves you for a long, long time, not just to play with, but REALLY loves you, then you become Real."
>
> Does it hurt?" asked the Rabbit.
>
> "Sometimes," said the Skin Horse, for he was always truthful. "When you are Real you don't mind being hurt."
>
> "Does it happen all at once, like being wound up," he asked, "or bit by bit?"
>
> "It doesn't happen all at once," said the Skin Horse. "You become. It takes a long time. That's why it doesn't often happen to people who break easily, or have sharp edges, or who have to be carefully kep'. Generally, by the time you are Real, most of your hair has been loved off, and your eyes drop out and you get loose in the joints and very shabby. But these things don't matter at all, because once you are Real you can't be ugly, except to people who don't understand."
>
> '[And] once you are Real you can't become unreal again. It lasts for always."

Surely, at least with the ones that love you and are loved by you, being Real is worth the wear and tear and hurt of the effort. Surely, the same can be said for the teacher-student relationship. What a liberating concept…to drop the protective mask and teach and live and behave genuinely. Becoming Real. Perhaps such a concept wouldn't work for actors or politicians, but what about teachers? And what, after all, are families for?

Anniversary

One week before Christmas in 2007, Evelyn and I celebrated our twenty-fifth wedding anniversary. Our silver anniversary. No picture in the newspaper. No elaborate party. Just a quiet lunch at Dumplin's and a lot of memories.

Mutual friends introduced us to each other in 1979. Then, we were reintroduced by other mutual friends a year or so later. We had an ice cream date in April, 1982, a whirlwind eight-month courtship, and then a Christmas wedding on December 18. We were married in Evelyn's home church, Calvert City's First Baptist Church, by her former pastor, Dr. Jerome Brown, and my father. A simple ceremony, appropriate for two lifelong Kentuckians who love Kentucky, especially the western end of the state.

Evelyn graduated with two degrees from Murray State, while I abandoned the commonwealth for five years to attend college in Tennessee and Texas. Our return to Murray in 1996 was a homecoming for Evelyn, back to a university that she loves and just down the road from her home.

After we married, Evelyn continued to teach fourth grade at Broadway Elementary School in Providence in Webster County. I was a teaching assistant at the University of Kentucky, where I took classes and worked toward a doctoral degree. I arranged for all of my discussion sections to be on Tuesday, Wednesday, and Thursday, so that I would spend those three days in the middle of the week in Lexington, a four-hour drive away.

We lived in a tiny cottage, with one downstairs room, a combination kitchen, dining room, and living room, and up the stairs a bedroom and bath. I would leave before daylight on Tuesday mornings, arriving in Lexington just in time to lead my first discussion section of American History, spend Tuesday night and Wednesday night in an efficiency Cooperstown apartment, and then drive back late Thursday evening, back to Providence for a late supper and a long weekend, before leaving again early the next Tuesday. Such was our routine that first semester of marriage.

After that semester, things calmed down a little as Evelyn continued to teach in Providence, and I taught and coached in high school and middle school, first in Providence and then in Dixon, still working evenings and weekends to complete a dissertation. We have lived in six houses, five different houses in Kentucky and one in Arkansas. We had two children, Wesley in 1988, born at Methodist Hospital in Henderson, Kentucky, and Cammie Jo in 1994 at St. Bernard's Hospital in Jonesboro, Arkansas. We have a wonderful life together, now for thirty-two years and counting.

My favorite photograph, other than photographs of my family and close friends, is included in John Egerton's book, *Generations,* about the Kentucky family of Burnam and Addie Ledford. The photograph shows Addie in her late 90s standing slightly behind a seated Burnam in his early 100s. Both are smiling, still vibrant and engaged, still obviously in love.

I love the photograph because it was taken on December 18, 1982, our own wedding day. The fact that Addie and Burnam Ledford were celebrating their 79th wedding anniversary on that day only adds poignancy to the photograph. 79 years! Addie died at 102, only a few years after that photograph was taken. Burnam lived to 106.

I do not believe that Evelyn and I will live to celebrate our 79th wedding anniversary (after all, I really don't think we will live to 106). But for now, thirty-two years and counting, for now, we can quote those lines from Browning's "Rabbi Ben Ezra":

Grow old along with me!
The best is yet to be,
The last of life, for which the first was made
Our times are in his hand
Who saith, "A whole I planned,
Youth shows but half; see all, nor be afraid!"

Part Two

Home

"Returning home by another way."

Top Left: Home in Murray, Kentucky. Top Right: Duane with Cammie Jo and Wesley petting a horse. Center Left: Bolin family front yard featuring snow-covered Leyland Cypress trees, c. 2012. Center right: Looking in the writing cabin from the porch. Bottom Left: Calloway County Courthouse, Murray, Kentucky. Bottom Right: Brick sidewalk featuring liriope, boxwood, and hosta plants.

Leaving Home

We had prepared for this day. We thought we had prepared for this day. We were not prepared for this day. During Labor Day weekend in 2007 we took our son Wesley to New Haven, Connecticut, to move him in for his freshman year at Yale. Wesley was thinking about majoring in history, and I think he thought it would be awkward for him to study at Murray State in the same department in which his father taught. When he was accepted at Yale, he decided he could not pass up the opportunity, so we were off to New Haven.

We borrowed Evelyn's father's new van, and we loaded it down, every spare space crammed with Wesley's clothes and books, a carpet, a computer, a television, linens, and whatever else is required to outfit a college dorm room these days. Evelyn's father reminded us that he took nothing but a duffel bag to college, but apparently times have changed. We loaded down the van and started on our two-day northern trek. We thought we were prepared, but we were not prepared.

I arranged for a trusted graduate student to take my Thursday classes, to give a quiz and lecture on the colonial period in American history. We took Cammie Jo out of school for three days, so her teachers prepared homework for her to complete on the trip. I took the dog to the vet for boarding, and Evelyn supplied the cats with enough food for the days we would be gone. We stopped delivery of the newspaper and the mail until we returned. We prepared in this way for the trip, but we were not really prepared.

Relying on Mapquest for directions, we headed toward Lexington, then Ashland, and then through West Virginia and a section of the panhandle of Maryland. We spent the night in Hagerstown, and then continued the next morning through Pennsylvania, New Jersey, and New York. We sort of made a horseshoe around New York City, and then finally hit I-95 into Connecticut. The traffic slowed to a crawl, but we finally made it to New Haven in the afternoon around four.

Unable to move in until the next day, we walked the campus, found Ezra Stiles College (Wesley's residential college), visited the Yale Bookstore, and then had supper (I don't guess they call it supper in the Northeast, but we had supper) at The Educated Burgher. We were able to move Wesley into Lawrence Hall on the Old Campus the next day, and it took some time to get everything situated in his room and in the common room that he shares with three suitemates. We thought we were prepared, bringing everything that we needed to bring, but we weren't really prepared.

The next day we went to an elaborate freshman assembly at Woolsey Hall, and then to a reception at the president's house on Hillhouse Avenue, a street that lived up to its billing as "the most beautiful street in America." Wesley had other meetings in the evening, so Cammie Jo, Evelyn, and I went back to the hotel to recuperate and to prepare for our leave-taking the next day. We still were not prepared.

The next morning, a Sunday, we attended church together at a church nearby the campus, went to the café at Atticus Books for a forlorn lunch, walked back past Skull and Bones to Wesley's room one last time to make sure everything was in order, and then went out to College Street to say our goodbyes. It was obvious that we were not prepared to say goodbye. Wesley had to walk away, not to be late for another meeting, but not prepared to leave just yet, we walked along College Street with him to the Hewitt Quad, croaked out another goodbye, and then watched him walk away yet again.

We had anticipated this day of leave-taking for weeks and months and even years; we had prepared for this day, but when the time came to leave, to drive away, to travel back to Murray, we were not prepared.

I remember the time, a few days after he was born in 1988, that we drove Wesley from Methodist Hospital in Henderson, Kentucky, home to Providence. We stopped on the way at my father's drugstore in Dixon to show him off to grandparents and friends. Now, instead of bringing him back home with us, we left Wesley at Yale to prepare for his first day of classes. As for us, we took the southern route home, down I-81 through the Shenandoah Valley in Virginia, across Tennessee to Nashville, and then northwest from Nashville to Murray. We returned to an empty house, still not prepared ourselves. We prayed that Wesley would flourish in the days ahead.

Birds of Kentucky

My father taught me early on to love birds. He loved to sit on a front-porch glider and listen for the sweet melodies and various chirps and warbles and squawks of cardinals, mourning doves, and mockingbirds. Evelyn's father maintained backyard feeders that attracted a wide range of Kentucky birds. The only birds he did not condone were common starlings, creatures that competed with the more polite and less aggressive species.

We have followed the example of our fathers by keeping bird feeders of our own, one in the backyard and one in a fenced-in area on the southwest side of our house. Last summer we attempted to grow vegetables along with beds of hostas and impatiens in our side garden in close proximity to the hanging bird feeder. Not a happy choice of location. The birds enjoyed the vegetables as much as the seed we poured into the feeder. They seem to enjoy the fruits of our labor. For me, it has been enough to watch cardinals and mockingbirds and blue jays vie for a place at the feeder/garden table. Like my father-in-law and his pesky starlings, I have come to resent the blue jays, those bullies. Despite their striking beauty, blue jays make it miserable for everyone else.

I must admit that my relationship with birds has had a fluttering history. Back in Dixon, Kentucky, where I grew up, we lived next door to the old Dixon school, the rooftop of which was a favorite roosting place for pigeons. I took my BB gun to the far side of the school for target practice, but when I made a rare hit, the small pellets bounced harmlessly off the breasts of the tough old birds. They looked down at me with mocking eyes. "Is that the best you've got?" they seemed to say.

One spring morning I took my BB gun and went on a more serious hunting expedition in the patch of woods behind our house. In midsemester of my Kentucky History class, taught at that time in the seventh grade, I was immersed in the life and legend of Daniel Boone, and I imagined myself a modern-day longhunter. Back in the woods, I sat down on the ground, my back to a tree, Boone-like, I thought. I located a gray bird perched on a tree branch, and although I could not identify the bird at the time, I now know it to have been a mourning dove. I took aim with my rifle and pulled the trigger.

The helpless bird fluttered to the ground, and when I went to make an inspection, I found the bird huddled on the ground, a single BB sized hole at its temple, if a bird has a temple. Still alive, the mourning dove sat there blinking at me. Overcome with remorse, I fashioned a bed of leaves, tried to make the dying bird comfortable, and, not knowing what else to do, walked back to the house.

When I trekked back to the woods later in the afternoon, all that remained were a few fluffs of gray-white down. The weakened bird had undoubtedly been unable to make its escape from a prowling cat. Filled with regret, I vowed that I would never again kill a helpless creature.

That event, along with my father's example, somehow transformed me into a lover of birds. And whenever I hear that distinctive, haunting, early morning wooing of a mourning dove, or whenever I spy a pair of mourning doves in the low branches of our backyard pines, I remember again one thoughtless act of youth, and I renew a grown-up, now middle-aged commitment to admire and respect and cherish Kentucky's most excellent creatures of flight and song.

Moving Bricks and Liriope

It has become a rite of March for Evelyn to dig out the grass clippers and borrow the neighbor's hedge trimmers to take on the laborious task of trimming the monkey grass. We have always called it monkey grass, but I think the proper name is lilyturf, or even more accurately, *Liriope muscari*. Sometimes, I use the more formal term, *Liriope*, because I love the way the word rolls off the tongue. *Li-ri-o-pe*. A beautiful word. Much more poetic than monkey grass. We have two varieties of *Liriope*, both a solid, dark green version, and a variegated brand, which we have planted in contrasting rows to line the ivied beds in front of our house.

I used to mow the rows of *Liriope* in the late winter—this was necessary to allow for the new growth—but now the clumps have gotten so large that a mower simply does not do the job. Now we must do the work by hand. It is tedious work, and I once completed the task, but for the past fifteen years Evelyn has volunteered for the job and I have not complained.

Our common monkey grass has a long and rich history. We first acquired it in Arkansas to help with the landscaping of our faculty house at the small college where we lived and worked from 1992 to 1996. We took a wheelbarrow and dug up the clumps from the president's house. This was not some daring prank, but rather the president had given us permission. He believed, erroneously it turned out, that the *Liriope* attracted mosquitoes, the Arkansas state bird, and when we found out that he planned to have the ground crew clear it out, we asked rather humbly if we could make use of the stuff.

The president cocked his head, looked curiously at his new faculty member, smiled knowingly in an odd sort of way, and then said, "Sure." So, one Saturday morning we went to the president's house, dug up his

Liriope, divided the clumps, and replanted it at our humble abode. We lined the beds to good effect in our front and back yards.

We had spent so much time and effort that when we decided to move back to Kentucky, we dug it all up again, loaded it in the back of Evelyn's father's pickup truck, and moved it, along with other plants, to Murray. Our neighbors, there in Arkansas and here in Kentucky, thought we were crazy, and rightly so, but we were not about to leave behind perfectly good *Liriope*. The good folks who moved into our faculty cottage in Arkansas promptly killed off a Gingko tree that we had planted. No telling what they would have done to the *Liriope*.

So we moved the *Liriope* to Kentucky, along with a truckload of old bricks we used for landscaping. The bricks we had moved from Webster County in Kentucky to Arkansas. There, we laid them down meticulously in a sort of houndstooth-check patterned walk. When we moved back home, we dug the bricks up again and copied the pattern at our first house in Murray. Then we dug up the bricks yet again, and yes, the *Liriope* too, when we moved several years ago to our present home. The bricks, like us, had been moved from Kentucky to Arkansas and back again.

Believe me, moving bricks and *Liriope* (common monkey grass) is backbreaking work, and trimming the slender, browning, wasted leaves of the *Liriope* is sure to produce sore, blistered hands, the first set of garden blisters in the new year. Just ask Evelyn. There is something very fulfilling, though, about seeing the results of hard work, even if the work involved moving bricks and *Liriope*.

Trimming the Ivy

Some jobs give more satisfaction than others. My mother insists that work is only fulfilling when you can see the results of your labor. Surely, we've all undertaken some laborious task, the results of which are not immediately evident—teaching, for example, or working at the university at my desk or in a committee meeting. How many times have I walked through the back door of our house, after a long day at the office, having been there from 7:30 a.m. until 5:00 p.m., working at who knows what, hunkered down at my desk, working solidly, intently? Coming into the kitchen, Evelyn asks me how the day has gone.

"Fine," I say. And then I realize that I have worked steadily throughout the day, and now, at the end of the day, I can't, for the life of me, remember one thing that I have accomplished. I can't remember one thing that I did, period. Did I counsel students? Did I answer e-mail? Did I conduct meaningful research? Did I even teach a class? I simply can't remember.

Trimming the ivy is not like that at all. So, every few months, I'll take my handy clippers, a ladder, and a black plastic garbage bag. I'll put on any old T-shirt and khaki shorts, along with my favorite gardener's hat, a tan pith helmet, and walk determinedly out the front door. Beginning at the front-door stoop on the front walk, I clip the encroaching English ivy vines in a straightedge line away from the walk. I make the turn by the planters with the begonias, and carefully, systematically, clip along the bed, being sure to expose the old bricks that we have placed as a border in front of the *Liriope*. I follow the gentle curve of the brick border, stopping at the picket fence at the side of the house.

Please don't write me off at this point, but we have allowed ivy to climb the brick walls of our house too, aware that some folks swear it will damage the brick and mortar. I was taken with the ivy-covered walls on a trip to Oxford, England, and I do, after all, work at Murray, Kentucky's Public Ivy University.

At first, we did not know if the ivy would take, but we've found from experience the old saying to be true: "The first year it sleeps, the second year it creeps, and the third year it leaps." Anyway, from time to time it is necessary to trim the ivy down from the top row of bricks just below the roofline, so that it doesn't engulf the house altogether. I have nightmares of neglected ivy covering the house, roof and all, kudzu-like, something that might happen when I get too old and infirm to perform the ritual of trimming the ivy.

With the trimming completed, I climb down from the ladder, gather up the strands of clipped ivy, return the ladder along with the clippers to the garage, wash off my face and hands, grab a large glass of ice water, and repair to a bench in our front yard to admire the job of work that is now completed. I lean back contentedly on the weathered wood bench, observe the manicured line of ivy on brick, sigh a satisfied sigh, and close my eyes, imagining English ivy in its original habitat, climbing some ancient stone wall of a venerable Oxford college or parish church.

Back in the real world, I open my eyes, glance back at the house to admire my handiwork, and then notice that the gutters have little trees growing in them. I shake my head, consoling myself with the fact that tomorrow I will have another job to do, the completion of which, unlike some other types of work, will bring an immediate reward.

Planting Trees

One of the more fulfilling and worthwhile December traditions for us has been the simple act of planting trees. We have planted trees at various locations where we have lived and with varying degrees of success. In Walnut Ridge, Arkansas, we planted a gingko tree in honor of my father. Dad had a mature ginkgo in his front yard in Dixon, Kentucky. That tree was especially beautiful in the fall, when for a brief time the fan-shaped leaves turned a brilliant yellow before carpeting the ground beneath. Our Arkansas gingko did not make it; when we moved back to Kentucky we learned that the tree failed to survive the neglect of subsequent tenants of our faculty house in Walnut Ridge.

At our first address in Murray, we planted a dogwood, a magnolia, a sugar maple, a red maple, and three hemlocks. The red maple didn't make it—I think it's hard to kill off a maple, but we did—and only one of the hemlocks survived. The dogwood, though, provided and continues to provide gorgeous white blossoms in spring. The magnolia has elegant, large, fragrant, white petals in the summer. The sugar maple displays brilliant yellow and orange leaves in the cooler days of fall. And the hemlock provides green branches throughout the winter, drooping branches laden with snow when the welcome winter storms come along. (At least the snowstorms are welcomed by schoolchildren anxiously lying in bed on frosty mornings to see if school would be called off for the day.)

At our present home, we tried to plant Arbor Day pine saplings along a back fencerow, but they didn't make it. Later, we planted four larger nursery-bought white pines and these now line up with three more mature pines, forty feet tall. At the front corners of our house we planted two foster holly trees. The dictionary defines the holly as "a small evergreen tree or shrub with glossy sharp-pointed leaves and bright-red berries." I prefer to call our hollies, even though they remain small, trees rather than shrubs, and they have indeed sported bright-red berries through the winter.

Only a few years ago we learned that December is a wonderful month for tree planting. Dr. Steve White, a retired biologist at the University and a tree expert, made us aware of this. We took his advice to heart, and we have found December, even in the last days of the year, to be exactly the perfect time. Just the other day we planted (or had our local nursery plant) three healthy, sprightly Leyland Cypress (*Cupressocyparis leylandii*) trees. We got the idea from the Leyland cypresses at the university. Clustered between two silver maples in our front yard, the new trees provide year-round color and, as our nurseryman put it, "winter interest." The Leyland cypress is fast growing and will reach a height of twenty-five feet or more. It has been reported that some Leyland cypress trees only live for twenty to twenty-five years, but we are hoping for the best, and if they die, we will try again (if we are living ourselves). It seems ironic that the bare-branched days of winter bode well for planting trees, but those last dying days of the year can be just the perfect time to plant trees, these constant reminders of the rebirth of life itself.

Lost and Found

The nine-year-old third grader at Oaklawn Elementary School in Fort Worth, Texas, had waited for this day. Oh how he had waited for this day. Usually, his father would come around at the end of the school day in the white Rambler station wagon to pick up the two brothers for the short ride—only six blocks—home. But now his brother, two years older, had been elevated to traffic guard at the school, and he was busy ushering students across the street at one of the four corners of the school grounds before he himself walked home. For a while the father picked up the younger brother alone.

The younger brother remembered the day the father had picked him up on November 22, 1963. The boy jumped, as always, into the front seat, not bothering in those days to buckle a seat belt. Instead, again as always, he flicked on the radio. On that day, though, the radio announcer revealed some truly dreadful, unfathomable news. "The President has been shot!" the announcer intoned. The boy could hardly take it in. The President! John F. Kennedy! Why, he was to be in Dallas, just thirty miles down the road. How could this be?

The boy learned as he watched the black-and-white television set in the front living room in the days ahead that the president had indeed been shot and killed. Those were frightful days.

But now it was spring, and the boy's parents had decided that it was time for the younger brother to walk home alone. It was just six blocks, after all. And the boy knew the route well, having often walked it with his mother to a grocery store nearby the school. He knew that after several blocks from the school a large, dark brick house surrounded by a chain link fence would rise on the hill to the right. Intimidating black Doberman pinscher dogs, three of them, always came barking down to the fence at the sidewalk. Although the fence was sturdy, the boy always walked a little faster by that house, past those dogs.

Anyway, it was at that house that the boy knew to turn left onto the safety of Collins Street, his street. The street was still gravel, still unpaved, but after making the turn, his house, a nondescript white frame bungalow with attached garage in front, stood only three doors to the right at 3310 Collins St. His house. His home.

So on that cool spring day, the boy waited patiently for the final school bell to ring. And when it rang, he gathered up his things, headed for the corner, crossed the street, and all by himself, headed home. He skipped along a block or two and then began to look for the large dark house with the chain link fence. He listened for the familiar bark of the dogs. He walked another block, and kept up his watch. Then, another block. And then, one more.

By this time he knew something was amiss. Had he missed a turn? Had he left the school from the wrong corner? What had he done? He wasn't sure where he had gone wrong, but he was sure of one thing. He was lost, utterly lost. He began to cry, and through his tears he saw across the street a tall man with a bag draped over his shoulder. The man wore a distinctive blue-gray uniform. The boy knew him for what he was, a mailman, a postman.

The boy looked both ways and crossed the street. He got the postman's attention, and still crying, tried to explain to him that he was lost. The boy explained that he had just left Oaklawn Elementary School a while ago, that his parents had allowed him for the first time to walk home alone, but that something had gone wrong. He was lost.

The boy has never forgotten what that postman did at that moment of his despair. The postman did not just point the boy back to the school with instructions to walk a few blocks in the direction from which he had come. Rather, the postman put his arm around the boy, left his own mail route, and walked with the boy step by step all the way back to the school.

Sure enough, back in the parking lot stood the boy's family, father and mother and brother, beside the white Rambler station wagon. The

Rambler had all the doors flung open wide, as if the car itself welcomed the boy back. The boy ran into the arms of his parents and they took him safely home.

I will never forget what that postman did for me that day. And I will never forget his face. And when I try to imagine what God looks like, I don't see a stern old man with a long-flowing beard. Instead, through tear-stained eyes, I see the kindly, smiling face of the postman who led me back home.

Let It Snow

Why can't it snow? Why won't it snow? We need a good, deep snow to purify the air, to clear the mind, to beautify the landscape. I tell people how I yearn for snow, and they look at me as they often do, with a mystified look of disbelief. I know they are thinking about icy, slushy roads, cleaning off windshields, shoveling walks and driveways, and those piles of scarves, coats, and wet socks and boots at the back door.

Instead, I choose to remember the delicious experience of a teenager, rolling over to listen to a local station on a bedside radio, the announcer reeling off school closings, in alphabetical order, schools called off for the day or if we were lucky, even longer. My high school was Webster County, so I had to wait patiently, expectantly, until the announcer finally made it to the "Ws." And then, if the announcer called my school's name, there was no better feeling in the world than to flick off the radio, pull up the covers, and hunker down for an extended winter nap on into the morning.

We were usually called in by the coach for basketball practice, anyway, but these snow-day practices were simply not the same as the usual after-school sessions. Exhilarated by the snow, we made it to the gym before the coaches, dressed quickly in an icy locker room, and goofily took the court, playing the fool until the coaches arrived. We heaved shots from the bleachers, threw basketballs up through the rafters, and tried Meadowlark Lemon hook shots from half court. Once, the head coach sneaked in and caught us. He witnessed our shenanigans, and promptly ordered us to the end line for two and a half hours of wind sprints and block-out drills.

We really didn't mind overly much. When practice was over, we headed out into the fading afternoon to a winter wonderland. We made circles—cutting donuts—in the empty school parking lot, skidding and sliding around in the snow and ice, before finally making it out to the cleared and salted main highway into town. Those were the days.

We gathered at someone's house to eat popcorn and watch television, all the while thinking about the next day. Had it snowed enough to call off school for another day? Winter snow days in western Kentucky were so much better than the snowless winters we spent in Fort Worth, Texas. During our five years there, it snowed only once, if you could call it that, a one-inch dusting that lasted all of a day, a dusting that still produced the all too brief magic of crystal beauty.

In Arkansas in January 1994, it came a huge snow the day Cammie Jo was born. We brought her back to our faculty house, stepping carefully across the uncleared driveway with our precious cargo. Back for a visit in Kentucky, it snowed one Halloween, and Wesley made a snowman in his grandparents' front yard to greet the trick-or-treaters. Those were the days.

But I remember a heavy snowfall one Easter morning in the 1960s. We gathered in the quiet hush of early morning for a community sunrise service. We sang "In the Garden," as the delicious smells of coffee and cinnamon rolls wafted up from the church basement. After the service, we partook in an Easter church breakfast. Then with the service and breakfast over, we filed out of the church into the pristine white miracle of Easter snow. Those were the days.

Now, as I write this essay, I look out my north-facing History Department window, and guess what? It's snowing. Right now, at least, it is "really coming down," as my father would say. As for me, all I can say is, "Let it snow. Let it snow, Let it snow."

My Little Town

I am haunted by the lyrics of the Paul Simon song, "My Little Town." I do not dislike the song when I hear it performed by Simon and Garfunkel. Rather, it is just the sort of sad and melancholic tune that appeals to me. But just because I enjoy the song does not mean that I agree with its message. Much like Sinclair Lewis's *Main Street*, "My Little Town" presents a biting commentary on small-town America, that life in such a place is shallow and even empty, void of action, void of life itself.

In Paul Simon's words:

In my little town
I grew up believing
God keeps his eye on us all
And he used to lean upon me
As I pledged allegiance to the wall
Lord I recall
My little town.

Well, I grew up believing the same thing, that God keeps his eye on us all, and I still believe this to be true. And I, too, pledged allegiance in school, not to a wall, however, but to a flag, the symbol of a country that I believed in. I still believe in that country.

As I recall the little town in which I grew up, my remembrances of that place were decidedly different than the memories of Paul Simon, who wrote:

Coming home after school
Flying my bike past the gates
Of the factories
My mom doing laundry
Hanging our shirts
In the dirty breeze.

Rather than ride a bike, I walked home from school, once getting lost before a kindly postman helped me find my way. And my mother hung out laundry, too, but the breeze that I remember was clean and sweet, much like the air we now breathe at home in Murray.

Simon's song becomes increasingly bleak in the last two verses:

And after it rains
There's a rainbow
And all of the colors are black
It's not that the colors aren't there
Its just imagination they lack
Everything's the same
Back in my little town

Nothing but the dead and dying
Back in my little town
Nothing but the dead and dying
Back in my little town.

In my experience, however, one's imagination can be exercised best perhaps in a medium-sized town such as Murray. This town, a college town, holds so many advantages over other communities of equal size (culture, music and the arts, entertainment and sports, business and educational opportunities) without the disadvantages of larger cities (rampant crime, congestion, pollution). Simon writes that there is "nothing but the dead and dying back in my little town," but to me our town offers instead life and hope and possibility.

Simon writes:

In my little town
I never meant nothin'
I was just my father's son.

To me, however, a town such as Murray allows for the opportunity to be someone, to be somebody who can make a difference. And, after all, it's not such a bad thing to be "my father's son."

If this essay has become a celebration of our town, I don't want you to get the impression that I believe everything is perfect here in Murray. We have problems to deal with, prejudices to overcome, injustices to address. But, still, we have the opportunity to grow, to make lives of purpose and meaning. Right here in our town. Right here in Murray.

Thoughts of Home

It is true that, just as we are about to take a journey, our thoughts turn most acutely to home. I am thinking about home this week. When Wesley came home from college for the Christmas break he put together a playlist of songs about home to play on his iPod on the plane and in the car, and as we drove home from the Nashville airport through Land Between the Lakes.

Wesley's list of songs included Simon and Garfunkel's "Homeward Bound," and "My Little Town," James Taylor's "Isn't It Nice to Be Home

Again," Frank Sinatra's rendition of "I'll Be Home for Christmas," and the UK pep band's version of "My Old Kentucky Home." Now, as I write this, we are facing a reverse trip to Nashville for Wesley to catch a Saturday flight to go back to college for the spring term. And we all are thinking of home, how blessed we have been to have been home together during this Christmas break. Simone Weil wrote, "To be rooted is perhaps the most important and least recognized need of the human soul." We all look forward to homecomings. Yet, this need to come home, to find home, often goes unfulfilled.

Although we have lived in several places, we now think of Murray as home. This collection of essays is called *Home and Away*, away meaning anywhere but Murray. Although we think of ourselves being rooted to one place—our home—a great store of literature suggests that we all feel from time to time an alienation, a sense of loneliness, or at least a longing or anxiety or restlessness for home. As one writer put it, our "restlessness is a yearning beyond words for the home to which we can no longer return." Thomas Wolfe asserted, "You can't go home again."

G. K. Chesterton said, "Man has always lost his way. He has been a tramp ever since Eden." Plutarch wrote, "It is truest to say that the soul is an exile and a wanderer, driven forth by the divine decrees and laws, and then, on an island buffeted by the seas." According to Seneca, "the human race is constantly rushing to and fro." And George Santayana asked, "Has anyone ever considered the philosophy of travel? It might be worthwhile. What is life but a form of motion and a journey through a foreign world?" The novelist William H. Gass believes that "life is itself exile, and its inevitability does not lessen our grief or alter the fact." We all yearn for home. (Os Guinness, *Long Journey Home* (Water-Brode Press, 2001)).

This sense of alienation, of homelessness, sometimes crowds out any assurance that we do indeed have a home, that there is a place we can always turn to that will provide rest and peace; a place to which we can return, safe from our roamings, safe at home.

People of faith come to the realization that we will never really be safe at home, this side of heaven. That sense of alienation to some extent will always be with us. The journalist Malcolm Muggeridge wrote, "The first thing I remember about the world—and I pray it may be the last—is that I was a stranger in it. This feeling, which everyone has in some degree, and which is at once the glory and desolation of homo sapiens, provides the only thread of consistency that I can detect in my life." According to Muggeridge, this sense of alienation, that we are indeed strangers, is one characteristic of being human.

The writer of Hebrews believed that our yearning can only be fulfilled in time: "For here we do not have an enduring city, but we are looking for the city that is to come." (Hebrews 13:14) We are "looking for the city that is to come," but as for now, Evelyn and I remain in Murray, however transient this home might be, waiting for the time when Cammie Jo and Wesley can return and Wesley can play again James Taylor's assuring tune, "Isn't It Nice to Be Home Again."

Keeping Christmas

Christmas is a time for remembering. So, this week before Christmas, I choose to remember Christmases past. And just as Mary gave birth to the Christ child, thus ushering in the Christmas moment, it has been three women in my life who have seen to the keeping of Christmas for me.

In our household, Evelyn is the one who faithfully organizes our Advent observances. She is the one, year after year, who makes sure we keep Christmas in a way that is appropriate, in a way that is based on family tradition. She is the one who orchestrates the hanging of wreathes, the trimming of the tree, and the placement of manger scenes around the house.

She is the one who begins, in consultation with her sisters, the gathering of gifts. Evelyn is the one who keeps the Advent calendar, making sure we don't miss church Christmas concerts, band performances, and the various gatherings of family and friends. The proper keeping of Christmas for the Bolins is only made possible by the determination of Evelyn, a determination based purely on love.

Evelyn gets it honestly. Evelyn's mother, Jossie Seaton (or Mama Jo as she was known by family and friends), taught her well. For Mama Jo, Christmas could only be observed properly when the family—the whole family—gathered to celebrate together; extended family, all four daughters and their families, cousins, aunts, uncles, and friends. Just as the Holy Family found themselves together on that first Christmas, only when the Seaton family gathered together could Christmas be observed properly. After Mama Jo died in April 2003, stores of quilts, made by her own hand, and other Christmas presents were found in a spare room, just waiting for the Christmas to come.

This will be the first Christmas in our family without my mother, Cammie Bolin, or Mama Bo. Our daughter is Cammie Jo; her name is a good southern name, but it is also the combination, a blending together, of the names of her paternal and maternal grandmothers.

Our children, both Cammie Jo and Wesley, inherit the combined traditions of the keeping of Christmas from their grandmothers. Notice, I haven't mentioned the grandfathers. They have observed benignly the celebrations with a knowing and, although they would be reluctant to admit it, an appreciative regard.

My mother concentrated all of her attention—and ours—on the coming of the Christ child. No Santa Claus here. Jesus was enough for children and adults alike. And for her, the best way, always the best way, to observe the coming of the Savior was through food, the best of food in the southern, Kentucky tradition. Turkey, ham, and all the trimmings: the best dressing in the world (absolutely the best), sweet potato casserole, mashed potatoes, giblet gravy, and pies of several varieties. After the feast, we always sat, stuffed and contented, waiting only until we could partake—after the opening of presents, of course—of evening turkey sandwiches and the rest of the delectable leftovers, all somehow better the second time around.

Of course, all of these celebrations were wrapped around church Advent services, office parties, and school activities. And so we have kept Christmas in such a way year after year. Now that Evelyn's mother and my mother are gone, it is not the same. But we learned from them the art of keeping Christmas, and we carry on, remembering Christmases past, and anticipating the observance of Christmases new.

The Day After Christmas

I was tempted to try my hand at a poem, perhaps "The Day After Christmas," along the lines of "The Night Before Christmas," but I decided that I couldn't pull it off. I love to quote poetry, but I must leave the writing of poetry itself to more talented writers such as Ann Neelon and Carrie Jerrell and Constance Alexander, the real poets of our community.

Lacking such talents of poesy, I will have to be content to describe in simple terms the day after Christmas in the Bolin household. I know that many of my friends work right through Christmas, maybe with one day of respite for the day itself. Then, it's back to work today, the day after Christmas.

On an academic calendar, however, my family has come to appreciate, or at least succumb to, the rhythms of the academic year: the mad rush of the beginning of each term, the flurry of testing and grading at midterm, the dog days of the semester before the teasing break for Thanksgiving in the fall and a weeklong interval in the spring. And then another mad dash to the end, to finals week, with more testing and marking and calculating of grades, followed by the satisfying communication between Faculty Hall and Sparks Hall to turn in the semester's grades, the accounting for an entire term of teaching and learning.

Only on the Monday after finals week can we turn our full attention to Advent (for the Christian), and to final touches of decoration and shopping and preparation for the flurry of gatherings of family and friends and to church Christmas programs, perhaps a Christmas Eve service, all leading up to the day itself, at home with Cammie Jo and Wesley and Evelyn, or sometimes a drive to another family get-together, and then back home stuffed and cozy around a family-room fire to savor memories, to read and reflect on the Christmas season we have just enjoyed.

Then, the day after, and already we are thinking of organization, of cleaning up the last scraps of wrapping paper, of how long to leave up the tree and the other decorations, when to box everything up to haul up the stairs to the attic for yet another year.

In some ways the day after Christmas is a lazy day, devoted to reading a prized book, or listening to new music, cherished Christmas gifts. But already we are anticipating, with a little dread, the first day of school. My classes begin on the 14th, so already on the day after Christmas I am thinking of syllabi, class outlines, and class notes in preparation for the beginning of another term.

Many of my friends and family go back to work literally on the 26th, but in a sense I am back at work too, a shift in thinking and attitude from leisure to lessons, anticipating new classes, with new combinations of students, new challenges, and new material to teach.

I suppose this is as it should be. After all, we are told that the shepherds, after seeing the Christ child, went back to the fields. As St. Luke puts it, "The shepherds returned, glorifying and praising God for all the things they had heard and seen, which were just as they had been told." (Luke 2:20) The shepherds went back to work, "watching over their flocks by night."

There was now a difference, however. They had visited the manger, and now after that experience, they went back to their work, to fulfill their calling with a new understanding, in a different light.

Home By Another Way

It is the Gospel of Matthew that records the visit of the Magi to the Christ child. After they had seen the baby, they heard of Herod's plan to kill him. So instead of returning to Jerusalem, we learn, "having been warned in a dream not to go back to Herod, they returned to their country by another route." The wise men went home by another way. Perhaps Evelyn's father took it from Scripture; whenever he took his family on a drive in the country or even to Paducah he always came home by another way.

I have taken this practice to heart too. When my neighbor found me passed out by the side of Fairlane Street on a Thursday afternoon in 2010, she and her husband for some reason were going home by a different route than they usually traveled. I am thankful that they came home by another way.

Evelyn talked with Lynda Purcell at our church about the well-worn paths we usually take to arrive at home. Lynda wondered what she had missed all these years by taking the same route home day after day. Writers from Robert Frost to William Zinsser know that taking alternative routes are sometimes lifesaving and life-changing. Frost wrote that taking the road less traveled "made all the difference." Zinsser wrote that "change is a tonic."

Travel writers such as H. V. Morton knew that great discoveries are often made off the beaten path. Neglected ruins, pristine brooks, and mysterious forests can be found only if one ventures off the highways and interstates. As comforting as familiar paths and terrains can be, the unfamiliar, the altogether new, can also bring joy. Someone asked Daniel Boone if he had ever been lost, and the Kentucky frontiersman said, "No, but I was once confused for several days." Boone always tried to search out the unfamiliar, crossing the Mississippi River to die in Missouri, away from his Kentucky home.

Some of the essays in this *Home and Away* collection concern my travels in Kentucky and beyond. But it is home that I yearn for. It is home that comforts me. I remember vacation trips that my father planned for us when I was a child. I remember the anticipation of those trips, but I also remember the palpable excitement and joy that my father had as we neared home at the end of the journey. Even though he might be exhausted after several days of vacation, his fastidiousness and grave concern at the beginning of the trip was replaced with a levity and even giddiness as we returned home.

Those vacation destinations, though, would never be forgotten: the Alamo, Galveston Beach, the Smokies, the California redwoods. It always seemed that we came home by another way because we had already been changed by the experience of the destination. We came home renewed; we came home changed. It was after meeting the Christ child that the wise men went home by another way. They returned to the east forever changed. We too will be changed and renewed, if we come home by another way.

Part Three

Away

"We shall not cease from exploration..."

T.S. Eliot

Top Left: James Wesley Bolin, c. 1942. Top Right: Camp Ridgecrest for Boys. Center: Cammie Jo (right) and Emily Morrell in Jerusalem, January, 2015. Bottom: Regent's Park College, Oxford High Table.

Summer Camp

I remember that summer as if it were yesterday. It was back in 1976, that bicentennial summer when I worked as a camp counselor for the Ridgecrest Camp for Boys not far from Asheville, North Carolina. I managed—well, that's not really the word for it—I survived a ten-week stint in charge of a rustic cabin filled with a dozen twelve-year-old boys. All of the boys in the camp were divided into Indian tribes, and we were the Shawnees—actually, we were the "Mighty Shawnees"—appropriate for me since I hailed from the Dark and Bloody Ground of Kentucky.

At the first mountaintop campfire, I was given my camp Indian name, Leaping Leopard, a name that was tied into the fact that I played basketball at Belmont University. That summer I also played on the Ridgecrest counselor's team. We played home games in our gymnasium, the largest log structure in North Carolina, against counselors from other camps and against players from little Montreat-Anderson College, student-athletes who stayed over the summer to take summer school classes and to hone their basketball skills.

We rose early in the morning for an assembly down by the flagpole before taking our breakfast in the dining hall attached to the gym. There we had the usual camp fare, cereal, bacon, and a Kool-Aid sort of drink that we called bug juice. After breakfast, a senior counselor inspected our cabins for order and cleanliness. This consisted of an army-type routine where dimes were dropped on taut sheets, lockers and floors examined for dust or stray debris. Our earnest inspectors never found a perfect cabin; there was always something wrong, some scrap of paper on the floor, some speck of dust on a windowsill. Still, we made it a point of pride to make our cabin as presentable as possible.

We filled our days with chores and "skill development" classes. I conducted a daily basketball clinic, along with some classes that had something to do with beads. I also led crews to clean the latrine and pick up around the grounds. On Thursday evenings, we all lined up, organized by tribes, and marched up to the top of a mountain to our council meeting. Each tribe—all decked out in feathers and war paint—performed, around a blazing bonfire, original songs and skits meticulously prepared the week before.

I'm quite sure none of this was politically correct, but we innocently did it all as a way to honor the Native American heritage of our country. It is still a thrill to think about those council sessions up on that mountaintop. It makes me feel young again. Leaping Leopard indeed!

The counselors had every other weekend off, and we always drove into town for Asheville's famous "Shindig on the Green," where we partook of another type of cultural experience with mountain music, clogging, and candied apples to eat. We came back to our cabins late at night, amazed to find the boys quiet, if not all asleep, tucked in by junior counselors in our absence.

I was not an accomplished outdoorsman, and to my shame I completely botched an overnight tent-camping trip when I brought the boys back down the mountain in the wake of a thunderstorm. To make a long story short, we didn't make it through the night on the mountain but came back to our cozy cabin, tracking in mud and streaming wet. I remember that our cabin inspection did not go so well the next morning.

That summer at Ridgecrest Camp for Boys proved to be a humbling experience for me in more ways than one. Some of the boys were sent to camp by loving parents who had scrimped and saved to give them an authentic summer camping experience, a ritual of growing up. A few wealthy parents, I am sorry to say, sent their boys to the camp for both sessions, the entire summer, as a way, the boys explained it to me, "to get them out of their hair." And so, summer after summer, unwanted and neglected, these boys came to camp away from home.

I liked all of those boys. I learned from them. I think, though, that I loved those neglected rich kids the best. Ignored at home, it was at the camp that they learned of their worth as human beings and of their potential as young men. I wonder where they are today.

Oxford: Come Full Circle

One December evening I sat down in the Helwys Dining Hall of Regent's Park College to dine with students and fellows of that University of Oxford college. The young student sitting to my right hailed from Northern Ireland. She studied English at Oxford. I soon learned that the young man to her right was an American. He came to Oxford to work on a postgraduate degree in history after attending undergraduate school in Minnesota. When he mentioned that his Minnesota alma mater was Bethel College, I immediately recognized it as the school of Paul Reasoner, a friend and teammate on a basketball team I had played on one hot and humid summer in 1978 in the Philippines, of all places.

In 1978, we had spent five weeks sometimes playing two or three games a day in Mindanao, the southernmost island. Paul happened to be the young man's philosophy professor at Bethel. So we enjoyed making this connection over our dinner of chicken and vegetables in the Regent's Park dining hall.

When I returned to my room after supper, I realized that a circle had been connected, or as we say it in western Kentucky, I had come full circle. For it was Paul Reasoner who at the end of our five-week summer basketball tour of Mindanao casually mentioned that I should read C. S. Lewis, one of his favorite authors. I had never read anything Lewis had written. I returned to my Kentucky home for only a week before taking off for graduate school in Texas.

That autumn term, in the intervals between writing research papers, attending seminars, and taking examinations, I read C. S. Lewis. I read C. S. Lewis and I read about C. S. Lewis and his tenure as an Oxford don at Magdalen College. Somewhere between his book *Surprised by Joy* and his children's series *The Chronicles of Narnia*, when I came under Lewis's spell, I also came under the spell of Oxford, never dreaming that I would ever really get to visit that "city of dreaming spires."

That was twenty-five years ago, and now a quarter of a century later, now in my own middle age, I visited that city with colleges founded in *the* Middle Ages. And it was all because of an offhanded remark, a reading suggestion, made by my friend and basketball teammate. I had come full circle.

Oxford: In Search of C. S. Lewis

We asked at the Oxford Information Center for the proper city bus to board to take us to The Kilns, the home of C. S. Lewis, the writer and Christian apologist and someone whose writings have had an enormous influence on my life. We walked to a bus stop, boarded the bus, and after a fifteen-minute ride got off on Kiln Lane. We walked to Lewis Close and then down that lane to the house. At first, I did not recognize the place, although I had studied many photographs of the house and gardens. Since Lewis's death on November 22, 1963 (remember another significant, tragic event occurred on that very day), other houses have been built all around. When Lewis lived there with his brother Warren, the house sat isolated on an eight-acre tract of land.

We took our obligatory photographs, and then I mustered up the courage to ring the doorbell. A young bearded man came to the door. I apologized before asking if it would be possible for two American tourists to see the rooms inside. He gave me a friendly, albeit resigned, smile, and explained that part of the deal to be allowed to live there included a willingness to show the place to tourists. And there were a great many tourists. He led us into a sitting room and went to get his wife, who would give us a private tour.

We waited in the room and looked at photographs of Lewis and his wife, Joy, the books on the floor to ceiling shelves, and a writing desk beneath a large window at the room's end. It was only a small room, but it provided the living space where Lewis would sit on weekend evenings, reading or writing. A young woman, the young man's wife, appeared at the door, and took us outside to see the pond where Lewis swam daily and sat on a stone bench close to the water to think and pray. We were taken back in the house to see the upstairs bedroom and study, and downstairs again to see a wardrobe (not *the* wardrobe of *The Chronicles of Narnia*, which is housed at Wheaton College in Illinois), the kitchen, and the dining room. We thanked our enthusiastic guide and headed off to the Holy Trinity Church, the parish church of Headington, where Lewis is buried.

The rooms in the house had been narrow and shabby, typical of English cottages, and the small Anglican church, where Lewis held membership from 1930 to his death in 1963, along with its churchyard, was tucked out of the way in a corner of the village, now a suburb of Oxford. Yet, despite the modesty of these places, and because of their simplicity, we caught a glimpse of his world and a better understanding of the influences on the writer himself. Invigorated, we marched off now in search of the grave of Lewis's friend, J. R. R. Tolkien, whose following is even more rabid than Lewis's. That day, we never found Tolkien's grave, but the home and gravesite of one great writer proved to be more than enough.

Oxford: Trading Places

In December 2004, I found myself in Oxford, England. I spent twenty days at Oxford's Regent's Park College, conducting research, writing, and exploring Matthew Arnold's "city of dreaming spires." Although I came back to Murray five days before Christmas, I missed many of the Advent activities back home: the Christmas parade, my children's various Christmas programs, and other festive occasions at my church, at the university, and in my community. Of course, Oxford had a charm of its own.

I visited Blenheim Palace, the birthplace of Winston Churchill, all done up for Christmas, and Oxford's Wadham College Chapel served as the site for what promised to be a memorable Christmas program. It was indeed a program that I will not forget. The college's Candlelit Christmas Concert featured four accomplished singers: a soprano, countertenor, tenor, and bass, all accompanied by an excellent pianist. The program included "Flocks in Pastures Green Abiding" from Bach's Cantata no. 208, "The Lamb" by John Tavener, Mendelssohn's "When Jesu, our Lord," more Bach numbers, and Witold Lutoslawski's "The Holly and the Ivy." Interspersed between the musical selections, readings from the works of G. K. Chesterton, Dylan Thomas, Kipling, O. Henry, Raymond Chandler, John Betjeman, and Thomas Hardy provided a nice complement to the beautiful music.

Candlelight flickered in the stone and wood Gothic chapel, a soaring stained-glass window hinted at dark hues of blue and green at one end of the room, and majestic organ pipes dominated the other end in the chancel. Decorated for the season, the chapel presented a picture-perfect Christmas scene. Such sights and sounds of Christmas I had before only read about in books or imagined in my dreams.

After the first Bach number, a distinguished reader, indeed a famous Oxford writer and personality, rose to read from Fanthorpe and Chesterton. It was Colin Dexter, the author of the Inspector Morse mysteries, set in Oxford and read around the world. The diminutive writer prefaced his reading from the chosen poetry about the Christmas story with, "Though I am not a believer myself, I am moved by the beauty of the story." While I appreciated his candor, and his rich English voice, I found the writer's words unutterably sad and ironic. As a believer in the Christmas story, I too am moved by its beauty—but not just the beauty of the words.

After the first reading, the singers continued the program with Tomas Luis de Victoria's "O Magnum Mysterium." "How great and wonderful a mystery," the translation begins. Rarely if ever have I heard voices like that!

But back home in Kentucky the night before, our son played his saxophone and sang with his usual excellence and verve in a high school Christmas performance, and our once-shy daughter sang and read with a crystal clear voice at a church program. Even though I was in England at the time, I knew these things; my wife and my mother called to tell me.

I learned a great deal during my Oxford sojourn. I learned from research in rare books, and I learned from visits to what were to me exotic places. I also learned more about myself. I learned, for example, that while the Candlelit Christmas Concert at Oxford, 4,000 miles away from my Kentucky home, was unlike any Christmas program I had yet seen or heard, I would trade it for a family-room fireplace, a simple but elegant Christmas tree in a front parlor, and the Advent celebrations of my son and daughter in Murray, Kentucky, any day.

Knowing Things

In October 2007, I found myself at the Ohio Valley History Conference in Bowling Green, Kentucky, having traveled there with colleagues and friends. I have attended scores of history conferences during my teaching career. At these conferences we renew friendships with colleagues from other colleges and universities, and we get to know our own colleagues better, seeing and talking with them outside the confines of history department offices, and even hearing about their own historical interests and researches, something that—now I know this will seem odd to you—we rarely take the time or make the effort to do back home in Murray.

At Murray State, we professors seem so caught up in our own routines, running from office hours to classroom hours to home hours, that we do not often make the effort to really get to know the folks whom we work with, whom we teach with, every day. This is a shame, really, having to go away to a set aside place at a set aside time to learn more about these members of our own department, our own university. But there you are.

And here we are at this conference. I am not sure that you know or even care how these history conferences work, but at such a conference we browse book exhibits where we also meet familiar faces to talk about books and history. We attend sessions where two or three papers are read on historical topics of interest to those particular historians.

The paper presentations are followed by brief comments, a brief critique, given by a predetermined "commenter," who has been sent the papers in time to read before the conference. Then, the audience is invited to make observations or ask questions.

I have served in all of these capacities: as paper presenter, as commenter, and as audience. I am always amazed at what I learn. I am amazed at the many and varied historical interests of the historians. I am sometimes amazed at how heated a historical discussion can become. Sometimes tempers flare. More often, new insights are gained about new topics. It is too much to say that a good time is had by all, but I usually come away from these conferences with a new appreciation for my colleagues and with a determination to become a better historian myself.

Now, I must say that some of the papers I hear at these sessions—on historical topics far from my own interests in Kentucky, American, sports, and religious history—are of little interest to me. And I am sure that papers I have written hold little interest or value for many of those who choose nonetheless to hear them. Still, I am always inspired to hear someone who has studied any topic, no matter how arcane, to such an extent that as a scholar he or she knows more about that topic than perhaps anyone else in the world.

From time to time, at these historical conferences, I meet such a person. To be someone who knows more about a topic than anyone else must, in a way, be a lonely experience. After all, to whom can you really converse about a topic that only you know about in such detail. But just think of it: To be able to become such an expert, to devote the time and energy to learn more about something than anyone else. Not a bad goal for any historian to seek, would you say?

A Destin Diary: Day One

Just yesterday I finished up all of my grading—marking essay examinations—for my summer school classes. I had not taught summer school for six or seven years, so this summer's experience was at once fresh and unexpected. I taught two upper-level history courses in a little over four weeks of four-hour sessions. I don't know if I will attempt such a thing again; I hesitate for my students' sake, and for mine.

To celebrate the end of summer school, we hightailed it to Florida for a short vacation in Destin. Cammie Jo has been campaigning for the Florida beaches for some time, so we did this for her, to be sure, but also for Wesley (before he goes away to college in two months' time) and also for Evelyn and me. As part of the celebration, I plan to write several essays in the form of "A Destin Diary," an essay for each of the four weeks of summer school. I will ruminate and reminisce; I will pause and ponder; I will consider and contemplate. "A Destin Diary" for this wonderful summer interlude.

We left out early—well, early for the Bolin family—on a Sunday morning. Dr. Gil Mathis graciously agreed to teach my Sunday school class, and Beth White covered for Evelyn in her Sunday school class. As for us, we communed together—with each other and with the Lord—tooling down Interstate 65 in a borrowed van, a new van on loan from Marlin Seaton, Evelyn's considerate and ever patient father.

With several stops along the way in Tennessee and Alabama, we checked into our place in Destin in plenty of time to dip our toes into the Gulf of Mexico. Well, Evelyn and I dipped our toes; Cammie Jo and Wesley dipped considerably more.

This is a beautiful place: white sand, sky-blue sky, darker blue gulf water, convenient and more than adequate bookstores nearby. The beauty, however, goes beyond the sights of the place. The sounds are especially intoxicating. As I write these words—Wesley and I sit on a patio overlooking the gulf, Wesley reading a collection of essays, me writing these words—the rhythmic wash of the surf and the muffled yet gleeful chatter of children in the distance threaten to lull me into a peaceful sleep. Only a scattering of families and pairs of lovers dot the line where the surf meets the sand. I see glints of flashlights down the shore to the east, only dim silhouettes of couples to the west.

A late seafood supper awaits, but for just these few brief moments, with pen in hand, I soak up these sights and sounds, and indeed the salt air smells, of this idyllic place. Gone are the cares of the academy. Washed away in the tide are the myriad worries, large and small, of the classroom, of the office.

I know that e-mails wait to be answered, that summer-school grades must be turned in to the registration office in Sparks Hall, that syllabi must be put together and classes planned for yet another fall semester. But, for now, for these few days, away with my family, away from classroom cares, away to these beaches of Destin, I can ruminate and reminisce. I can pause and ponder. I can consider and contemplate. I can imagine and dream again.

A Destin Diary: Day Two

On this morning in Destin, we woke to the sight and sound of the breaking surf. While other members of my family went down to the beach early to look for shells, I stayed behind to make coffee and begin this diary entry. Already I feel inhibited; writing a diary is after all much more private than a column or essay. But because this diary is also serving as a newspaper column and eventually in an essay collection, I must be at once introspective and candid, a hard thing to pull off.

Looking out at the Gulf of Mexico reminds me of the first time I saw the gulf. With my father in seminary, my family spent five years in Fort Worth, Texas, from 1960 to 1965. Each summer we took a short vacation, it seemed, either to Six Flags Over Texas or to the Alamo. The Texas heroes of the Alamo became my personal heroes—James Bowie, Sam Houston, Colonel William Barret Travis, and especially Davy Crockett.

As a boy I once wrote a letter to the director of the Alamo, telling him of my interest, and he sent back all manner of copied letters and memorabilia about those Texans who had died there. In our backyard I took a stick and dramatically scratched a line in the dirt, imagining how Colonel Travis had drawn a line in the sand, inviting all those Texas freedom fighters wishing to stay and defend the Alamo—and to die—to cross the line. Everyone crossed the line, and so did I.

So we visited the Alamo on our summer vacations, but one summer, our mother and father took my brother and me all the way down to Galveston, and that is when I first experienced the gulf. A chronic worrier, my mother did not allow my brother and me to venture very far into the tide, but I still remember the power and the majesty of the gulf.

We did the usual things, collected shells and built sand castles, while our mother and father watched. We have photographs showing my mother in a dress and my father in dress slacks and a white shirt with the sleeves rolled up, watching over us patiently. I guess they took pictures of each other since neither appears in the same photograph.

Now, by the gulf in Destin, a row of blue chairs and umbrellas have been placed conveniently for guests, and these same gulf waters, albeit farther to the east of Galveston, are as inviting as ever. I situate myself, thinking that beyond the horizon to the east lies the west coast of Florida, and miles to the west, beyond Mobile, New Orleans and Houston, lies Galveston, that magical place I have not seen since I was ten years old. But Destin holds a magic all its own.

Much has changed in these more than forty years. Evelyn and I have a teenage son and a teenage daughter. Our vacations, sometimes to our children's chagrin, have through the years tended more toward "academic vacations," rather than amusement parks and beaches. On vacation, Evelyn does not wear dresses, and I do not wear dress slacks and long-sleeved white shirts. We seem to read more than we play. (On this trip, we brought, each one of us, stacks of books from Murray, and we visited a convenient Barnes & Noble last night to procure a fresh stack of volumes.) Our children have decidedly more freedom than my brother and I had in the early 1960s.

Some things have remained the same, however, since my first look at the Gulf of Mexico. Today, we seem to have about the same allotment of worries and cares in this new age of terrorism as we did during the days of the Cuban Missile Crisis and everything else that went with the Cold War. We also have, and I know this to be true, just as much love for each other as my mother and father showed to my brother and me all those years ago.

A Destin Diary: Day Three

Writing at the beach is a rather free-form exercise, and one that I enjoy. It's not exactly stream of consciousness, like James Joyce's *Ulysses*, but freewheeling thoughts do flow, remembrances of times past, future hopes.

My view from our patio overlooks the Gulf of Mexico, which I know empties into the Atlantic Ocean yet is hemmed by South, Central, and North America. But from my patio view no land appears. The vastness of the gulf seems unfathomable; almost overwhelming, much like time and history as they, too, appear to be contained only within the pages of a history textbook. But to actually experience time and history, to live it, sometimes seems unfathomable, too.

The poet T. S. Eliot captured the idea of this notion in the "Burnt Norton" portion of his "Four Quartets:"

Time present and time past
Are both perhaps present in time future,

And time future contained in time past.
If all time is eternally present
All time is unredeemable.
What might have been is an abstraction
Remaining a perpetual possibility
Only in a world of speculation.
What might have been and what has been
Point to one end, which is always present.

One link that I have found that ties time and history, past and present, is teaching.

Sitting here overlooking the gulf, I get the sense of what Eliot tried to convey. Other writers have grappled with the enormity of time, space, place, and history. The southern writer Pat Conroy wrote that "the water is wide," and from my vantage point with Central and South America beyond, Conroy's statement certainly rings true. The water is indeed wide.

In "The Rime of the Ancient Mariner," Samuel Taylor Coleridge wrote that there was "water, water everywhere, nor any drop to drink." We need not drink the gulf water, although yesterday I swallowed more than I needed of the salty stuff. But if we look carefully, it is amazing what we will find, as Henry David Thoreau observed.

Thoreau wrote that "time is but the stream I go fishing in. I drink at it, but while I drink I see the sandy bottom and detect how shallow it is. Its thin current slides away, but eternity remains." Yes it does. Another writer suggested that what matters is that we, while fishing, come up with some surprises.

Life is filled with surprises and pleasures. My daughter Cammie Jo and wife Evelyn have opened this gray, overcast morning with a walk on the beach in spite of the threat of rain. A storm settled in late yesterday afternoon, and the forecast for today is for scattered thunderstorms and rain. As I write this, we are badly in need of rain back home, but here we are hoping it won't rain.

Maybe we should pray that the rain will simply move inland to Kentucky. As a boy I used to pray fervently that no rain would fall until after our Little League baseball game had been played. But I also prayed that my team would win just as other boys must have prayed that their teams, too, would win. I wondered how God would decide. That season my team had a losing record. I had my answer.

Cammie Jo and Evelyn have returned from their walk and Cammie Jo and our son Wesley have already plunged into the gulf this morning, the first along our stretch of beach to do so. Not long ago I would have joined them but am now content on the patio with coffee and pen and paper. Maybe this shadows what Eliot was writing about.

We all confess to being bored from time to time, but observers, those who really look, will find surprises: interesting, heart-rending, fascinating things. That is, after all, what teaching and learning is all about.

A Destin Diary: Day Four

The skies are still overcast this Wednesday morning (actually June 20), but the forecast calls for only a thirty percent chance of rain, so I suppose we will be able to spend a goodly portion of this, our last full day in Destin, on the beach. The beach boys are even now drilling holes in the sand, all in a row, to put down blue beach umbrellas for vacationing guests. Now, they're bringing out matching blue lounge chairs from the storage bins at the back of the beach. They carry out eight at a time—I don't know how they do it—and they remind me of hermit crabs as they scurry across the sand with their loads.

Yesterday, we bought flavored shaved ice concoctions from these same two young men at a snack shack on the beach. What a life they must lead! They spend their days from early morning to late afternoon on a beach. No business suits, just shorts and shades. I suppose they live here year-round, but they could be college students who, shunning a high stakes internship, have chosen to spend a summer in a more relaxed environment. Before the day is through, I will try to ask them about home.

Home. We cherish home, but at the same time we are bound to wonder if we have chosen to live in the place we were meant to live. When we travel to some vacation destination, we always wonder about the "natives" of the place. In the restaurants and the shops, are any of those folks locals, or are they all from afar, vacationing here for a few days before returning to their homes in Ohio or Minnesota or Kentucky? Does anyone really live here? We asked around, and sure enough—hard to imagine—there are families who call Destin home. We even saw a low, long brick building with a sign that proclaimed "Destin Middle School."

Of course, we know of several couples in Murray who spend several winter months each year in some Florida locale, south of the snow and slush. They maintain these second vacation places, but they still call Murray home. Evelyn and I and our children have come to call Murray home. Evelyn grew up living in Calvert City, in one place since she was two years old. My family moved from place to place in the following order: Arlington, Kentucky; Jefferson City, Tennessee; Fort Worth, Texas; Oregon City, Oregon (for two months); College Grove, Tennessee; Parsons, Tennessee; and then Dixon, Kentucky.

I lived at three different colleges: Belmont University in Nashville; Baylor University in Waco, Texas; and the University of Kentucky in Lexington. Since Evelyn and I married, we have lived in six different houses: three in Providence, Kentucky (where Wesley was born down the road in Henderson); one in Walnut Ridge, Arkansas (where Cammie Jo was born in nearby Jonesboro); and two in Murray. We have lived the longest in Murray, and Murray is our home.

All of these places! I remember that when we decided to leave Kentucky for Arkansas in 1992, I went to tell the president of Madisonville Community College, where I then taught, about our decision to move. I expressed concern that we would be leaving the only home that Wesley, then at four years old, had ever known. The wise president assured me that home for Wesley would always be in his father's arms. We know that in a few more weeks Wesley will be leaving home for college—all the way to Yale in New Haven, Connecticut—and then in five years it will be time for Cammie Jo's college years as well. We also know that beyond college they both will eventually establish homes of their own. Evelyn and I hope and pray, though, that for Wesley and Cammie Jo, they will always feel at home in their parent's arms.

Well, so much for this Destin Diary. Tomorrow, we head back to Murray, or as the southern writer Willie Morris put it, "north toward home." I never got around to asking those beach boys about their homes. I bet though, for them as for all of us, the old cliché holds true: Home is where the heart is.

Horizons

On a vacation trip to Florida, my thoughts were drawn to horizons. Several of my colleagues at the university asked me how long we vacationed in Destin. They kidded me that I had, after all, been writing for four weeks about that Florida vacation. I had to explain to my colleagues that we were only in Destin for four days. I tried to write an essay a day about what we were experiencing there. Each day we sat in beach chairs facing south toward a distant horizon on the Gulf of Mexico. Unlike Kentucky horizons, disturbed by hills or a line of trees, a straight line of water and sky formed a pristine horizon in Destin, unbroken save for the occasional boat. One morning, facing south, I scanned the horizon beginning to the far east moving my gaze steadily, but slowly, westward until I reached a point where condominiums rose along the shore just at the point where sky and water met a point of land. Only two boats, one small, one large, broke the long, straight line. In Florida, I could only imagine what lay beyond the horizon, although I know from a lighted globe that my family bought for me one Father's Day that it must be Central and South America, and beyond that Antarctica.

In hilly western Kentucky, horizons are not too distant, unless you are lucky enough to be on a pontoon or fishing boat on Kentucky or Barkley Lake some enchanted evening. Even level farmlands planted in corn or wheat have horizons broken by a fence line of trees. I don't know whether I prefer a distant horizon or a near one, the long view or the short view. Either way, we often wonder what lies beyond the horizon, what lies ahead, what will transpire in the years beyond what we think will happen in the next few hours or days or weeks. Of course, beyond this existential moment, we really don't know.

In Florida, we visited Seaside, that beautiful, planned community of pastel beach houses, inviting front porches, and white picket fences. At Cammie Jo's insistence, the night before we left for Florida we watched "The Truman Show" because much of the film had been shot in Seaside. The movie is about an elaborate television show, the ultimate reality show, centered on Truman Burbank (played by Jim Carrey), a man who was filmed live from birth—no, even before birth—through his school and college years and marriage, all unbeknownst to him.

Everyone else, hundreds of actors, and thousands upon thousands of television viewers, are in on the ruse. The show's producers plan for him every step: his wife, his best friend, his neighbors, and acquaintances. This all takes place in a huge biosphere located next to Hollywood. The show is watched around the clock by viewers all over the world. Only Truman is unaware that he is the star of a television show, that the script is his life, that each continuous episode is planned out.

Everyone else knows the script, as much as it can be known. Only Truman is in the dark.

Finally, as an adult, Truman catches on and plans his escape on a boat, only to have his boat, after a manufactured storm at sea, bump into the wall of the biosphere. In the end, Truman steps out a door into...well, he doesn't know. He chooses the unknown for the known, the planned, made-up (for him) world he has lived in since conception.

Isn't that the way we would have it? If we could, would we want to know how our lives pan out? Would we want to have the ability to see into the future? Would we want to see beyond the horizon? I suspect not. As daunting, as scary, as the future may be, when it comes to the future, we prefer the unknown to the known. Along with Truman, we would reject a life lived as if going through the motions, according to a script that everyone knows, even ourselves. For people of faith, we prefer the old sanctified truth: We don't know what the future may hold, but we know who holds the future.

All the Way to China

My mother was a masterful storyteller. And how could she be anything but, with two boys two years apart to rear. She told us stories to put us to bed at night. She told us stories as we waited for Dad to come home from work in the late afternoon. And she sometimes fabricated stories just to find a few minutes peace in those long mornings before we were old enough to go to school.

For example, I remember that she would sometimes arm me with an old kitchen spoon and suggest that I find my favorite "digging place" in our backyard. "Remember," my mother would say, "if you dig long enough and deep enough, you'll come out in China on the other side." For the first half hour of the enterprise, I was always determined, and it didn't hurt that I had visions of a small, black-haired, almond-eyed Chinese boy just my age poking the ground with chopsticks on the other side of the world. I figured we would eventually meet somewhere in the middle.

And we finally did meet, not as five-year-old boys, but fifty years later, and not in the middle of the earth, but on the streets of Beijing and Xi'an when Therese St. Paul, Kathy Timmons, Tom Timmons, Dicky Turner, and myself spent two weeks representing Murray State University in China. We left on Tuesday, May 31, on an early morning flight from Nashville, flew to Chicago, and then spent thirteen hours flying straight over the Great Lakes, the Arctic Circle north of Alaska, down through Siberia, Mongolia, and then China, to Beijing. I had not been on a journey such as that since I traveled to the Philippines as a twenty-two-year-old. Of course, then, I thought I could do anything.

Now, in Beijing, it seemed that everything was done for us. Mr. Hu, our driver, had chauffeured the Olympic Committee in 2008. He proved masterful at navigating the Beijing streets, where it was not unusual for a car to go the wrong way on a roundabout or to use a sidewalk to pass another vehicle. The streets were cluttered with pedestrians, bicycles, motorbikes, electric buses, motorbuses, taxicabs (one was a Peugeot), and cars—high-end cars such as Audis, Mercedes, BMWs, and Peugeots). Drivers seemed to rely on luck, and Tom and Dicky suggested that traffic patterns almost looked like great choreographed motorized dances. Drivers sporting new automobiles would tie red cloth from exhaust pipes and rear view mirrors, red being the color for good luck, to ward off fender benders or more serious crashes.

But Mr. Hu was above all that as he floated over the city's streets between the impressive glass-and-steel skyscrapers or down the narrow lanes of the old neighborhoods or hutongs. No GPS for Mr. Hu; none was needed. He knew Beijing like the back of his hand. And that is no small accomplishment when you consider the fact that Beijing is a city of at least fifteen million people. Some estimates suggest a more accurate count to be twenty million. Here is a city with a population three or four times the population of the commonwealth of Kentucky.

Yet I never feared for my safety. Crime is low, and when a crime is committed it is dealt with swiftly, with little thought or concern for innocence until proven guilty. I guess my first impression of Beijing was the juxtaposition between the modern and postmodern with the ancient: the crass commercialism that we are so familiar with here in the United States with a deep reverence for the old ways, for the elderly. For the next few weeks, I hope to write with respect and love for the Chinese people. Their history is venerable. Their culture is admirable. There is much to be learned if we will make the effort. In a short story in the most recent issue of *The American Scholar*, John Rolfe Gardiner paraphrased that old imperialist Rudyard Kipling: "What knows he of America who only America knows?"

Encountering the Other

When I visited China several weeks ago through the auspices of the Discover China program at Murray State University and the People's Education Press, I was prepared to encounter an alien culture, so different from my own in western Kentucky. And that, of course, was one of its charms. Why visit another country if it was exactly like our own? James Axtell, a longtime professor at William & Mary and a recent author of a brilliant history of Princeton University, referred to the value of "encountering the other."

I was recently dismayed when at a family reunion I heard a relative tell me that her grandson, a bright and accomplished young man, his school's valedictorian, had refused to apply for Murray State's top scholarship because it required a study-abroad experience. "I don't want any part of that," he said. I immediately thought of the John Updike quote: "billions of consciousnesses silt history full, and every one of them the center of the universe." How many of us go through life without seriously attempting to encounter the other? Surely, when we find that we are so wrapped up in ourselves we make very, very small packages.

Anyway, even as I was prepared to encounter the other in China, I brought back with me something else—the realization that human beings are really very much alike wherever we go. Yes, we ate different food in different ways. When we sat down to a meal at the beginning of the trip, determined to eat with chopsticks, my attempts invariably brought a rushing waitress with a fork for the fumbling American. By the end of the trip, I nimbly picked up peanuts with my chopsticks… sometimes flawlessly.

Other signs of culture—automobiles, architecture, clothing, cellphones—had become disappointingly globalized, at least in the cities. Only in the country and in the villages did Chinese farmers live the old way, harvesting wheat by hand, carrying water on foot, and burying the dead in the fields where they had worked throughout their lives.

I learned to admire other qualities of the Chinese people. It was not unusual, for example, for four generations of family members to live in one house or apartment. Great care and respect are given by family members for the elderly. In the cities, on the other hand, the government, not the people, owns the land, and people can only own apartments for seventy years, at which time the apartments are no longer really livable anyway. In the cities, there is a one-child policy; couples are fined if they have another child (twins are the exceptions). Unfortunately, boys are more cherished than girls.

Again, in the country, unlike the cities, property is passed down through the families generation after generation, and the one-child policy does not apply. The Chinese people are embarrassingly polite. We were told not to ask someone where we could buy a watch such as the one they were wearing or they would insist that we take theirs. The Chinese people are elaborate gift givers. When the Magi came from the East bearing gifts for the Christ child, it is not hard to imagine a contingent of Chinese ambassadors traveling along the Silk Road bearing expensive gifts.

With all of the cultural and historical and political differences, among the people there is a transcendence of human dignity that brings us together, that helps us communicate, and through this transcendence, we learn from each other and about each other, and we learn so much more about ourselves. T. S. Eliot said it best:

> We shall not cease from exploration
> And the end of all our exploring
> Will be to arrive where we started
> And know the place for the first time.

Thank you, Murray State University, for the opportunities you give students, faculty, and staff to encounter the other, and, in the process, to encounter ourselves.

Part Four

Teaching

"What matters is if I reach a few students at a level that transforms them and gets them to see the world in a different way."

Perry Lentz

Top Left: Overladen bookshelves in my Murray State University history department office. Top Right: Pogue Library Reading Room, Murray State University. Center: Hugh Ridenour, history teacher extraordinaire. Bottom Left and Right: 16-year-old Duane Bolin guarding Jerry West, LA Laker Superstar.

A Silent Classroom

For me it is a humbling and inspirational experience to sit all alone in a silent classroom. I often seek out one of my classrooms at Murray State University after the end of a term or before the beginning of a new semester. I have tried to recapture that wonderful but frightening smell—some combination of freshly painted walls and lockers, old textbooks, and floor wax—that I remember when walking through the halls of the old Dixon school building in my hometown in Webster County.

After Dixon, Clay, Sebree, and Slaughters consolidated to form Webster County High School in 1964, the old high school buildings continued to serve students in kindergarten through eighth grade, until new elementary and middle schools were built. We lived next door to the old Dixon school, and my mother, an elementary teacher, and I would find her classroom to put up bulletin boards and position desks in the late summer before the students returned for the fall term. Janitors and teachers and the principal would already have been at work and although the ancient building was in decay, their efforts to prepare the place for yet another school year produced that distinctive aroma that I will continue to long for.

My university classrooms in Faculty Hall, a 1970s structure, produce a different smell altogether, but the aura of the empty, silent classroom is still there, and it is still inspiring to me. I unlock the door, decide not to flip on the lights, and sit at the desk at the front of the room in the semidarkened space.

Six rows of desks, seven seats deep, line up before me, and a prominent wall clock ticks off the passing minutes. I have seen paintings of the interiors of one-room schools where the benches and seats hug the four walls, and my high school history teacher always arranged his desks in a U shape only two seats deep so that he would roam the area down the middle and confront students directly. The typical university classroom these days line up the desks in rows, however, although some innovative teachers still go to the trouble of moving seats around.

School bells, some ensconced just outside the school door and some hand-held and hand-rung by the teacher, called students to their scholarly work in the old days, but today students rush into class, glancing nervously at the wall clock before plopping down backpacks and books and cellphones and sometimes drinks and candy bars.

I have a sneaking suspicion that the familiar rows of desks, along with the wall clock, appeared after the Industrial Revolution. Classrooms came to mirror the factory system. Assembly-line workers clocked in and clocked out, and in a sense the school became a factory as well. Today, the nobility of a plant worker, as well as a teacher, has been insured by better working conditions, but the vestiges of industrialism remain as students line up in straight rows of desks and as they are bound to fixed shifts of class time—fifty minutes for Monday, Wednesday, and Friday classes, and an hour and fifteen minutes for Tuesday and Thursday classes—to learn what there is to be learned.

But sitting in this empty, silent classroom, I envision what will take place here when the seats are filled (as they now are) with undergraduates and graduate students. I imagine the excitement of learning and the surprise of understanding a concept for the first time or in a new way. I think about the free exchange of ideas, and I anticipate the unbelievable potential of young and active minds in the pursuit of learning.

Now, as I write this, classes have begun in a new semester at our university. The seats are occupied in overflowing classrooms, the halls are crowded, and office hours are filled with appointments. The reverie of sitting in an empty, silent classroom is over and the nervous thrill of walking into a packed classroom is here. My hope is that I will not squander away this opportunity, for my students and for myself, that the memory of the excitement and inspiration of that silent, empty classroom will encourage me and strengthen me through the course of the semester.

Getting Started

Although classes started last week, preparation for those classes began when professors turned in their grades last May. Although I chose not to teach this summer, I thought and worked throughout the summer on my upcoming fall classes. How did my students respond during last spring's semester? What worked? What do I need to change? What assignments and activities should I discard? How can the learning experience of my students be deepened? We think on these things. These are the questions we ask at the end of every semester.

Then, in the middle of the summer, we take on the hopeful but laborious task of preparing syllabi. The syllabus provides a plan for the class, complete with a class schedule or outline, course objectives, grading procedures, attendance policy, and a listing of readings we will tackle in the course. This semester I will teach four classes, including HIS 361 Teaching History, a methods course for those students preparing to teach history on the high school level someday, HIS 100T Freshman Transitions, for those first-year students planning to major in history, and two sections of HIS 221 American Experience Before 1865, a survey course in American History.

I prepared and made copies of the syllabi for each of these classes about a month ago. Although the number will change through the add/drop period, it looks like I will have some twenty-two students in Teaching History, twenty-two in the transitions class, and over thirty in each of the survey courses.

According to the syllabus, we will meet fifteen times—once a week—from 6:00-9:00 on Monday evenings in the Teaching History class. Freshman Orientation is a one-hour course, so we will plan to meet a lucky thirteen times from 2:00-2:50 on Tuesday afternoons. I teach the survey courses back-to-back on Tuesdays and Thursdays from 9:30 a.m.-10:45 a.m. and 11:00 a.m.-12:15 p.m., thirty-one sessions in all through the course of the semester.

These are the hours when students meet together in a classroom experience, but, hopefully, I will encounter students on campus, at the residential colleges—my particular college is Regents College—and in office-hour visits outside the classroom walls. This semester I have set aside office hours from 8:00 a.m.-9:30 a.m. on Tuesdays and Thursdays, 9:00 a.m.-noon on Mondays and Wednesdays, and 2:00 p.m.-3:00 p.m. on Thursdays. I leave Fridays open to write and to make visits to public schools in the region. At home I try my best to keep up with my own reading and to squeeze in time to work on a current book project and to write newspaper columns. On Saturdays and Sundays, I write some more and spend time at home or at band contests, ball games, or other school, church, or family activities with Evelyn, Wesley, and Cammie Jo.

Let me say that in the course of a week I will spend many more hours on campus in committee meetings, workshops, and seminars beyond the designated office hours reserved specifically for students. My family and my faith come first, but hours are spent in preparing for class lectures and class discussions, as well as in the preparation and grading of assignments, quizzes, and examinations.

A semester of opportunity has begun. What will we make of it? What will we learn together about each of the various subjects? What will my students learn from me, and what will I learn from my students?

Talks to Teachers

How can teachers "get through" to students? How did the influential teachers that taught me in elementary school, middle school, high school, and college get through to me? What were their devices? How did they practice the science or the art of teaching? I discuss these things with my students who are preparing to teach history in high school. Is teaching a science or an art? And is it possible, after all, to teach someone how to teach? We discuss these things.

Just last week I plucked from my bookshelves at home a worn volume, published in 1914. Nothing but the cutting edge of research for me! The pragmatic psychologist William James published a series of "talks" he had given in 1892 as public lectures at Harvard. The author of the influential *The Varieties of Religious Experience* now turned his attention to the topic of teaching in *Talks to Teachers on Psychology: And to Students on Some of Life's Ideals.* James applied his understanding of psychology to the art of teaching.

James made it clear where he stood on the question of whether teaching is an art or a science. "Psychology is a science," he wrote, "and teaching is an art." Furthermore, he stated, "sciences never generate arts directly out of themselves." Now, I realize I am out of my element here. My colleagues in the Department of Psychology or over at the College of Education know and teach the literature on teaching and learning. Still, William James makes a great deal of sense to me when he asserted that "the science of logic never made a man reason rightly, and the science of ethics (if there be such a thing) never made a man behave rightly."

We teach certain scientific principles in our various disciplines. For example, in the discipline of history we teach how to collect and analyze data from primary and secondary sources. In history, we applaud the rigor of scientific analysis. According to James, the most a science "can do is to help us to catch ourselves up and check ourselves, if we start to reason or to behave wrongly; and to criticize ourselves more articulately after we have made mistakes."

James continued, "A science only lays down lines within which the rules of the art must fall, laws which the follower of the art must not transgress; but what particular thing he shall positively do within those lines is left exclusively to this own genius. One genius will do his work well and succeed in one way, while another succeeds as well quite differently."

I am not sure that my teachers are geniuses, but I do know that they had a genius for opening up the world to me. I am sure they learned how to do that not in a college class such as my Teaching History course. I am sure, instead, that they learned the art of teaching on the fly, in the classroom and at home as they prepared for each new day. Or as James put it, "The art of teaching grew up in the schoolroom, out of inventiveness and sympathetic concrete observation."

To know history, or any other discipline, to have a head knowledge of the subject matter is not enough. The teachers who inspired me knew their history and literature and science and mathematics, to be sure, but they also knew something else. They knew how to animate the subject. Or as James put it, teachers "must have an additional endowment altogether, a happy tact and ingenuity to tell us what definite things to say and do when the pupil is before us."

William James spoke from his own experience, but this has been my experience as a student as well. "In teaching," James said, "you must simply work your pupil into such a state of interest in what you are going to teach…that every other object of attention is banished from his mind; then reveal it to him so impressively that he will remember the occasion to his dying day; and finally fill him with devouring curiosity to know what the next steps in connection with the subject are."

I do not remember much of the subject matter that my teachers taught me years ago (although I must have absorbed more than I think), but "to my dying day" I will remember how the women and men who taught me so well worked me up "into such a state of interest" that I was thirsty for more. I am still trying to quench that thirst.

The One Who Made the Difference

Last week my high school history teacher drove a couple of hours from his home just to speak to my HIS 361 Teaching History class at Murray State University. A master teacher for over two-and-a-half decades at Webster County High School, Hugh Ridenour is a master teacher still, in light of his performance to my students the other night.

When I sat in his history classroom in the 1970s, he opened up to me a whole new world of possibility and opportunity. In the years since his "retirement," Hugh Ridenour has gone on to publish books and articles on a range of historical topics, and to make historical presentations for the Speakers Bureau of the Kentucky Humanities Council. His teaching goes on, now outside the classroom.

We, all of us, can remember one—at least one—teacher who made a difference in our lives. Mark Edmundson, a burly professor of English at the University of Virginia and before that a football player at Medford High School in Massachusetts, wrote a book about Frank Lears, an unlikely philosophy teacher during his senior year. Edmundson decided that although popularity, evidenced by positive course evaluations and a steady rise in rank, had accompanied his own years of teaching at "Mr. Jefferson's University," "virtually no one, from what I could tell, was changed by taking my classes." Edmundson contrasted his own sincere but uninspiring teaching with the teaching of Lears, who, fresh out of Harvard, found a way to connect with the students at Medford High. "I had been changed by Frank Lears, no doubt about it," Edmundson stated in his book, *Teacher: The One Who Made the Difference*. Edmundson wrote:

> In America today we treasure a long-standing myth of the great teacher: call it the Mr. Chips—Robin Williams myth, if you like. The teacher of this myth is infinitely kind, infinitely benevolent; he loves his students first and last, almost more than he loves himself. He memorizes their names on the first day. He tells amusing, self-deflating stories that make everyone feel at ease. He is a source of [wise] socially sanctioned advice: be kind, be good, be true. If he challenges anything, it is orthodoxies that are already dead in the world at large and have reared their heads in one last corner. Most of all he adores—and is adored—by students.

Edmundson challenged this rendition of the great teacher myth. One of his goals "is to remind readers that great teachers—and perhaps the great teachers who matter the most—do not always come in this all-benevolent mode." "The two great teachers we know in the West, Socrates and Jesus," Edmundson wrote, "were not without kindness, to be sure, but both had a sharp edge. Jesus asked people to do the impossible. He wanted them to give up all of their possessions and follow him, to change their lives utterly around. Socrates asked one badgering question after another about why his contemporaries behaved as they did. In the end, society could not tolerate either of these men, and did away with them."

From time to time, my family and I watch or re-watch movies centering on teachers and teaching, among them *Dead Poets Society*, *Mr. Holland's Opus*, and *A Beautiful Mind*. Each of the teachers in these three films was dismissed or resigned from their positions: John Keating or Robin Williams, for inciting students to question authority; Glenn Holland played by Richard Dreyfuss, whose position as a music teacher was eliminated, considered superfluous in the face of a budget crisis; and John Nash or Russell Crowe, who was simply terrible in the classroom anyway, because of increasingly erratic behavior brought on by debilitating schizophrenia.

Despite these setbacks, all three teachers made a difference, their teaching living on in the lives of their students. More than mere facilitators, a popular present-day moniker used to describe something other than real teaching, "My Captain" Keating and Mr. Holland and even John Nash, who won a Nobel Prize for Economics in 1994 over forty years after writing the theory for which the prize was won, made contributions based on pure inspiration. The purpose of Edmundson's book and this essay is, according to Edmundson, "to give teachers… a measure of encouragement at a time when many forces are trying to make them members of the service economy—people who provide *skills* [and] marketable knowledge…but not inspiration, not the wherewithal to change a life around."

Now, lo, those many years ago, through his inspiration and example, Hugh Ridenour "changed a life around," and for that I remain forever grateful.

Gift Exchange

From time to time, my students come to me bearing gifts, gifts that any history professor would appreciate. One student brought to me a copy of an old family letter, a description of a great-great-grandfather's experience in the trenches on the Western Front in World War I. Another student brought to me a Civil War bayonet, an artifact that I continue to show to my students each semester. Yet another student brought to me ration stamps from World War II. I cherish these gifts from students, and I share them with my other students year after year. Students, though, have showered me with gifts of another sort, gifts that characterize the real value of the teaching/learning experience.

I have been on the receiving end of many gifts throughout my life. What a gift my family has been to me! What joy they bring to me each day. My home has been a gift that has brought to me a sense of place and a haven of rest. Throughout my life, teachers—Evelyn, my son, my daughter, my parents, my brother—have taught me what it means to give and receive love. And it is the idea of gift exchange that has caused me to strive to teach better in my university classroom. After all, my calling as a teacher is a gift in itself.

I think of my own teachers: Mrs. Bradford in a seminary kindergarten; Mrs. Eubanks in first grade; Roy Pullam, in his first year of teaching, whose excitement for the profession was infectious; Mr. Harding, a victim of polio who inspired me in the seventh grade to learn history; Hugh Ridenour, who inspired me in high school to teach history; my teacher/coaches, Eddie Ford, Harlan Peden and Dick Campbell; Dr. C. Pat Taylor, Dr. Wardin and Dr. Chamlee in undergraduate school, all models of caring professionalism; and Dr. Garrett and Dr. Nelli in graduate school, who took a special interest in me and saw in me something that I did not see in myself. These teachers showered me with gifts, gifts of learning and inspiration. How I wish I could tell them thank-you in a way that would convey to them the depth of my gratitude.

What if I could go back and be a student again, listening to a story on the oval braided rug of my kindergarten classroom, running down the hill of the playground at Oaklawn Elementary School, walking the halls at Webster County High, soaking in the lectures in undergraduate school, or talking with my professors in corner offices in graduate school. How much more I could learn! In P. F. Kluge's *Alma Mater*, the author went back to teach at his old school, Kenyon College in Ohio. There he had lunch one day with a new colleague, an English professor, who opened the conversation with the observation that "this is my twenty-second year of teaching 'Tintern Abbey.'" The English professor bore the repetition by making each reading in each new class fresh, and by looking on teaching as a gift exchange. "I have this romantic idea of teaching as gift exchange," he told Kluge. "What matters is if I reach a few students at a level that transforms them and gets them to see the world in a different way. Gift exchange.

Sure, teaching is method and information, but it's something else, a gift, an enrichment of your life, a transformation that you spend the rest of your life discovering."

I still benefit from the gifts given to me by my old teachers. But now the gift exchange continues still. Now, I find myself unwrapping gifts from my students: new perspectives, the excitement of learning, the awe of discovery. Now, my students come to the classroom or to the office bearing gifts, gifts described by the Kenyon professor as "an enrichment of your life, a transformation that you spend the rest of your life discovering."

Classroom Demeanor

I entered into my calling to teach with trepidation, and I still get shaky when I walk into the classroom each day. Don't get me wrong. I love teaching. Each week I am able to enter a room filled with young scholars. I unlock the door to the Faculty Hall classroom—the door remains locked when not in use because of the high-tech computer equipment contained within—and unload my books and folders and artifacts on the adjustable desk at the front of the class.

The desk is complicated; one side is made up of an adjustable desktop that the professor, if astute enough, may position at just the right height to accommodate bifocaled eyes. I can just see myself one day, having failed to master the contraption, attempting to adjust the desktop to a suitable level, only to have the thing slam precipitously down on my finger. I will step backwards in pain, planting my right foot into the trash can located conveniently behind the desk. By the time I can extricate myself from the trash can, the stunned students will sit there transfixed, observing the intricate dance by the middle-aged wonder at the front of the room. Surely their tuition dollars had not paid for such a spectacle. All this was extra.

Well, although I have yet to present just such a spectacle to my students, I can surely imagine it. I know from my own real-life experience just how precarious a classroom performance can be. I walk into the class with my notes neatly arranged in a folder and my thoughts rigidly ordered in my mind. I notice when I walk into the room that a fresh packet of chalk is arranged in the tray under a freshly dusted chalkboard. Everything seems to be in order. I take up a pristine piece of dustless chalk and, with the first swipe at the board, break it into five or six shards. I can never get the hang of writing with chalk, yet another reason why I should become more technologically savvy.

Things could be worse. I could replay my first day of student teaching at Bellevue High School in Nashville. On that day I marched into the classroom all full of myself, not much older than the eighteen-year-olds I was to teach. Today, I know how much I need to learn about technology; my children teach me every day that their father is indeed a Neanderthal, or Luddite, or both. In 1978, I just knew that I was on the cutting edge of the use of technology.

After all, I had decided to abandon the chalkboard for the high-tech overhead projector. I placed an outline of the day's history lesson on a transparency on the overhead and then made notes with a non-permanent marker as I taught. With such a system I could remain facing the class, rather than risk a barrage of spit wads with my back turned toward the students.

On that first day of student teaching, however, I walked confidently into the classroom in coat and tie, only to find the overhead placed on the floor beneath the chalkboard. To place the thing in its proper place on the stand I bent down—and here was where I made my first teaching mistake on that first day of student teaching, a day that the real teacher, Ms. Fanning, had entrusted her world history class to me, a senior student teacher from Belmont University—I bent down, back end facing out to the class. That was when I made my second teaching mistake of the day.

The too-loud ripping noise as the seat of my too-tight pants ripped open caught my attention, I think, before even my students could fathom the moment. Of course, in due time they did fathom the moment to great hilarity. For the rest of that first day of student teaching, I wrapped my sports jacket around my waist and taught very carefully, making sure to face my audience all the while. Of course, I had the overhead projector in front of me and did not have to resort to the chalkboard behind. Such is the inauspicious beginning of a teaching career. So you can see how I entered into my calling to teach with trepidation, and you can see why I still get shaky when I walk into the classroom each day.

Office Hours

In the life of a college professor, a portion of each week is taken up in what is referred to in academe as "office hours." In our college at Murray State, the College of Humanities and Fine Arts, faculty members are required to keep ten office hours per week. Oh, you should know that we are working in our offices much longer than ten hours per week. If not in class, we are preparing for class: planning discussions; writing lecture outlines; grading essays, book reviews, or research papers; or reading books and articles for background and context.

We also prepare for and participate in those dreaded committee meetings: search committees, curriculum and planning committees, or just plain department meetings. And although useful results often come out of the "committee experience," these tedious meetings take up time and energy. Each faculty member is assigned to one of the eight residential colleges, so sometimes we find ourselves at one of the residence halls—in my case Regents College—talking with students or sponsoring a student meeting, or maybe in Winslow Cafeteria for a meal with members of the college. Sometimes, we drive out to an area elementary, middle, or high school to talk with the teachers or give presentations to students.

At Murray State, we once had "Roads Scholars" teams, and I was a member of the Webster County team, so that I was able to make visits to Webster County High School, my old school. All of my old teachers have retired, but now when I go back to Webster County, I can not only visit with students, but also with some of my old high school chums, who now teach there. I often meet students in my Murray State classes who are the sons and daughters of my old high school classmates, and sometimes it is hard to keep a straight face in the presence of these students because I remember the old hijinks I shared with their parents.

As faculty members, we also take to the road to present papers or attend conferences. At these conferences, we read papers that we have labored over, and we hope we will get constructive feedback so that we can strengthen the papers and eventually transform them into published articles and books.

Back at the university, I teach my classes, this semester American History classes and a section of the History of Kentucky. Sometimes, I feel let down, because the class did not go as well as I had imagined, as I had dreamed and hoped it would go. Sometimes, I walk out of the class invigorated by my students; their ideas have caused me to think of the subject in a new way, from a different point of view. Either way, I return to my office, loaded down with books and papers. I dump them on my desk and begin the familiar, laborious process of organizing my notes and thoughts for the next class.

Back in my office, I sit before a computer screen, trying to make progress on a research project. I stare out a north-facing window for inspiration. Sometimes I try to write during my official office hours, but that seldom happens. I sit at my desk, with my office door open. And then—I never know when—something miraculous happens. A student politely, sheepishly taps on the door, peers in, and asks if I am busy. I learned something from a former colleague; whenever someone darkened his door, he immediately dropped anything and everything he was doing, straightened up in his chair, and gave the student or colleague his undivided attention. So, now I try to drop anything and everything that I am doing, straighten up in my chair, and turn my attention to the reason I am here in the first place. I invite the student in, nod toward a chair in front of my desk, and then settle in for a delightful discussion about history, future career plans, or just life in general. Murray State students are invariably polite, even if they sometimes wonder, and even complain, about a lower than expected grade. Usually, however, these outside-of-class meetings provide insight for professors and clarity for students. Office hours are saved by these serendipitous encounters with students, and on any particular day, if only one student comes in to chat, I am always encouraged and blessed by the experience.

The Best Guide in England

For the last three weeks, students have lined up at my office door for advising conferences. They seek out guidance, and for better or worse, their assigned college advisor is to be the guide. It is that time of the semester when Murray State students can preregister for classes for the spring semester. Yes, we are already thinking of the spring semester! Before students are allowed to register, they must meet with an advisor to chart out their courses. By last count, I had some forty advisees.

It is always a daunting task to sit down with a student to chart out courses, to chart out a life. Some students know from the first day they step foot on our campus what they wish to major in. Others will change majors multiple times during their undergraduate careers. This is a crucial time in a student's life, a time of seeking out one's life calling. And here am I, trying to dish out advice to young, impressionable young people. Here am I, someone who is so often in the dark, trying to help students see the light.

I suppose one of the most frightening things to discover in life is that one's mentors are less than perfect, even flawed individuals. Oh, the horror of finding out that a teacher or coach or minister is, after all, human. We would like to think that those we have trusted to be our guides are everything that we have unreasonably built them up to be. But then, when the years have diminished that aura of goodness or greatness, that patina of invincibility, we come to find out that even our most trusted guides have struggled with the vagaries and meanness of life just like everyone else.

At the end of his tour of England, and at the end of his book, *In Search of England*, H. V. Morton encountered near Kenilworth, just northwest of London, "on one of those hot sleepy midsummer afternoons, when the heat throws a haze low over the meadows," the ruins of Kenilworth Castle. Upon his approach to "this rambling, chocolate-red ruin," Morton "met an elderly man in a black coat who was saying goodbye to a crowd of American trippers. He waved his stick in the air and stamped his feet on the ground, and instead of smiling at his vehemence, they appeared to treat him with considerable deference." Morton was to learn that the old man served as the official guide to the castle ruins, and that he deserved his reputation as "the best guide in England."

The old man collected another group of tourists, some of whom, "having no proof as yet of his virtues, laughed behind his back as he waved his dramatic stick." Soon, though, it became clear that this tour would be one like no other, for "this old man," according to Morton, had "soaked himself in Kenilworth." "He lives Kenilworth, he loves Kenilworth." At one point, Morton wrote, "from the mouth of this extraordinary guide flowed a magnificent oration. He built up the tattered walls of Kenilworth for us, [and] he took us through the Middle Ages....There was not a sound now from his flock." He seemed to embody the ruins; he seemed "to our astonished eyes," Morton recalled, "to be the spirit of the place."

According to Morton, "it had been a remarkable *tour de force*. He left us rather bewildered, rather like children when the story had been told." For in one brief hour's tour, the guide had taught the group "about the long pageant of history that is England, the evil and the good that have marched side by side down the centuries." "England!" he finally cried out to the tourists. "You now stand in the heart of England. Are you proud of her, of your share in her?…I know that I am." What a performance! What a guide!

After the performance, Morton followed the guide back to the gate. There he was, already waving his stick at the next group preparing to take the tour. Morton complimented the elderly guide "on the dramatic genius of his address." "Ah," the old man said as he peered out at Morton. And it was only then that Morton saw that the guide was partially blind. "I am glad that you feel like that. I was an actor once…but"—and "here he pointed to his eyes"—"my career ended before it began!" Morton then realized that "the best guide in England" was all but blind, and that it was his failing sight that allowed others to see so well.

Speaking Anxiety

Here I sit. Sweating palms. Knees a-tremble. Staring out my office window, trying to collect my thoughts. In thirty minutes I will walk down a flight of stairs to my Faculty Hall classroom to teach two back-to-back sections of American History. Although I have been planning and organizing and rewriting notes for days, I try to reserve the thirty minutes before each class to sweat, to tremble, and to collect my thoughts.

This speaking anxiety has remained a constant in my life for over twenty-five years of classroom teaching. I am always especially anxious the first day of class each semester, and for some reason the last class session of each semester, but I go through the same routine, I experience the same sense of anxiety, each time I step into a classroom. Once the class begins, I eventually calm down, but as I walk through that door to face a classroom full of eager (or not so eager) students, I always enter the class a little shaky.

I don't think many of my colleagues in the Department of History experience this speaking anxiety. In my department at the university, Dr. Kathy Callahan, Dr. Bill Mulligan, Dr. Charlotte Beahan, Dr. Zack Heern, Dr. Brian Clardy, Dr. Bill Schell, Professor Ted Franklin Belue, Professor Taufiq Rashid, Dr. Terry Strieter, Dr. James Humphreys, Dr. David Pizzo, Dr. Aaron Irvin, and Dr. Marjorie Hilton are inspirations to me, teachers who know how to interest and inspire students. They are each accomplished speakers who make it look so easy.

And here I sit. Sweating palms. Knees a-tremble. Staring out my office window, trying to collect my thoughts. This is nothing new for me. When I played basketball in middle school, high school, and college, I became sick in the locker room before each game, literally sick, as I worked myself into a frenzy before taking the floor for warm-ups. Now, my anxiety has been transferred from a hardwood court to a chair-lined classroom.

As a professor, from time to time I am also asked to speak at history conferences or to groups of teachers or to various civic groups. Teaching my students is one thing, but speaking to my colleagues and peers raises the anxiety meter to new heights. At my church, I teach a large Sunday school class, and I go through the same routine (thirty minutes of sweating, trembling, and collecting my thoughts) at home each Sunday morning.

And this month, I am conducting Wednesday night prayer meetings at my church. This involves planning a thirty-minute devotional, a Bible study, each Wednesday night. For these devotionals, I have found that my thirty-minute exercise of sweating, trembling, and collecting my thoughts has stretched through the whole of Wednesday afternoons and evenings. Again, it is one thing to teach 18- and 19-year-old students, and it is another thing to speak to colleagues and teachers and peers, but it is something altogether more daunting to speak to my brothers and sisters in church. I look out at the kindly faces assembled in the chapel, a sea of saints, who have taught me through their words and deeds so much about the mysteries of faith. And I sweat, I tremble, and I try to collect my thoughts.

I don't think it will ever be different with me. As long as I teach and speak before an audience of any size, I will experience speaking anxiety. Perhaps, if I ever walk into a classroom or conference room or church chapel calm and collected, I will know then that it is time to retire.

God's Message to the World

We have a copy of the letter in the Bolin family archives. I think a distant aunt or cousin has the original. I cannot remember when I first saw the letter, but now a framed copy of it hangs on my History Department office wall. Before going out the door to class, I always glance at the letter for the purpose of inspiration, to inspire me to value the worth of each one of my students, to inspire me to care for them.

The letter was written on April 10, 1893, to my grandfather, Wesley Lafayette Bolin, a student at Clinton College in Hickman County in far western Kentucky. Founded in 1873 as an academy for young women, Clinton College graduates often found their way to Wellesley. Later, the institution became coeducational, but, with declining enrollments, it closed in 1915. In 1893, however, Clinton College still flourished, and Amanda Melvina Hicks, a cousin of Abraham Lincoln, both taught there and served as the college president, a remarkable achievement for a woman at a denominational college in far western Kentucky in the 1890s. Hicks served as president of Clinton College from 1880 to 1894.

Then in the spring of 1893, President Hicks wrote this letter to my grandfather. Although she sent the letter to my grandfather, the missive really concerned my great-uncle Eugene, also a student at Clinton College and the "character" of the Bolin family. I grew up listening to stories my father would tell about his "uncle Gene," and despite his uncle's shenanigans, my father, another Wesley, had a twin brother named Eugene after his uncle Gene. So, my great-uncle Gene must have had some qualities worthy of emulation. Anyway, Amanda M. Hicks seemed to be especially concerned about the prospects of one Eugene Bolin. Read the letter, and see for yourself:

> Clinton College, Apr. 10. [18]93
>
> Mr. Wesley Bolin—
>
> My dear pupil.
>
> I am very anxious that Eugene should hear the lecture tonight. The subject is "God's Message to the World." It may do Eugene a great deal of good to hear it. He told me he would stay at home and that you were coming. If you can so arrange that he can come I shall be much pleased even if <u>*you*</u> have to stay at home. I say this because I am so much concerned about his soul.
>
> Your friend and teacher
> Amanda M. Hicks

A great deal of mystery surrounds this letter. I never found out if my great-uncle Gene made it to the lecture that evening. And I never knew what the speaker said in his lecture, "God's Message to the World." There is a great deal that I do not know.

I do know, however, that here was a teacher who cared so much for one of her students that she took the time to write to the student's brother—my grandfather—asking him to make a sacrifice for the sake of his brother. In short, the teacher wanted young Eugene to come to the lecture because she was "so much concerned about his soul."

I don't know if Amanda Hicks inspired Eugene to come to the lecture, or to attend to his schooling or his soul, but I do know that she inspires me today. She inspires me to care for my students more, to recognize in them seeds of worth and even greatness.

Mr. Walker, Mr. Harding, and My Friend Eddie

When I think back to the years of my adolescence in Dixon, Kentucky, there are so many things to be thankful for; a loving family, neighborly neighbors, and close friends all made my Dixon days in Webster County idyllic. At least that is the way I choose to remember them. One fall day—it could have been a half-century ago—I worked the front register for Dad at Bolin's Drugstore. I balanced on the ledge behind the counter by the Greyhound Bus ticket box. The cash register there at the front of the store was smaller and less elaborate than the one at the back by the prescription counter. The back register had a crank on the side, and I loved to watch our father ring up a prescription. He jabbed down the buttons for the proper amount of dollars and cents and then with a flourish turned the crank on the side to ring up the sale. He always turned the lever just two times; that's all it took. A bell clanged, and he tore off the paper ticket all in one smooth motion.

The front register, minus the crank, also rang up the sale and produced a paper ticket that I tore off as well, just not quite as smoothly. I read a comic book and felt slightly irritated when a customer interrupted me to buy a candy bar or a bottle of perfume. On this day, I kept an eye on the famous yet notorious Cass Walker. A retired lawyer and, I think, a judge, Mr. Walker now lived in the shabby apartment directly above the drugstore. Everyone said he was a millionaire, but he wore the same three-piece suit every day and walked up and down Main Street looking for cigar butts on the sidewalk. At least one, maybe two times, a day he came into the drugstore to steal candy or ice cream. He tucked the prize deftly beneath his vest and brazenly walked out the front door.

My father always followed him out and reminded him that he hadn't paid. He would come back in, fumble around his vest pockets for change, and grudgingly lay down just the right number of coins on the counter. On this day, I watched Mr. Walker carefully. His suit was unusually soiled. He mumbled a greeting and headed for the ice cream box, taking an ice cream sandwich from the case. He walked directly in front of the register where I sat and out the front door. I admired him so much for his gall. He walked on down the street with his head down so as not to miss a cigar butt or coin. I watched him amble down the street toward the hardware store. I decided Mr. Cass Walker would have a free ice cream sandwich that day.

I resumed my reading of Richie Rich, only to be disturbed again, this time by a member of the "courthouse gang," one of the regular courthouse bench warmers. I loved these men. The courthouse benches on each corner of the square were occupied each day by the same dear fellows. Mr. Frazier and his son, Eddie, always sat on the south corner, while another group whittled sticks and chewed tobacco on the north side.

Eddie was in my grade at school. Every day in the seventh grade, Mr. Harding, my Kentucky History teacher, began class with the same routine. Mr. Harding had suffered from polio and now walked with two canes. The whole class was already seated when Mr. Harding appeared at the door, where he paused dramatically. Then he would pantomime ringing up Eddie on the telephone. He said in a loud voice, "Helloooo, Eddie." Eddie would pick up an imaginary phone in the back of the classroom where he sat and answered back, "Helloooo." "How are you today, Eddie." "Oh, just fine," Eddie said. "Eddie; why don't you come on up to the board." "Okay," Eddie said. He got up from his desk and walked to the front of the classroom.

He didn't have to be told to pick up a piece of chalk. Mr. Harding picked up another stump of chalk and illustrated how to draw a square on the board. "Now, you try it," Mr. Harding said. Eddie took his chalk and began drawing large circles on the board. "Now, Eddie," Mr. Harding pleaded, "let's draw a square, not circles." He took Eddie's hand and traced the outline of a square on the board. "Now, you do it." Eddie drew more large circles on the board. "All right, Eddie; you can go back home now." Eddie smiled and walked back down the aisle to his desk. Even though Mr. Harding repeated the routine day after day,

Eddie never drew a square. Never. Always circles. He drew fine circles though. And he loved to talk on an imaginary telephone.

Now I teach Kentucky History each spring semester to students at Murray State University. I remember how much excitement Mr. Harding had for Kentucky History, and I remember how he caused me to love the history of my state. But I remember something else too. I remember how he took time each day, at the beginning of every class, for Eddie. I remember how he made Eddie feel special. And in the process, he made me feel special too.

End of Semester Blues

I've got those lowdown, guilt-ridden, desperate-feeling, anxiety-inducing, essay-grading, committee-meeting, desk-unloading, library-hopping, coffee-shop-haunting, student-commiserating, e-mail-reading, excuse-making, steamrolling (thank-you James Taylor), mind-blowing, professor-rating, no-time-left, what-have-I-done?, end-of-semester blues. The end of a semester at any college or university is grist for the blues, although I have failed to find purely academic themes in the lyrics of Bessie Smith or Muddy Waters or Robert Johnson or B. B. King. The end of a semester is made for the blues.

I hear the blues from my students toward the end of every semester: When can I take that makeup test? Will you still accept my book review? Will you please read over my book review again? Sorry about missing class; did we do anything? Will you accept my doctor's excuse? Can I come by your office to talk about my grades? I have three finals on the same day; can I take yours on a different day? Will the final exam be comprehensive? Will you drop my lowest grade? Will this be covered on the final? Will that be covered on the final? Can I still drop this class? Will there be any true/false on the final? Will there be multiple choice on the final? Please no essays on the final! Do you give extra credit? Will there be a review sheet for the final? Will we review in class for the final? Can you have an evening review session for the final? Can you read over my class notes? Do you have any suggestions about how to study for the final? Do you give makeups? Why not? Why? How? When? Where?

End-of-semester questions from students are quotidian. Equally repetitive and exhaustive are the questions and concerns of professors: I am so far behind in all of my classes. Can I catch up this last week of class? What must I include in this last class session? What can I leave out? Is this committee meeting really necessary? Should I extend my office hours? Can I squeeze in a lunch with Evelyn today? Can Evelyn squeeze in a lunch with me? How will I find time to grade all of these research reports? When can I write out my final exams? Do I include this on the final? Do I include that on the final? Oh, I've got to make out a review sheet. Will I include possible essay questions on the review sheet? I've got to respond to all of those e-mails. I must block out time to speed grade all of those final exams. When can I tally up the grades? When are grades due in the Registration Office at Sparks Hall? When will I put together the syllabi for my summer courses? How can I find time to write? Is there time for a cup of coffee before the next class? How? When? Where? Why not? Why?

Students and professors alike ask endless questions at the end of each semester. Students and professors alike sing the blues. There always seems to be too little time at the end of any academic term to do justice to everything that justice needs to be done to. So here's to the end of the semester, a time of endings and new beginnings. But for now…I've got those lowdown, guilt-ridden, desperate-feeling, anxiety-inducing, essay-grading, committee-meeting, desk-unloading, library-hopping, coffee-shop-haunting, student-commiserating, e-mail-reading, excuse-making, steamrolling (thank-you James Taylor), mind-blowing, professor-rating, no-time-left, what-have-I-done?, end-of-semester blues.

Part Five

Learning

"There are times when the haunted waters of the past lift us up and inspire us to wade on, somehow buoyed by what has already been endured."

Top: Dr. Richard O. Davies, Evelyn and Duane Bolin at the Dr. James W. Hammack, Jr. Banquet, 2014. Center: Cammie Jo seeing Wesley and Daddy off to school in Walnut Ridge, Arkansas, 1997. Bottom: View of the Quad from the 6th Floor of Faculty Hall, Murray State University.

A Poem for the New Semester

For years now, the first day of class for any of my university history courses has been given over to the reading of a poem. In fact, the first thing that we do as a class and the last thing that we do as a class involve the analysis of a poem. On the first day of the semester, I enjoy watching the students' quizzical glances to friends in the next row and frantic consultations of class schedules to make sure they are not in an English Department class as we put off the syllabus for a time to consider the lines of an Ella Wheeler Wilcox poem instead.

I first heard the poem years ago at, of all places, a high school basketball camp in western Kentucky. I remember that Tom McMillan, a sensational left-handed forward for the University of Maryland and our guest instructor for the day, talked more about life than how to perfect a jump shot or block out effectively. He talked about how we had a responsibility to make something of our lives, and he urged us to live lives of service. There I sat—a fifteen-year-old freshman—perched on the first row of the wooden bleachers, drinking it all in. McMillan made a deep, profound impression on me, and it has not surprised me that he went on to live a life of service as a member of the US House of Representatives after his basketball days were over. Here is the poem that he recited in that stifling gymnasium in Madisonville, Kentucky in July, 1970:

> One ship drives east, the other drives west
> With the selfsame winds that blow.
> 'Tis the set of the sails
> And not the gales
> Which tells us the way to go.
> Like the winds of the sea are the ways of fate,
> As we voyage along through life:
> 'Tis the set of a soul
> That decides its goal,
> And not the calm or the strife.

I committed the poem to memory, and with my first college teaching job, I recited it to my students on the first day of class. A creature of habit, I have continued the practice ever since. We analyze the poem. What hidden themes, themes that we will encounter in the course, can we find in the lines of the poem? Students are usually very astute, and they suggest, for example, in an American history course, that ships are used for warfare, and that surely we will discuss various wars in American history. Someone else chimes in that ships are also used for commerce and that we will discuss the ebb and flow of the American economy in the course. Yet another student states that the ship sailing west suggests the significance of westward expansion in American history. We go on, playing with these themes and topics, and before long students have a pretty good grasp of what the course is all about.

Then, after a time, I ask the students to personalize the poem. What does the poem have to say to you as a student in this course? What does it have to say to you as a person? What motivates you? What particular challenges do you face? What do you want out of life? After all, "'Tis the set of a soul that decides its goal, and not the calm or the strife."

So, we went through the ritual yet again in the first class session of each of my courses this semester. The poem never becomes stale, at least for me. Of course, I recite the poem for selfish reasons too. It serves as a useful tool to keep me on course, to help me remember that while I most assuredly teach the discipline and the subjects of history, I teach students as well.

Syllabi and Life

Again this semester I want to consider a sampling of activities engaged in by students and teachers in and out of the classroom. You will observe that many of these everyday activities are very ordinary and perhaps should not merit the space of this essay, but, nonetheless, these are activities in which I am involved, and, for better or worse, I can only write about those things that I know. Please allow me these moments of reflection about the mundane affairs in the life of a teacher.

One of my tasks as a teacher, a task that I have recently performed, is the preparation of a syllabus for each of my classes. This is a job that I always undertake with a measure of excitement. I begin this task soon after the completion of each semester, when the successes and failures of a term of study are fresh on my mind. Perhaps there is something I can change in the syllabus for the next semester that will keep me from repeating the mistakes of the past.

A syllabus is a document, handed out to students in the first class session, which explains the course and defines the parameters of the course for students and professor alike. I never encountered a syllabus (at least I don't remember seeing one) until I was a freshman at Belmont University, but now I notice that our son in high school and our daughter in middle school have been given a syllabus for each of their courses.

The syllabus includes the course number, title, and catalog description. It also includes statements about the purpose of the course, a listing of course objectives, identification of the required textbooks and outside readings, a description of the writing component of the course, all testing and grading procedures, the academic honesty policy, the attendance policy, and finally a class-by-class schedule of readings and discussion topics. Every class session is accounted for. The class schedule helps the student (and the professor) prepare for each class session. Hopefully, students (and the professor) will have digested the readings for that day and will be willing and even eager to contribute to the class discussion.

Although there are sometimes unavoidable digressions, it always amazes me how we are able to adhere so closely to the class schedule of the syllabus. By the end of the term we will, hopefully, accomplish what the syllabus has outlined. And, again hopefully, each student will fulfill the requirements for the course, as the syllabus has dictated. At the end of each semester, we wrap up the course in a neat package, I deliver the grades to the Registration Office in Sparks Hall, and then put together a syllabus for the next semester, to start the process all over again. With each new syllabus, there is always the anticipation of success, the hope that students will be furthered along in their academic journeys, that real learning and real progress will be made.

I have learned that life is not like a syllabus. Life does not come prearranged or prepackaged. As much as we try to plan ahead, it is impossible to put together a "life schedule" like a class schedule in a course syllabus. The course of life is much too complicated. Of course, a college class always offers up many surprises, pleasant and unpleasant. But life itself is all too messy. So much of life, it seems to me, is out of our hands. Life often throws us a curve, or as the theologian and writer Frederick Buechner put it, "Life works us all over before it's all through." In life, as in a college course, however, there is always the hope of success, that we will be able to complete the course requirements in good order and in good fashion. The apostle Paul said it best in a letter to his friend Timothy. At the end of his life syllabus, he said, "I have fought the good fight, I have finished the race, I have kept the faith."

Spectators and Participators

It is a teacher's delight when students actively participate in a class. Students participate by reading—actually reading—assigned texts, by keeping up with writing assignments, and by chiming in during class discussions. Oh, the joy of a dynamic class session when students are really engaged, when they actively participate in the learning process. At such times, real learning takes place.

Garrison Keillor told the story of how the residents of Lake Wobegon, Minnesota, celebrated Flag Day in a unique way. You are familiar with Lake Wobegon, I hope, where "all the women are strong, all the men are good looking, and all the children are above average." Keillor's Lake Wobegon is filled with unforgettable characters and with everyday happenings that are just as unforgettable. I remember the story of this one particular Flag Day when the town fathers got together and decided to order red, white, and blue baseball caps, just the right number for the few hundreds of Lake Wobegon citizens. Everyone had a cap. The idea was to create, when viewed from above, a human American flag on Main Street. You know, red caps for the red stripes in the flag, white caps for the white stripes and stars, and blue caps for the blue background.

The cap orders were made, and on that memorable Flag Day, all of Lake Wobegon—women, men, children—came out to participate in the big event. It took an hour or two to get the folks organized. Just the right number of red, white, and blue caps were passed out, and organizers lined everyone up. On a given signal, Lake Wobegoneans placed the caps on bald, gray, brown, black, red, and blond heads. And there they were. They had created, in all its glory, a human American flag.

What a sight! They stood there at attention, all grinning, eyes shifting from side to side. But then the grins turned quizzical. There they stood, but one by one, they began to realize that because everyone in Lake Wobegon made up part of the flag, no one was there to see the thing. Murmuring residents soon produced a plan. One or two at a time would leave the human flag, walk up the steps of the courthouse and onto the roof, so as to view the masterpiece. And so they began. The slow procession away from the flag continued, up the courthouse stairs, out onto the roof for an admiring perusal of the scene below, and then the slow climb back down.

But the scene below on Main Street began to change; the vision of the flag blurred. As the minutes and indeed the hours passed, the human American flag became a sitting flag and a kneeling flag. Suddenly, exhausted and frustrated, one whole corner of the flag broke away in a sprint to try to get a glimpse of the spectacle before it fell apart completely.

When that happened, of course, the flag disintegrated. Keillor explained that the flag disintegrated, fell apart, when Lake Wobegon's residents stopped being participants, and, instead, became mere spectators. As mere spectators, the flag disintegrated before their eyes.

I haven't had a class disintegrate completely yet, but I do know that the teaching/learning endeavor is far less successful when my students choose to be mere spectators rather than active participants. Only when they participate fully do they really learn. And only then is the class a success.

A River Runs Through It

It is already mid-September and the semester at the university is into its fifth week. I have given and graded several quizzes, and students in my American History classes have read about and discussed America's beginnings: the period before Columbus, the European Age of Discovery, the Colonial Period, and the American Revolution. The first major examination is looming.

In my Teaching History class, students have prepared oral and written reports, and next week we will discuss *The Elements of Teaching*, a book written by James M. Banner, Jr. and Harold C. Cannon about characteristics or "elements" displayed by teachers: learning, authority, ethics, order, imagination, compassion, patience, character, and pleasure. In my Freshman Transitions class, eager first-year students continue the process of adjusting to college life: classes, dorm life, cafeteria food, and, oh yes, classes.

Orienting oneself into any new environment is at once challenging and exasperating. Perhaps it's not too early (or late) to begin thinking about a more settling and peaceful activity to calm our nerves from the trials and tribulations of a hectic semester at Murray State. I speak of fishing, of course, something that I know little about, except for what I have read and experienced from my friend, the writer Gary Garth, an outdoors columnist for the *Louisville Courier-Journal* and other publications. I have also been instructed by a beautifully crafted book about woods and waters, a book that was made into a motion picture.

Norman Maclean did not write the novella, *A River Runs Through It*, or any of his other stories, until he was in his seventies. The book, nominated for a Pulitzer Prize, is about history and the tragedies and hurts inevitable in the passage of time. Two brothers, both fishermen because of their minister/father's love for angling, grew up to take decidedly different directions in life. Both of the sons became writers, but the younger of the two, the brawling, drinking, freedom-loving, prodigal son, made fly-fishing into an art form before dying young.

"In our family," Maclean wrote in the voice of the older brother, "there was no clear line between religion and fly fishing. We lived at the junction of great trout rivers in western Montana, and our father was a Presbyterian minister and a fly fisherman who tied his own flies and taught others. He told us about Christ's disciples being fishermen, and we were left to assume, as my brother and I did, that all first-class fishermen on the Sea of Galilee were fly fishermen, and that John, the favorite, was a dry-fly fisherman."

I love this book, not because of fly fishing, although I have a secret dream—well, it's not a secret anymore—to wade out into the waters of Casey Creek in Trigg County, an exotic bamboo fly rod in hand, casting out in perfect rhythm a fly tied with my own expert hands. I have friends that have done that very thing, but I can only dream, and I know that even if I waded out into Casey Creek I would not and should not be successful, for as one of the sons stated in *A River Runs Through It*, "If our father had had his say, nobody who did not know how to fish would be allowed to disgrace a fish by catching him." Oh well, I can still dream.

And I can still learn from the eloquent writing in this elegant book. In the closing scene, Maclean writes these achingly beautiful lines: "Eventually, all things merge into one, and a river runs through it. The river was cut by the world's great flood and runs over rocks from the basement of time. On some of the rocks are timeless raindrops. Under the rocks are the words, and some of the words are theirs. I am haunted by waters."

I too am haunted by the waters of the past. Sometimes the past weighs us down, in the sense that the late great southern historian C. Vann Woodward referred to as "the burden of history." Surely, at times we must seek to overcome the past, to throw off the burden of history. But then, there are times when the haunted waters of the past lift us up and inspire us to wade on, somehow buoyed by what has already been endured.

Spring Break

I write these words with the prospect of an academic spring break ahead, and as you read this essay, students, faculty, and administrators are absorbed in the middle of a week when the usual schedule of classes, office hours, committee meetings, and campus activities are temporarily suspended. This is not to say that work is suspended, because spring break week often provides needed time and freedom for faculty members and administrators, at least, to play catch up, to concentrate on overdue projects or looming deadlines.

Many students, like professors, chairs, deans, vice presidents, and the president, spend the week in serious work. Not all students head for the beaches in Florida. Some students tend to take off early, stretching spring break week to a week-and-a-half or two. I maliciously scheduled a major examination last Thursday, just before spring break, to keep my American History students on campus a while longer, but some professors postponed examinations until after the break.

Imagine all those students at Daytona Beach, brushing sand from the pages of biology and calculus textbooks, taking a few minutes from their ruminations every two hours or so to frolic in the surf! Well… maybe not, but diligent students will nonetheless be greeted back on campus with exams, quizzes, and research paper deadlines.

Students in my History of Kentucky class have told me that they plan to conduct research on Kentucky county reports over the break. There they are, whiling away hours in museums, libraries, and archives. Other students are spending spring break away from studies and parties, choosing instead to serve on campus ministries' mission trips or other volunteering activities. Still others have gone back home to spend time with families and old high school friends.

For me, spring break week is a mixed affair. Our teenage children enjoy only a minibreak, attending school on Monday and Tuesday, with Wednesday, Thursday, and Friday off. Cammie Jo has track practice even on her days away from class, and Wesley is headed today to Washington, DC, on a band trip where he and other students and teachers will visit the Holocaust Museum, the Smithsonian, and all the memorials.

I always look forward to spring break with giddy delight, a week away from the usual routine of classes and committee work. I realize now, though, that my determination to schedule examinations the last class session before spring break has backfired, requiring me to grade the things during this week of supposed peace and tranquility. And then there are those two stacks of book reviews hanging over my head.

Spring break fails to alleviate these burdens of the teaching trade. Instead, these anxieties still remain, and I peck away at the grading burden in the mornings at the coffee shop or in the afternoons at home in my study. After all, "no man ever sank under the burden of the day," wrote George MacDonald. "It is when tomorrow's burden is added to the burden of today, that the weight is more than a man can bear."

Oh, there is one other problem keeping me from the successful completion of my burden of work. One's children can be brutally honest—can't they?—especially with their parents. Last Sunday, I remarked to my son, rather innocently, that all week I had experienced trouble in preparing my Sunday school lesson. I try to teach a large, vibrant group of the faithful at my church, and now just a few minutes before heading out the door for the fellowship hall where the class meets each Sunday morning, I simply mentioned to Wesley that "the lesson had just not come together" that week. (I think that's the way I put it.) Wesley shot back immediately, "Daddy, there is only one reason for that." "And what is that, Wesley," I asked. "March Madness!" he replied.

Writing Bloopers

Kids say the darnedest things. And, sometimes, students write the darnedest things. An essay response is required on every examination that I give in my history classes at Murray State. Students often produce well-reasoned, well-organized, and well-written essays within a fixed block of time, one hour and fifteen minutes for a Tuesday/Thursday class. This is no small achievement.

From time to time, however, the pressure of the clock and a lack of preparation cause students to state ideas with less clarity. Sometimes, faulty sentence structure, poor word choice, and fuzzy thinking (all problems for which I have been guilty) produce sentences that I wince at and savor all at once, sentences that I am quick to include in a growing "student blooper" file.

Bloopers are not limited to student essays, of course. Sunday school provides a venue for children to utter their own interpretations of the Bible. A recent e-mail I received revealed a few "Bible Facts from Kids." One young Bible scholar assures us that "Lot's wife was a pillar of salt by day but a ball of fire at night." Another stated confidently, "Solomon, one of David's sons, had 300 wives and 700 porcupines." Yet another offered one concept of biblical marriage. "Christians should have only one wife," the youngster said, before quickly adding, "This is called monotony."

Church bulletins sometimes reveal less-than-enduring truths. One bulletin announced, "Thursday at 5:00 p.m. there will be a meeting of the Little Mothers' Club. All those wishing to become little mothers, please meet with the minister in his study." Another bulletin proclaimed, "This afternoon there will be a meeting in the south and north ends of the church. Children will be baptized at both ends." In one announcement for a church charity function, it was revealed that "the ladies of the church have cast off clothing of every kind and they may be seen in the church basement on Friday afternoon."

My favorite bloopers come in the written offerings of history students. I grade essays for style as well as content, and sometimes students resent such meddling. On one of my course evaluations, one student moaned (and I quote directly): "This is a History class not an English class I do not feel me English down fall should make me loose points. Even English class was give more than 5 min. after answering 40 problems to write 3 pages with no gram. & spelling mistakes." Oh well.

In an examination essay, one of my very own students stated that "the biggest gold rush in the 1880's was the 1849 gold rush." My students are not the only culprits, however. Richard Lederer, a teacher in Concord, New Hampshire, is the editor of *Anguished English*, a book in which he compiled some favorite bloopers from his students at St. Paul's School.

One of Mr. Lederer's students wrote, "Ancient Egypt was inhabited my mummies, and they all wrote in hydraulics. They lived in the Sarah Dessert and traveled by Camelot." In a unit on ancient Greece, a student revealed, "Socrates was a famous Greek teacher who went around giving people advice. They killed him. Socrates died from an overdose of wedlock. After his death, his career suffered a dramatic decline."

In American History, one student elaborated on the early years of Abraham Lincoln. "Lincoln's mother died in infancy," the student wrote, "and he was born in a log cabin which he built with his own hands." My favorite blooper came from the pen of a student contemplating the achievement of Sir Francis Drake when the explorer circumnavigated the globe. Perhaps the student was confused when he or she wrote, "Sir Francis Drake circumcised the world with a hundred foot clipper." Oh me.

Classically Trained

We often hear that accomplished musicians or painters are classically trained. This gives these artists a certain stamp of approval that they have received the very best preparation for what they have come to be. Sometimes the term is used when an artist has veered from the path for which they have been "classically trained."

Perhaps, for example, the artist has become a popular musician or joined a rock band. A newspaper reporter will write that "despite being classically trained," the charismatic rock star decided to use his or her talents for other rewards. A staid audience at a performance of a symphony orchestra simply did not satisfy in the way that thousands of screaming, sweating fans could feed the ego of one seeking fame and fortune. Still, the fact that the performer was "classically trained" somehow gave chops to the musician. That shirtless bad boy could not just scream and prance around a stage. He was "classically trained."

To be classically trained meant that one had studied with the best, with a master. That student had had the very best instruction at that particular craft, either at college, university, or in private lessons. Cezanne learning from Pissarro. Yo Yo Ma at Harvard in a master class with Rostropovich. Ben Sollee in Kentucky at the University of Louisville.

Or…Duane Bolin as a teenager in Webster County, Kentucky, in the 1970s. Folks, let me tell you. I was classically trained in so many different ways, and I am so, so grateful. Let me tell you exactly what I mean.

In Dixon, Kentucky, I was classically trained in the art of Kentucky county politics. In Dixon, Duane Clark lived across the street from me. We traded baseball cards on our front porch on long summer afternoons, and when we did not trade baseball cards, he taught me how to play basketball, the signature sport of Kentucky. Duane's father, C. B. Clark, was the Webster County sheriff. Moving to Kentucky from Texas by way of Tennessee, I thought it odd that, as Kentuckians, we paid our local taxes to the county sheriff, but, sure enough, we did.

C. B. Clark would later become the Webster County judge-executive, a position he would be elected to for four terms before he died tragically in 1992 in an automobile accident when he swerved to avoid a backhoe partially blocking highway 132. "It's a shock to the entire community," said Jim Townsend, a Webster County magistrate who would later follow Clark as county judge. "The people of that county have lost a great leader," said Henderson mayor Bill Newman. Indeed they had.

I just remember C. B. Clark as Duane's and Teresa's father and Mrs. Melba's husband, and the kind man who always smiled at me and wished me well. I knew from my conversations with him how much he loved his family, his wife, his son, his daughter. I also knew that he was on my side, and with Clarks in our family tree, my father always thought we were related to the Dixon branch. I also remember C. B. Clark as the man who gave me a classical education in Kentucky county politics, a subject I teach every year in my university course, History of Kentucky.

Folks, I have been classically trained in Kentucky history and Kentucky politics, especially of the local variety. I know all of the nuances, all of the variations. I have been the recipient of its political, unmerited good graces, and I have been on the other end as well. I have seen Kentucky politics as one of the "ins" and I have experienced it as one of the "outs." In short, I have been "classically trained" in the art of Kentucky politics.

In addition to this personal, up-close experience, I studied Kentucky history in the seventh grade with Roy Harding, I gained a great education in many aspects of Kentucky history in high school with my high school mentor, Hugh Ridenour, and then in graduate school at the University of Kentucky, I studied with the master historian of Kentucky counties, Dr. Robert Ireland (see his classic, *Little Kingdoms*), and the director of my dissertation that became my first book on Kentucky politics, Dr. Humbert Nelli. Folks, I have been classically trained.

Do I want, like my son, Wesley Bolin, to be a part of it all? OH NO! Do I want to continue to observe it and teach it? Oh yes. It is an honor, a privilege. For after all, I have been classically trained.

Integrating the Curriculum

My high school history teacher remembers an assignment he gave in one of his history classes. He wanted to incorporate or integrate geography into his history class to show how intimately related the two disciplines are. He gave each of his students a blank sheet of paper, and he asked them to draw a map of the route from the school to home. Just a simple assignment.

The students got to work, and the teacher noticed that one student, his problem child, sat at the back of the class with his head on his desk, his usual pose. The teacher walked to the back of the classroom, tapped the student on the shoulder, and asked him why he was not at work on the assignment. The teacher will not soon forget the student's reply. "I don't know the route," the student responded. "I ride the bus."

The fact that the student literally had no idea of the route home convinced the teacher that he needed to include more geography in his history classes. I too need to work to integrate the curriculum. I need to include not just history, but geography, political science, economics, sociology, music, literature, and art in each of my classes. Students always benefit when they see the big picture, how everything is tied together.

R. F. Delderfield's *To Serve Them All My Days* is one of my favorite novels about teaching. The narrator of the novel described the teacher at a private boarding school as one who had no qualms about integrating the curriculum: "He was still inclined to be a drifter in class and the boys knew it, and took shameless advantage of it, but that didn't bother him overmuch. He had never seen any specific subject as water-tight, so that his English had often spilled over into history, geography and even divinity, and sometimes, when the bell sounded, he would again remind himself he had learned more than he had imparted."

The best course that I had in undergraduate school at Belmont University was a course called The Western World. It was good for six hours of credit, and the class met every day of the week, Monday through Friday. On Mondays and Tuesdays, Dr. Albert Wardin, a history professor, would come in to lecture on some period or topic in Western civilization. On Wednesdays and Thursdays, Dr. Virginia Chaney, a literature professor, would discuss with us the literature of the period or topic that had been discussed on Monday and Tuesday. Then, on Friday, Professor Wardin and Professor Chaney would come into the classroom together to team-teach the session. Those sessions were always my favorite, because they would somehow weave the history and the literature together to show how the one informed the other.

Based on the examples of Hugh Ridenour in high school and Professors Wardin and Chaney in college, I have tried to incorporate as many different disciplines as possible in my own classes. I have especially enjoyed the analysis of art and music with my students. In my History of Kentucky course, students read a Kentucky novel to introduce them to the rich literary heritage of the state. In each class period, students hear Kentucky music, written or performed by Kentuckians, to learn about the equally rich musical heritage of the commonwealth. We analyze campaign songs in my American History survey courses. I use maps extensively in all of my classes. How can you teach history without maps? We study politics, and we study economics, too, even though I really know very little about economics.

I agree with Delderfield's protagonist in *To Serve Them All My Days*. At the end of class, at least at the end of a good class, I remind myself that I have learned more than I have imparted.

The Last Class of the Semester

The students filter out of the classroom, and I gather up my books and notes, turn off the lights, and close the door, wondering what we accomplished and what we failed to do. This is a bittersweet time of the year for me, if not for my students. This past week, students came to a Faculty Hall classroom to attend the last class of the semester. Oh, there are still final examinations for the students to take (and for the professors to grade), but the last regular class session represents the last time each term that one unique group of students will meet in one place in that exact combination of personalities and abilities and motivations to discuss ideas, to pose and tackle questions, and to simply enjoy the academic delights of the act of learning.

I doubt that students would describe the classroom experience in that way. For some students, classes constitute a fifty-minute session (for Monday, Wednesday, and Friday classes), or an hour and fifteen minutes (for Tuesday, Thursday classes), or two hours and forty minutes with a ten-minute break (for once-a-week evening classes). For some, these required meetings include furtive glances at a classroom clock, careful checking of day planners for the more important appointments of the rest of the day, and mind-wandering and mind-numbing whiling away of the minutes until the class is mercifully over. For other students, however, university classes provide an opportunity to delve into important and profound ideas, to explore exciting and relevant issues, to find out more about who we are.

In my American History and Kentucky History classes this semester, I am confident that I learned as much as or even more than my students. I know I learned more about the discipline of history and more about the historical subjects *from* my students. My students also taught me more about myself.

I react to the last class each semester with a mixture of one part anxiety, one part regret, and one part relief—anxiety because of the approaching final examinations and because I approach every class session with a measure of worry, regret for all that I failed to do as a teacher during the course of the term, and relief that we made it through yet another semester relatively unscathed.

At least, we have had—professor and students together—a concentrated time to think about history. What is history? Why study history? And how does one go about studying history? We have also had time to think about what Mark Edmundson, a University of Virginia professor, considers even more important questions: "Who am I? What might I become? What is this world in which I find myself? How might it be changed for the better?" Or as Socrates put it after one of his teaching/learning exchanges with a student, "This discussion is not about any chance question, but about the way one should live."

Now, after this last class session of the semester, we take a break from such crucial and intense exchanges. We look forward to all that the summer holds, all that the summer will bring. For the professor and student alike, the summer break involves rest and relaxation, to be sure, but also serious preparation for another school year of promise and hope.

So, the students filter out, and I gather up my books and notes, turn off the lights, and close the door on an empty classroom, wondering what we learned, what we accomplished, and what we failed to do.

Final Exams

Nothing makes me more nervous during the course of a semester than final examinations. For me, final exams mimic life itself. I think

I remember my anxiety as a student years ago, four years as an undergraduate and then several more years as a graduate student, enduring the anxious anticipation and then the fretful week itself. I remember giving up on study-group sessions; it always made me nervous when a fellow student seemed to know it all already or when friends joked and jostled, all slap-happy from too few hours of sleep.

So I would hunker down in my dorm room or in a lonely corner of a library or perhaps, at the end of a spring term, in an isolated nook outdoors in the quadrangle. There I would pore over classroom notes, neglected textbook chapters, or stacks of note cards all arranged chronologically or topically. I committed these cards to memory, a practice few students seem to use anymore. And I tried to anticipate essay questions, forming in my mind and in scribbled outlines a possible plan of attack.

I think that once I was in that zone, that intense study mode, all pepped up on steaming cups of coffee laced with cream, un-showered and unkempt, eyes glazed over outwardly, but mind active and even burning inwardly, once I found myself in that state, I actually enjoyed myself, though I would never admit it.

And then when the time came for the examination itself, if I had prepared properly, if I had committed the time required, if I had covered all the bases of textbook reading, note-taking, and organization, then it all came pouring out in one mad exhilarating rush. Finished, I breathe again, place my pencil on the desk, look over the thing one more time, check my name at the top right side of the first page, gather up my book bag, and unload the examination on the professor's desk at the front of the room.

Now, on his or her side of the desk, he or she sat, reading calmly sometimes, or working on who knew what, or simply staring vacantly out over the room. I used to imagine a slight smirk on the professor's face or a look of bored but satisfied control. Now I know better. Now that I sit on the professor's side of the desk, I know that the professor, all pepped up on steaming cups of coffee laced with cream, is anticipating lonely hours in a coffee-shop corner, or all holed up in a home study or in a campus office, poring over the students' offerings, administering a combination of justice and mercy, and waiting, like the student, for the holiday break, a welcome respite from days of anxious toil and worry and busyness.

I don't know which side of the desk has made me more anxious, but I do know this: Final exams are like life itself. And I do know this: Final exams always presage new beginnings.

Graduation

For several days, "clothing of celebration" has hung from a secretary/bookcase in the entry hall of our home. Wesley picked up a rental tuxedo for the junior/senior prom two days before the big event, and his graduation robe came in several weeks before this Friday's commencement. The prom and the commencement represent two different types of celebration. Both occasions, however, mark times set aside for significant moments in the lives of young people and older people (mothers and fathers celebrate along with sons and daughters). We will repeat this ritual with Cammie Jo in only a few years.

In times such as these, true insight sometimes is revealed. Abraham Heschel, a Jewish rabbi, remarked that "true insight is a moment of perceiving a situation before it freezes into similarity with something else." The writer of one of my Sunday school lessons paraphrased the rabbi's statement. "Celebration," he wrote, "is a moment of perceiving a situation before it freezes into similarity with every other experience in our past."

Celebrations help break up the humdrum tick-tock of our lives. We set these times aside to remember the past, to revel in the present, and to anticipate what the future might hold. In a sense, a celebration serves as a culmination of all that has gone before. The prom represents the social event of the junior or senior year. A graduation or commencement is the academic culmination of four years of homework, research papers, and examinations.

Dr. Harry Spalding, a Kentucky family doctor and at one time the mayor of Bardstown, was also a poet. His collection of poetry, "Tales of a Kentucky Town," includes a poem about the last days of the old Bardstown Preparatory School for Boys. My former student, Jen McPherson, quoted from Spalding's "The Last Prep Man" in her research report on Nelson County in my History of Kentucky class. The poem gives a note of finality at the last commencement of the venerable institution:

And now he was the very last
Of all that he'd then known;

The faces, the names, the glow
In friend's eyes, the teachers past
The span of time, the truth they'd shown,
And the voices that echo, echo, and echo.

Certainly a sense of finality as well as celebration pervades the pomp and circumstance of both proms and graduations. And yet, there is at the same time an understanding that there is so much more to experience and to learn. "You cannot help but learn more as you take the world into your hands," wrote John Updike. "Take it up reverently," he advised, "for it is an old piece of clay, with millions of thumbprints on it."

So, to high school graduates and college graduates alike, take up the rest of your lives reverently. You will encounter millions of other thumbprints as you proceed, but you will also leave your own mark, a thumbprint like no other.

You Are Not Special

When David McCullough, Jr., an English teacher at Wellesley High School in a suburb west of Boston, gave that school's commencement address on June 1, 2012, he almost instantly became a media celebrity. Before his address, most of the notoriety in the McCullough family had been reserved for his famous historian father, David McCullough Sr. the author of best-selling books such as *Mornings on Horseback* (on the pre-presidential years of Theodore Roosevelt), *Truman*, and *John Adams.*

The younger McCullough later wrote that by June 2, however, "from Berlin to Beijing, Facebook, Twitter, and the blogosphere went crazy." The video of the Wellesley High School commencement had gone viral, McCullough's e-mail in-box had exploded, and his voice-mail had filled up. Limousines appeared in his driveway. "All because of a twelve-minute speech," McCullough wrote. Rabbis, ministers, and priests continue to draw heavily from his talk. And come the month of May, even newspaper columnists cannot resist. Writers find fodder for essay collections in books.

What did the popular English teacher actually tell those graduating Wellesley teenagers? As they were about to go out into the world to change the world, those elite, upper-middle class students, favored above so many others in the United States, what words did he send them out with exactly?

Well, he told them, first of all, that the symbolism of the commencement ceremony was entirely appropriate. Take, for example, your ceremonial costume, he said, "shapeless, uniform, one size fits all. Whether male or female, tall or short, scholar or slacker, spray-tanned prom queen or intergalactic Xbox assassin, each of you is dressed, you'll notice, exactly the same." And then your diplomas, he said, "but for your name, exactly the same." And then their beloved English teacher delivered the kicker. "All this is as it should be," he said, as he peered out at the robed graduates, "because none of you are special." "None of you are special." "You are not exceptional."

He then hammered his point home. Despite what your seventh-grade report card indicated, despite what Mr. Rogers told you, despite what "your batty aunt Sylvia" said as "you've been pampered, cosseted, helmeted, bubble-wrapped…as capable adults with other things to do have held you, kissed you, fed you, wiped your mouth, wiped your bottom, trained you, taught you, tutored you, coached you, listened to you, counseled you, encouraged you, consoled you, and encouraged you again. You've been nudged, cajoled, wheedled and implored. You've been feted and fawned over and called sweetie pie." "Yes, you have," McCullough assured the graduates.

"But do not get the idea that you're anything special," he said. "Because you're not."

McCullough backed up his claim with statistics. "Across the country," he asserted, "no fewer than 3.2 million seniors are graduating about now from more than 37,000 high schools. That's 37,000 valedictorians…37,000 class presidents…92,000 harmonizing altos…340,000 swaggering jocks…2,185,967 pairs of Uggs." "But why limit ourselves to high school?" he continued. "After all, you're leaving it. So think about this: even if you're one in a million, on a planet of 6.8 billion; that means there are nearly 7,000 people just like you." "And consider for a moment the bigger picture: your planet, I'll remind you, is not the center of its solar system, your solar system is not the center of its galaxy, your galaxy is not the center of the universe."

McCullough's point was, of course, that "your galaxy is not the center of the universe," and NEITHER ARE YOU! Because. You. Are. Not. Special.

The wise teacher concluded his address with this: "And then you too will discover the great and curious truth of the human experience is that selflessness is the best thing you can do for yourself. The sweetest joys of life, then, come only with the recognition that you're not special. Because everyone is."

This is a truth that I need to learn for myself first before I try to teach it to my students.

Part Six

History

"Remember the house of thy father, Remember the paths of thy peace."
Alfred Noyes

Top Left: Linda Neville. Top Right: Three generations in 1989: James Wesley Bolin (69), James Duane Bolin (34) and Wesley Seaton Bolin (1). Center: President Jimmy Carter with the Bolin family, c. 1999. Bottom Right: Duane and Coach Adolph Rupp, Memorial Coliseum, Lexington, Kentucky.

What is History?

When I began teaching history over 25 years ago, I made a determination that my students would have an opportunity to answer three questions: What is history? Why study history? How does one study history? My desire to do such a thing is the result of an experience that I had in my first graduate seminar in history.

I had a very charismatic history teacher in high school; he instilled in me a desire to study history. And I had three college teachers of history who developed in me a desire to deepen and expand my knowledge of history. I cannot remember, however, any of my teachers asking me point-blank the loaded question, What is history?, until I walked into a graduate seminar at Baylor University taught by Professor Hugh Davis.

That seminar room was dominated by a long oval wooden table. The walls of the room were paneled in dark wood. The room looked just like a university seminar room should look. There were only eight or so chairs around the table, all of them, save one, occupied when I walked into the room a little late. Now, I try to get to class or any meeting a few minutes early, but then, as a green graduate student from a town of 500 people in western Kentucky and fresh out of Belmont University where I had completed a bachelor's degree in history, I didn't know any better. I came to the class a few minutes late.

And the only seat left empty in the room was at the table's end, down the length of the table from where Professor Davis sat directly opposite. This was the first day of class, so we did the usual thing; we introduced ourselves to the professor and to each other. One member of the class had come to Baylor straight from Oxford University. Another student was actually the dean of a Mennonite college in Canada, on sabbatical to complete another master's degree. When it came my turn, I told them about my roots as a small-town boy in western Kentucky and about my recent graduation from a small college in Nashville, Tennessee, the music capitol of the world. Neither my fellow students nor the professor seemed impressed.

Without further ado, Professor Davis now began class in earnest. And without blinking an eye he looked down the length of that table—and, I might add, down the length of his formidable nose on which were propped bifocal lenses—to me, the muttering small-town kid with the obvious inferiority complex. He looked directly at me, and then he asked, "Mr. Bolin, what is history?"

Well, I froze. I had loved history in high school. I had majored in history in undergraduate school. But, apparently, I had never considered this important question that every aspiring historian must consider. I looked away at the wood-paneled walls. I looked down at the Ticonderoga pencil in my right hand. I looked, I am sure, like a deer in headlights back toward Professor Davis at the other end of the table. Finally, knowing not what else to do, I mumbled out the word "past." I said something about history being "the study of the past."

My timid response did not seem to satisfy Professor Davis, because for the next hour and fifteen minutes he lectured me personally (I am sure he was not talking to anyone else in the room; only to me) about how history was much more than the past. He lectured me that the discipline of history was much more complicated and that the study of history was much more complex.

I left that seminar room in a daze. After I had recovered several days later, I made a promise to myself. I promised myself that if I ever got to the other end of the seminar table, or if I ever stood at a podium as a teacher at the head of a class, I would ask my students, on the first day of class, the question, "What is history?" I also decided, based on my own experience, that I would add one stipulation: I would ask my students to define history without using the word "past." I have followed this practice at the beginning of each semester, year after year.

I am always amazed at the answers my students give. Their answers are always better, much more profound, than my mumbled response all those years ago.

Why Study History?

Here again are three questions that any student of history must think deeply about: What is history? Why study history? How does one study history? In a previous essay I discussed my own struggles to define history, to answer the question, What is history? Just as challenging, perhaps, for a teacher or a student of history, is the question, Why study history?

In my Teaching History class at Murray State, a methods class for students planning to teach high school history, I encourage my students to find a way to articulate clearly a response to the question, Why study history? After all, when they teach in their own high school classrooms, they will be bombarded with variations of the question:

Why do we have to study this stuff? Why do we have to read about all of these dead people? Why must I read these history books? Will this crazy stuff be on the test? Why do I have to take this history class? Why study history? Why, why, why?

Apparently, teachers of history have already been convinced that it is indeed important to study history, or they wouldn't have made it their life's work to convince others. But a teacher must be able to articulate to skeptical students—students often unconvinced and unwilling to make a concerted effort to study history—what the teacher already knows to be true.

When I ask this question to my own students, I get the usual response: "We study history because it is a University Studies (a general education) requirement here at Murray State." More perceptive students might even venture to add, "We study history so that we will not repeat the mistakes of the past." But what about the successes of the past; shouldn't we study for inspiration, to find positive as well as negative examples by which to live? Shouldn't we study history so that we will be better citizens, and better human beings?

Polybius (c. 203-120), a Greek historian, believed, "History offers the best training for those to be involved in public service." And Leonardo Bruno (1374-1444), a Florentine humanist, wrote, "The careful study of the past enlarges our foresight in contemporary affairs and affords to citizens and to monarchs lessons of incitement or warning in the ordering of public policy." "From History," Bruno wrote, "we draw our store of examples of moral precepts."

More recently, Sir Kenneth Clark, in narrating the 1970 television series, "Civilization," concluded, "At this point, I reveal myself in my true colors as a stick-in-the-mud. I believe that order is better than chaos, creation better than destruction. I prefer gentleness to violence, forgiveness to vendetta. On the whole, I think knowledge is better than ignorance, and I'm sure that human sympathy is better than doctrinaire ideology." Clark then focused in on his primary point, a point I want to emphasize in this essay. Clark said, "I believe that in spite of the recent triumphs of science, men have not changed that much in the last two thousand years, and in consequence, we must still try to learn from history."

I too am a stick-in-the-mud. I agree with Sir Kenneth Clark that what motivates men and women today—love and honor or lust and greed—motivated men and women hundreds of years ago as well. In that sense, human beings have not changed that much in the last two thousand years. And we must still try to learn from history.

Shaking Hands with History

Jeremy Shoulta, a graduate of Georgetown College and the Baptist Seminary of Kentucky and the son of our former pastor in Webster County, is now the senior pastor of the Maranatha Baptist Church of Plains, Georgia. Yes, that Maranatha Baptist Church. Yes, that Plains, Georgia. It is indeed the church of Jimmy Carter, the former president of the United States.

One summer Evelyn, Wesley, Cammie Jo, and I drove to Plains, Georgia, to attend Sunday school and the worship service of the Maranatha Baptist Church, the home church of Jimmy and Rosalyn Carter. It was an experience we will not forget. And since Evelyn and I used to rock Jeremy (the president's new pastor) and his twin brother Josh to sleep at night, we hope we will be able to visit the church again soon.

The Sunday school class was held in the sanctuary, already full when we arrived. So we were ushered into a smaller adjoining room to watch the class on a big-screen television monitor. The president walked in—with secret service agents close behind—to chat with our group before proceeding into the sanctuary to begin the class.

After a well-taught lesson, Rosalyn joined the president for the worship service. The sanctuary had cleared out after the Sunday school lesson, the main attraction of the morning, but the former first couple stayed on, sitting on the third row from the front, only a few rows in front of where we found a seat.

After the service, the president stood at the corner of the church as a line formed for pictures. We waited patiently, and when it was our turn, we asked a fellow tourist to take pictures with our camera. After the pictures were snapped, Evelyn did something that I did not think to do. She took the hand of President Carter and shook it firmly. Evelyn was determined to shake hands with a former president.

My father remembered shaking hands with Cornelius McGillicuddy Sr. or Connie Mack, the baseball manager of the Philadelphia Athletics. It was a point of pride for my dad. Dad remembered how Mack, the manager of the Philadelphia club for the first fifty years of the team's existence, wore suits in the dugout. He had been determined to shake hands with that living baseball legend. He touched history.

When a young man and his wife shook an aging Winston Churchill's hand in 1958, he later said to his wife, "Now think of it; that hand you shook today held a saber at Omdurman." At Omdurman in the Sudan in 1898, a young Lieutenant Churchill of the 21st Lancers took part in one of the last cavalry charges in British history. No matter that he actually held a Mauser pistol, rather than a saber. The young woman had shaken Churchill's hand—she had touched history.

So did Evelyn, like the young woman, and like my father before her. In that churchyard next to the peanut fields in Plains that summer day not too long ago, she shook hands with a former president of the United States. She touched history.

Walking Into the Past

In 1992, we left Kentucky for an Arkansas sojourn, for me to teach in the history department of a small liberal arts college. We returned to the Bluegrass State after four years away; we loved that fine Arkansas school, but we missed terribly the rolling hills of western Kentucky. If anything, our exile in the pancake-flat, mosquito-ridden delta rice fields of northeastern Arkansas taught me the intimate connection between the past, present, and future, something that any history teacher should already know.

Students—students of history at least—should also know how to make these connections. What is history? Why is it important to study history? How does one study history? These are questions that I have been wrestling with for some time. These are questions that my students discussed last week in class. My Murray State students will continue to consider these questions throughout this semester.

When we left Kentucky those many years ago for "the land of opportunity," the Natural State, as tourism brochures proclaimed, Ron Watson, a resident of Hopkins County and a very fine poet, himself a native Arkansan, gave to me a farewell poem that made the connections clear in language that a small-town boy from a western Kentucky county seat town could understand. The poet described a father and son experiencing together the eerie sensation of "walking into the past." The experience took place in an old general store, no sprawling Walmart mind you, but the sort of place where old gentlemen in overalls gathered in the late afternoon to play dominoes around a coal stove:

It's Saturday
and we stop at the Dalton Store
before putting in on the river.
Oldtimers are holding down a bench
that hasn't changed in 20 years
and somebody shot Homer Bailey's dog
for running deer is what we hear
as the screen door squeaks open
and slams shut
and swallows us into the general store
that is always darker than outside.

A fading red Coke machine
is defining nostalgia against a wall
and kids we might have been
are standing on a footrail
at the counter. We hope
it is black licorice and Moon Pies
but they could be buying anything.

We try not to hurry
and for a moment begin to blend
as easy as shade into the slow scene,
to soak up the almost forgotten something
we once were.
Paid-up, the kids spill toward us
in a stream that we divide. We turn
to watch it reconnect down the dark aisle
that points like a chute in the cool dimness
toward a door that opens like a tablet of light.

I have tried to picture a father and his small son standing hand in hand in the middle of the store's darkened aisle soaking in "the almost forgotten something we once were." Standing in the present, the father and son gaze into the darkened interior at "kids we might have been," standing at a counter buying perhaps "black licorice and Moon Pies," only to have the representative group from the past "spill toward us in a stream that we divide." And even as the past comes hurtling into and through the present, the familial pair "turn to watch it reconnect" into the future, "toward a door that opens like a tablet of light." These connections between the past, present, and future also link together an understanding of history and ourselves. "As far as we're concerned, there's no such thing as a dead past," Kentucky's Historian Laureate Thomas D. Clark told an interviewer in 2001. Dr. Clark, who died at 101, knew whereof he spoke. "You're part of the past," he said. "Everything you do, everything you touch in some way has an intimate association with the past.... Even human prejudices are age old." Now, what can we—students, teachers, writers, and readers—learn from that?

Empathy and History

In the discipline of history, historians write books, publishers send the books out to scholarly journals, journal editors send the books out to other historians, who in turn write book reviews to be published in the journals. To be reviewed in a scholarly journal or in a newspaper is helpful in getting out the word (even if the review is negative), boosting book sales, and (especially if the review is positive) boosting the reputation of the author.

Usually, reviews are complimentary; the reviewer recognizes the achievement of the historian, the long months and maybe years of research and writing. Sometimes, though, reviewers are indeed critical. It can get especially nasty if someone's research is called into question, or if a historian's integrity is held to be suspect. That's what happened to the eminent Harvard historian Samuel Eliot Morison, the biographer of Christopher Columbus.

I remember that my mother had secretly called Dr. Gladys Bryant, one of my history professors at Belmont University, to ask for advice on a good book of history to buy as a Christmas present for her history-major son. Dr. Bryant, surely caught off guard by my mother's phone call, had suggested Morison's *The European Discovery of America*. I have that Christmas-present book on my shelves and through it I came to admire Morison's work.

In one of Morison's books on Columbus, however, the historian got himself in a pickle with a reviewer when he made what he must of thought was an innocuous statement about one of the discoverer's voyages. Morison simply stated that on one particular day in 1492, the captain [Columbus] had "staggered to the deck of the ship." The conscientious book reviewer questioned the statement. After all, he asked, how could Morison, who surely wasn't there in 1492 to witness the event, know that Columbus on that day had staggered to the deck of the ship?

Morison responded that in his research he had consulted the ship's log, and on that particular day, the captain [again Columbus] had been ill. Furthermore, the captain noted that on that day there was a storm at sea. With that evidence, the historian had reasoned that with a storm at sea, an ill and weakened captain would not have walked to the deck of the ship; he would have staggered.

That explanation did not satisfy the critical reviewer. How could the historian know for sure, based on the evidence? What, after all, did the evidence reveal? Morison made one more stab at an explanation. He said that he himself had sailed on a scale replica of the Santa Maria. He assured the reviewer that based on his own experience, a sick captain, in a storm at sea, would have staggered to the deck of the ship. He knew from his own experience!

Well, now! What do you think? Samuel Eliot Morison, this renowned historian, had certainly developed an empathy for his historical subject through his research. We often encourage our students to empathize with those long-dead individuals in their history textbooks. What must it have been like to live as they lived, to think as they thought, and to act as they acted? "Put yourselves in their shoes or moccasins," we tell students in our history classes. "What was it like to have lived back in those long ago days?"

But what role does empathy play in historical research and writing? Perhaps this is another example of history as an art, rather than an exact science.

Letter from an Iraqi Refugee

Each fall semester students in my American History classes read about and discuss the American Revolution. It must have seemed odd to them that I started class one day by reading from a copy of a letter from an Iraqi refugee that I had clipped from the editorial page of a major newspaper. In the letter—the clipping already yellowed with age—the highly educated writer commented on the trial of Saddam Hussein, remembering his tyranny and the years of abuse under his rule.

The writer minced no words as he revealed in minute detail an era of terror and horror. Let me quote directly from the letter; the intent of the writer will be made clear. He wrote, "When a long train of abuses and usurpations, pursuing invariably the same object, evinces a design to reduce [us] under absolute despotism, it is [our] right, it is [our] duty, to throw off such government, and to provide new guards for [our] future security. Such has been our patient sufferance."

With this introduction, the letter writer then listed specific examples of Saddam's past abuse: "He has refused his assent to laws, the most wholesome and necessary for the public good." "He has dissolved representative houses repeatedly, for opposing, with manly firmness, his invasions on the rights of the people." "He has affected to render the military independent of, and superior to, the civil power." "He has plundered our seas…burned our towns, and destroyed the lives of our people."

"He is at this time transporting large [armies]…to complete the works of death, and tyranny already begun with circumstances of cruelty and perfidy scarcely paralleled in the most barbarous ages, and totally unworthy the head of a civilized nation." "He has constrained our fellow-citizens…to bear arms against their country, to become the executioners of their friends and brethren, or to fall themselves by their hands," he wrote. The writer concluded his letter by remarking, "a [ruler] whose character is thus marked by every act which may define a tyrant, is unfit to be the ruler of a free people."

Strong words indeed, but what would you expect from someone who had suffered so much for so long? OK. So much for the ruse. You, O reader—along with the most perceptive of my students—are too intelligent, too sharp, too well read in the essential primary documents of American history, to be fooled. Of course, you knew that I did not quote from a letter from an Iraqi refugee sent in for publication on an editorial page in a daily newspaper. You knew, O perceptive one, that I read instead from Thomas Jefferson's Declaration of Independence, penned 239 years ago in 1776.

So, what's the purpose of the deception? Well, O gentle reader, it is to illustrate how the past resonates in the present. For, if truth be told, the words of the Declaration *could* have been the words of a distressed refugee in this uncertain, unbalanced present world. Our students need to read the Declaration of Independence. Our teachers need to read it too.

In one of the great ironies of American history, Thomas Jefferson, the nation's third president and the author of the Declaration, died within hours of John Adams, the second president of the United States and Jefferson's one-time political enemy. They both died on July 4, 1826, the fiftieth anniversary of the signing of the Declaration, the document from which I quoted under another guise a few lines above.

John Adams uttered on his deathbed his last words: "Thomas Jefferson still lives." Adams was wrong in his facts, not realizing that Jefferson had already died a few hours earlier. Or was he? For surely Jefferson lives on in the words that he wrote down in 1776, words that still resonate, not a few old dead words about a long-dead past, but words that live on and continue to inform and inspire today.

Tearing Down

Quite a scene is unfolding down below my north-facing, sixth-floor Faculty Hall office window. I have a wonderful view of the northern tree-lined horizon, and the only thing that breaks that clean line of trees is the white cupola of the new Clark College, the top decks of Hester, Hart, and Elizabeth colleges (with an America flag taut in the wind above Hester), the press box and lights at Stewart Stadium, and one lone distant water tower.

I often spare a few moments' time before a class session to gain inspiration from the changing panoply of tree branches and leaves, and just now the leaves are changing hue, not as brilliantly as usual because of the long, bone-dry summer, but beautiful nonetheless.

Another scene unfolds, or, more accurately, is unlayering below my window, however, and this scene is anything but beautiful. It is a scene of shattered skeletons, of piles of debris, of ugly, unsightly ruin. It is a scene of tearing down.

The university is tearing down the old Boy Scout Museum, along with all of its various appendages. Many still remember the still-older Murray Training School which stood on this site. But now the building that housed a newer school, the Boy Scout Museum before it moved to Texas, and more recently various federally funded programs and even ROTC offices, is being torn down to make room for more parking. It is interesting to imagine what buildings or landscaping will be placed on this site in the future. No telling, with the university expanding—and becoming more beautiful—with each passing year.

The old sometimes gives way to the new. But sometimes something new is made out of something old. Isn't that how we should consider the study of history—building something new from the best of the past, from the vestiges of the past?

My family has watched old episodes of the television series, *Joan of Arcadia*. The show, now with all of the seasons out on DVD, is a modern version of Joan of Arc. Joan of Arcadia talks to God, too, and God talks to Joan, appearing to her in various guises. In one episode, Joan's mother, an art teacher in Arcadia's public schools, has designed an art project for her students. She asks her students to bring in artifacts from home: old ceramic bowls, toys, jewelry, whatever they can find that reminds them of their childhood.

The students dutifully bring in the items and place them before them on the art room's worktables. Then, the art teacher does something interesting (and a little dangerous I think). She gives the students hammers and instructs them to break the objects into pieces. She then explains that she wants them to make works of art out of the broken pieces. They are to glue the broken pieces into collages, using the old broken pieces to create new works of art.

When a student questions the art teacher about this madness, she explains the process in simple language. "Just think of it this way," she says. "You are breaking up the past to create something new. You are using the past to create something new."

I am thinking of that *Joan of Arcadia* episode now as I look up from my keyboard, casting my gaze to the destruction site below. I am looking down upon the mess, the detritus of the past. The old Boy Scout Museum is all broken up into pieces of steel and concrete, waiting for the dump trucks to haul it away. As for now, from my sixth-floor perch, this is indeed an ugly sight.

I must admit that I am a preservationist. I think it is important to preserve the past. I hate it when old, stately buildings are torn down to build a strip mall. But, believe me, unlike the old Murray Training School, this windowless fortress of a building is not stately. From the first, it had no aesthetic value, as far as I could see. So, now, surely, this is a time to tear down the old to create something new. I can't wait to see what is in store for the university in the future, as we retain the best of the past, and tear down what should, by all accounts, be torn down ...to create something new.

Re-membering

During the first day of my American History classes last week, I talked with my students about the importance of developing a "sense of history." The way historians go about their work changes with each passing generation.

We seek to understand the past, to make connections with the past, to make sense of the past. Individuals and groups, long left out of our textbook histories, have now found a voice in the so-called new history. It seems that the writing of history has been rendered in increasingly fragmented segments. Writing for the *New York Times* on August 26, 2000, David Oshinsky called the discipline of history the "Humpty Dumpty of Scholarship." "History has broken into pieces," Oshinsky wrote.

According to Oshinsky, "By the 1980s an explosion of historical categories—race, gender, ethnicity, sexuality—had supplanted the more traditional fields of political, diplomatic and intellectual history. Those formally on the margins of American society now got the lion's share of attention." In my opinion, much good has come from the recovery of these lost voices. All individuals and groups need to learn from the past. And we all need to learn from the past of others, especially those unlike ourselves.

I know that I have contributed to this fragmentation of the past in my own history classes. In addition to American History, I also teach classes in Kentucky History, Sports History, and Teaching History. Within those classes my students often discuss social history, political history, diplomatic history, military history, intellectual history, and economic history. We discuss the history of women, the history of various racial and ethnic groups, the history of art and science and religion. All of these histories have a place at the history table. All of these voices must be heard.

Still, there is a danger in the increasing fragmentation of the past. What about the big picture? What about the grand narrative of the historical past? Oshinsky wrote, "Critics of the new history have worried about the fragmentation of the past, with each group telling its own story, on its own terms, in its own authentic voice. And even advocates wondered at times about the place of these categories in the larger scheme of things."

I worry about this as well. Have we lost the ability to tell the story of America's past, for example, in a way that can be understood by everyone, not just historians specializing in increasingly smaller subsets of the past? Oshinsky asked the same question. "So is there a way to combine the diversity and specialization of today's history with the grand narratives of the past?" he wrote. "Can professional historians win back a broad audience?"

Surely, we need popular historians such as David McCullough, Barbara Tuchman, and Stephen Ambrose who have the ability to make sense of the past for a lay audience. After all, the art of doing history is really the art of "re-membering" the past. I want you to notice the hyphen in my rewriting of the word "re-membering." History is certainly about remembering the past, but it is also about "re-membering" as opposed to "dis-membering." When we dismember something, we pull it apart; when we remember something, we put it back together again, seeing the whole.

I hope that the discipline of history is not the Humpty Dumpty of scholarship. By remembering the past, we make sense of our lives. We see how we fit into the big picture, the whole scheme of things.

The Past is a Foreign Country

Sometimes I forget as a teacher of history how difficult the study of history often is for many of my students. In *The Past is a Foreign Country* (Cambridge University Press, 1985), the historian David Lowenthal likened the study of history to a study-abroad experience. Lowenthal took his title from the first line of the L. P. Hartley novel, *The Go-Between*: "The past is a foreign country: they do things differently there." The past is so different from the present, just as visiting a foreign country for the uninitiated is such a different experience from living at home.

According to Lowenthal, "The past thus conjured up is, to be sure, largely an artifact of the present. However faithfully we preserve, however authentically we restore, however deeply we immerse ourselves in bygone times," he argued, "life back then was based on ways of being and believing incommensurable with our own." "The past's difference," he wrote, "is, indeed, one of its charms: no one would yearn for it if it merely replicated the present. But we cannot help but view and celebrate it [except] through present-day lenses."

People did do things differently "back then." So, the problem for the student of history is to try to figure out what they did, what they thought, how they lived, and then to make some sense of all that for ourselves, for our own situations. Making a connection with the past is sometimes hard, sometimes easy. Surely, for example, a study of the Bible and the Qur'an will help us understand the deep divisions in the Middle East today. Surely, a study of the presidential administrations of Andrew Jackson and Teddy Roosevelt will help us put into context George W. Bush's uses of power. Surely, a study of the beginnings of the Great Depression of the 1930s will give us pause, warning us of similar trends in our economy today.

But sometimes, students of history must simply admit that we just do not know, that we just cannot understand fully, how folks lived in the past. I know that I have learned to state those three words often in my history classes: "I don't know."

In *The Everlasting Man* (Image Books, 1955), G. K. Chesterton wrote eloquently about the limits of doing history. "The other day," Chesterton wrote, "a scientific summary of the state of a prehistoric tribe began confidently with the words 'They wore no clothes.' Not one reader in a hundred probably stopped to ask himself how we should come to know whether clothes had once been worn by people of whom everything has perished except a few chips of bone and stone. It was doubtless hoped that we should find a stone hat as well as a stone hatchet." "It is not contended here that these primitive men did wear clothes any more than they did weave rushes," Chesterton concluded, "but merely that we have not enough evidence to know whether they did or not."

Sometimes, we have to admit that we just don't know. But still, we search the archives of the past to enlighten, to educate, and even to refresh us. Recently, Marie Taylor, a great musician and an inspiration to me, as well as to her family and her many friends and admirers, sent a quotation along. In her thoughtful e-mail, Marie wrote, "Tonight, I opened a new box of Celestial Seasonings natural tea. For whatever reason, the following quote was included. I thought of you and decided you might add to your 'archives' in case you haven't already read it."

I have indeed added the quote to my archives, burgeoning file folders filled with quotations, clippings, and articles about the study of history. Now, I add the quote as a fitting end to this essay: "To look backward for a while is to refresh the eye, to restore it, and to render it the more fit for its prime function of looking forward." There it is. However difficult the study of history, however like it is to visiting a foreign country, just think of the refreshment and the excitement we always receive when we travel abroad.

Wherever You Go, There You Are

"Remember, wherever you go, there you are." A close friend read the quotation on the Internet, and it reminded him of me. Indeed, I have used the quote as a humorous remark and as a way to get at a deeper meaning for over thirty years. I once read the quotation scrawled on the wooden wall of a tiny restroom in High on Rose, a restaurant (and dive) at, yes, the corner of High and Rose streets in Lexington, Kentucky.

The restaurant no longer exists, I don't think, but during my graduate school days at UK it was popular for its Mexican food and liquid libations. Apparently, some wag, having partaken of a liquid libation or two, scratched out the quotation on the restroom wall one raucous (or maybe doleful) evening: "Remember, wherever you go, there you are."

When I saw the quotation for the first time, I took out my pen and copied it onto a paper towel, so as not to forget. In the years hence, I have tried to dissect the phrase, to see if there is any profound meaning there. After all, the sentence begins with the verb, "Remember," and that is what the study of history is all about. Historians remember their own experiences, and then, through primary and secondary sources, historians remember vicariously through the collective observances and remembrances of others.

The rest of the sentence is more problematic: "wherever you go, there you are." How can historians, or anyone else, make sense of that? Well, wherever we go, wherever we find ourselves, however we came to that place, through whatever circumstances, by whatever history, we have arrived at a place, whether we think of that place in historical, geographical, emotional, intellectual, philosophical, or spiritual terms. There we are.

And *that* is what history is all about, to make sense of our present state, our present condition, through the study of our individual and collective pasts. How did we arrive here in our present condition? Why do we find ourselves—as individuals, as members of a family, as residents of a town, a county, a state, as citizens of a nation, as inhabitants of a world—how do we find ourselves today?

Come May, we will invariably hear graduation speakers quoting from Dr. Seuss's last book, "Oh the Places You'll Go":

Congratulations!Today is your day. You're off to Great Places! You're off and away! You have brains in your head. You have feet in your shoes You can steer yourself any direction you choose.You're on your own. And you know what you know. And YOU are the guy who'll decide where to go.

Dr. Seuss seems to be more concerned with where one is going, rather than the place where one has already arrived, but "remember, wherever you go, there you are." Booker T. Washington instructed African Americans to "put down your buckets where you are." Jeremiah instructed those exiled Israelites in Babylon to "build houses and plant vineyards" even as they hoped and prayed to return home in the future.

We, all of us, are to make the most of our present circumstances, to make contributions wherever we find ourselves. If we are to prosper, to lead meaningful lives, we have no other choice. "Remember, wherever you go, there you are."

The Lessons of History

It is that time of the year when I take stock. Of course I am concerned about what lessons my students have learned in my history classes this semester, but I am also concerned about what lessons I have learned. What have I learned from my students? What have I learned about American history? What have I learned this semester about life? I try to teach history, but do I practice what I teach? What does history "have to say about the nature, conduct, and prospects of man," as one scholar of the lessons of history puts it?

I have on a bookshelf in our front parlor at home eleven thick volumes written by Will and Ariel Durant. This husband and wife historian team spent some four decades of their married lives researching and writing this massive work, *The Story of Civilization*. I can't fathom such an undertaking, but then, I can't imagine sitting each morning across a breakfast table from another historian. Ughh!!!

Anyway, the Durants accomplished this phenomenal feat (eating breakfast, I assume with each other, and writing this massive work): eleven volumes, averaging close to a thousand pages each, telling the story of civilization from *Our Oriental Heritage* through *The Age of Faith* and *The Age of Voltaire* to *The Age of Napoleon.* A monumental accomplishment, to say the least. But the Durants were not finished. They also wrote a short 117-page postlude, a thin volume, titled *The Lessons of History*, in which the historians "distilled for the reader the accumulated store of knowledge and experience" gained from the research and writing of the other heavy volumes of the work.

To these famous historians, history was "not merely a warning reminder of man's follies and crimes, but also an encouraging remembrance of generative souls…a spacious country of the mind, wherein a thousand saints, statesmen, inventors, scientists, poets, artists, musicians, lovers, and philosophers still live and speak, teach and carve and sing." The Durants believed that "the present is the past rolled up for action, and the past is the present unrolled for understanding." After years of study and after decades of publishing volume after volume of *The Story of Civilization*, what was the value of the enterprise in the end? What conclusions could be reached? How do you make sense of it all? What are, after all, the lessons of history?"

The Durants wrote this last little volume to answer these questions, and at the end of the book's opening chapter, a chapter aptly named, "Hesitations," the authors came to this profound conclusion: "Since man is a moment in astronomic time, a transient guest of the earth, a spore of his species,…a composite of body, character, and mind, a member of a family and a community, a believer or doubter of a faith, a unit in an economy, perhaps a citizen in a state or a soldier in an army, we may ask under the corresponding heads—astronomy, geology, geography, biology, ethnology, psychology, morality, religion, economics, politics, and war—what history has to say about the nature, conduct, and prospects of man. It is a precarious enterprise, and only a fool would try to compress a hundred centuries into a hundred pages of hazardous conclusions." And then the Durants added one more telling two-word sentence to this hesitant opening chapter. They wrote simply, "We proceed."

And so should we. We should try anyway. As daunting as the task may be, we must at least make the attempt to learn from the past, for our own sakes and for our futures.

Distant Voices

The rhythms of the academic term end for me in a bittersweet spasm of relief and regret in the semester's last day of class. The end of the semester inevitably brings with it thoughts of my mother and father, those two saints who watched with me—over me—through my own undergraduate and graduate travails and triumphs. The approach of Christmas certainly promises a time of joy with family and friends, but this Christmas will be the first since my mother's death. So for today I will tell you how I always reserve the last day of class in a semester to remember my parents and the home they made for me and my brother, Stephen.

When my mother died last August, 2006, my father had been gone for over twelve years. James Wesley Bolin died on June 6, 1994, the fiftieth anniversary of D-Day. My father served in the Pacific Theater during World War II as a pharmacy mate on a troop transport ship. Of course, World War II was a watershed event in my father's life; he rarely left his home county in Tennessee before signing up for the navy before Pearl Harbor.

My father stayed on board that troop transport ship for two-and-a-half years, carrying US troops to exotic places such as Tongataboo and Okinawa. During that time, he only set foot on dry ground for shore leaves two times, once in Sydney, Australia, and once in Wellington, New Zealand. In New Zealand, Dad wandered into an old used-book shop and picked up a volume of the *Selected Verse* of the English poet Alfred Noyes.

That small leather-bound book is now one of my most prized possessions, and it contains the poem "Distant Voices," a poem that my friend and fellow historian, Dr. Kenneth M. Startup, read at my father's funeral. And this is the poem that I read to my students on the last day of class with each passing semester:

Distant Voices

Remember the house of thy father,
When the palaces open before thee,
And the music would make thee forget.
When the cities are glittering around thee,
Remember the lamp in the evening,
The loneliness and the peace.

When the deep things that cannot be spoken
Are drowned in a riot of laughter,
And the proud wine foams in thy cup;
In the day when thy wealth is upon thee,
Remember the path through the pine-wood,
Remember the ways of thy peace.

Remember — remember — remember —
When the cares of this world and its treasure
Have dulled the swift eyes of thy youth;
When beauty and longing forsake thee,
And there is no hope in the darkness,
And the soul is drowned in the flesh;

Turn, then, to the house of thy boyhood,
To the sea and the hills that would heal thee,
To the voices of those thou hast lost.
The still small voices that loved thee,
Whispering out of the silence,
Remember — remember — remember —

Remember the house of thy father,
Remember the paths of thy peace.

I read the poem for my own sake, to help me remember the home and the life that my mother and father marked out for me. But I also read the poem for the sake of my students. During this week of final examinations, my students will remember many facts—dates, names, events—of history. They will ritually spit those facts back to me in their essays and other examination responses, and then they will forget them within a few days time. I know how it goes, from my own past experience.

If, however, my students could go away from my class with the understanding that remembering is important, that the act of remembering is crucial for their own well-being, for their own sakes; if my students will only come away from my class with that understanding, then these minutes that we have spent together this semester will have been worthwhile.

Part Seven

Reading

"I cannot live without books."

Thomas Jefferson

Top: Wesley Seaton Bolin, US Congressional Candidate, First Distirct Kentucky, 2014. Center: Wesley freshman year at Yale by Brittney Kajdacsi. Bottom: My Murray State University history department office, with more books.

"I Cannot Live Without Books"

My daughter's reaction embarrassed me at first. I was not embarrassed by my daughter, mind you. I was embarrassed at me. It was just that she laughed out loud. Evelyn and Cammie Jo had dropped off Wesley and me at a large out-of-town bookshop, while they checked out another store before looking for books themselves.

After thirty minutes or so, I saw them coming through the front door, but it was too late. There I stood red-handed, uh, book-handed, with an already too high stack of books under my arm. Cammie Jo took one look, and that was when she laughed out loud. And then she simply said with an inflection that only she could give, "Daddy!?!" I guess it was the fact that I had only been in the shop for a few minutes, and already I had found a pile of books that I could not live without.

Thomas Jefferson wrote, "I cannot live without books," and I know what he meant. I cannot, however, understand how Mr. Jefferson could have given up two whole libraries of books, even for the reason of establishing the Library of Congress. What a selfless man!

Books meant a great deal to Desiderius Erasmus too. "When I get a little money, I buy books," the reformer wrote, "and if there is any left over, I buy food and clothes." Well, I don't miss many meals, and my wardrobe is adequate, but Evelyn's mother used to nod knowingly and say that we were "book poor."

Such literary poverty is not such a bad state to be in. Books threaten to flow into the hall at my History Department office at the university. At home, books greet visitors at the front door and line the walls of our front parlor, our family room, the study, and even our bedrooms. We have an overflowing collection of books in our kitchen. We have found, along with James Axtell, one of my historian friends, that book-lined walls provide excellent insulation, warmth for body and soul on cold winter evenings.

An eloquent tribute to books can be found on the dust jacket of Garrison Keillor's volume of stories and letters, *We Are Still Married*. Keillor includes:

> "...a few lines about the great and ancient invention you hold in your hand, the Book itself. Slow to hatch, as durable as a turtle, light and shapely as befits a descendant of the tree. Closed, the *objet d'book* resembles a board. Open, its pale wings brush the

> fingertips, the spore of fresh ink and pulp excites the nose, the spine lies easily in the hand. A handsome useful object begotten by the passion for truth. The apostle Paul was not the host of a talk show, or else we'd be worshiping famous people on Sunday mornings; he wrote books, a Christian thing to do. The faith of Jews and Christians rests on God's sacred word, not on magic or music, and so technology burst forward into publishing, Gutenberg…making books similar to ours in the fifteenth century. Ages before the loudspeaker and the camera, came this lovely thing, this portable garden, which survives television, computers, censorship…and rotten authors. Along with the Constitution, the blues, and baseball, the democracy of letters is a common glory in our midst, visible in every library and bookstore. These stacks of boards contain our common life and keep it against the miserable days when meanness operates with a free hand and save it for the day when the lonesome reader opens the cover and the word is resurrected. The day can come next month or a hundred years from now, a book will wait."

The shelves at our house and at my office, all full of books, represent a lifetime of reading. When a student asks me, "Have you read *all* of those books," I respond simply, "I have read *some* of all of them, and *all* of some of them." I learned that line from my friend, Dr. Melissa McEuen, a professor of history at Transyvania University.

Now, it was Wesley's turn to laugh at me. He laughed just last night when he saw the foot-high stack of books on the nightstand by our bed. My nightstand stack represents a holiday ahead of reading pleasure.

Garrison Keillor said, "The day can come next month or a hundred years from now, a book will wait." A book can wait, but can I?

The Pleasures of Reading

The act of reading, the experience of it, can itself be rendered into an art form. And the art of reading is one of the great creative pleasures of life. The pleasures of reading go far beyond simply running one's eyes across the print of a page. The pleasures of reading go beyond the great worth of the accumulation of useful knowledge. We read newspapers to get the news. We read magazines to learn about new products of clothing or food or home décor, or to divert our attention while sitting in a barbershop or a doctor's office or in an airplane. We can read books in all of those places, of course (and maybe for all of those reasons) but we also read books for the sheer joy and pleasure of the act itself.

We derive pleasure from reading regardless of the nature of the book: fiction, poetry, history, biography, autobiography, memoir, or inspiration. It doesn't matter. We enjoy them all, depending on the mood we're in. We read library books against a deadline when they must be returned or "renewed," but even more wonderful are those books that we buy, or maybe one is given to us as an elegant gift. We buy them from Amazon.com or from Barnes & Noble online, or from another used-book Internet outlet. Even better, we go to a bookshop for a particular volume we have heard about, or we happen upon it while scanning the delicious rows of bookcases, sometimes sitting on the floor in the aisle to peruse the lower shelves more readily. We buy these books because in ownership we can keep them and mark in them and read them again and again. We get the precious volume home, and we inscribe our name inside the front cover or stamp a distinctive bookplate there to mark the book as our own. Although some connoisseurs disdain the practice, I make a book my own by underlining key passages or by placing a handwritten star or an asterisk in the margin, a reminder that I might want to recall that thought again. When I pick up a once-read book after years have passed, I wonder why I marked a particular passage, but it doesn't matter because I will undoubtedly find something new and fresh upon this second reading. Sometimes, we purchase a venerably worn used volume and find on the pages within exciting marginalia, the mysterious markings of a previous owner in another time and place.

During an academic semester, the stacks of books in my study and the stack of books on my bedside nightstand have gotten taller. Bookmarked with only a thin slice having been read, these stacks of books represent at least the possibility of a time for unfettered, joyful, restful, peaceful examination, reading with no strings attached, no immediate deadlines to meet. Large blocks of time in the red easy chair in the study, legs extended on the matching red ottoman covered up with a luxuriously soft navy blue throw, a cup of steaming tea with honey near at hand on the library table. Or by a crackling fire in the family room, in the recliner angled just so, making it possible to see the fireplace, but impossible to view the television screen, children lounging on the sofa or love seat watching said television screen, Evelyn in the other chair or sitting cross-legged on the floor, reading. In such a room I find that I can still concentrate on the book of the moment, even between frequent glances at the scene before me and even with the incessant hum of the television. We live in a postmodern world after all. Away from home I sit snugly and comfortably at my favorite table at Fidalgo Bay coffee house, with a medium-roast, black, of course, at my elbow.

This act of reading is an art, a creative act that we enjoy amid the hustle and bustle of all that goes on around us. We just open a book to immerse ourselves in another world, in another time and place, and in the process, in this creative act, we enrich and enliven the world we know as our own.

A Bookish Gift

One of the main goals in any humanities-based course—such as history or literature—is to foster a student's appreciation for the written word. This semester, students in my American History survey classes must write formal book reviews. Students choose books on American history topics that interest them, and then they analyze the books they have chosen. They identify and critique the author's thesis and major arguments, the author's use of source materials, and the author's writing style.

The whole exercise is designed to further specific skills that budding historians must master: critical thinking, critical reading, and clear, cogent writing. It is also hoped that the exercise of book-review writing will somehow spur on an interest in how books are written, how ideas make it to a printed page. Students in humanities classes—and all students for that matter—should learn to love books. Such a love enriches one's life no matter what field or occupation or calling one decides on.

In 2004, Raymond Danowski presented a gift to Emory University. A gift of books. Not a book, mind you, but books. Sixty thousand of them! The *New York Times* reported in a September 29, 2004, article that as a disgruntled teenager growing up in the Bronx, Danowski worked after school shelving books in the Burgess-Carpenter Library at Columbia University. It was there that he learned to love and cherish books. "The corridors were lined with books," he said, "and there were reading rooms with large tables, and windows looking out on trees." Along with other student workers, Danowski remembered that "we'd push carts around and then we'd disappear and start reading. I'd read for an hour and then get caught, and go back to shelving, and then find another place and read." "It was the first time," he said, "that he understood books to be a sanctuary." "It was like an oasis for me," he recalled.

As an adult, Danowski continued to cultivate his love for books, not just reading them, but collecting them, thousands of them. Eventually, he collected what has been described as the largest English-language poetry collection ever put together by an individual. The collection includes works by T. S. Eliot, William Butler Yeats, Emily Dickinson, William Carlos Williams, and James Merrill, and an 1855 edition of Walt Whitman's *Leaves of Grass*. Danowski especially loves W. H. Auden and his collection includes over a thousand Auden volumes, considered the most complete collection of that poet's work ever assembled. Danowski did not just collect the books to be collecting them. He had a larger, more important plan in mind. He wanted to give them away! He wished to provide assistance for others, for students intent on reading and studying the riches between the covers, the treasures contained in the pages, in the words. "A teaching library, one that a grad student could use for doctoral research," Danowski revealed. "That's what I set out to make."

Winston Churchill has written, "If you cannot read all your books, at any rate handle, or as it were, fondle them—peer into them, let them fall open where they will, read from the first sentence that arrests the eye, set them back on the shelves with your own hands, arrange them on your own plan so that if you do not know what is in them, you at least know where they are. Let them be your friends; let them at any rate be your acquaintances."

History and literature and other humanities-based classes at Murray State help students develop a lifelong love affair with books. "If you cannot read all your books, at any rate handle…[them], peer into them." Or like Raymond Danowski, give them away.

An Inspirational Library

There's no place like a library. My family haunts the public library on Main Street. I love to walk over from my Faculty Hall office to Waterfield Library to—yes, I know this is weird—smell the books. I read them too, but the smell of musty books is indeed intoxicating. I browse the shelves, sometimes plopping down in the floor before an especially enticing row.

When I enter Waterfield, students are lined up at the computers just to the right of the entry doors, but I bypass the computers and head straight downstairs to the stacks. Even better is to saunter over to the magnificent Reading Room at Pogue Library, the most beautiful space on our campus. There I read or meditate or pray. What a room!

During a trip to Oxford, England, I made a pilgrimage to one of the great libraries of the world. We made our way down Broad Street past the site of a cross embedded in the road's pavement, marking the spot where the Archbishop of Canterbury Cranmer was burned at the stake during the reign of Queen Mary in 1556.

We walked on past the Sheldonian Theatre with its row of huge stone busts of Roman emperors written about by Thomas Hardy in that most depressing of Oxford novels, *Jude the Obscure*. We then walked across a gravel courtyard through a gate by which a sign was posted, "Silence Please." We entered yet another courtyard, and walked past the impressive statue of the Earl of Pembroke. Finally, we made it into the library itself, or at least one portion of it. This was the Bodleian, a most inspirational library.

Just through the doors, there before us was the Divinity School chamber with its rows of barreled vaulting. We turned to the left, flashed our precious Bodleain reader's cards, acquired a few days earlier, and made our way into the Lower Reading Room. Although we had obtained our cards on a Tuesday, it took us until Friday to figure out the system by which the library could be used. Oh, we weren't there just to gaze upon the shrine, we were determined to make use of this great repository of books, books that we could find nowhere else.

Named after Sir Thomas Bodley, a sixteenth century benefactor, the Bodleian is a copyright library; publishers must send to it a free copy of every book published in the United Kingdom. Its several different buildings include over five million books, sixty thousand manuscripts, and fifteen thousand five hundred charters.

As travel writer Jan Morris stated, the Bodleian "is partly built up, like a huge mosaic, out of dozens of separate collections including the original Duke Humphreys' Library, named after Henry V's brother, the Duke of Gloucester, the quintessential library room with its hundreds of university crests and floor-to-ceiling books, the room's original book stacks, with ancient leather-bound books." C. S. Lewis used to read in this room, and he once wrote to his father, telling him, "I spend all my mornings in the Bodleian.... If only one could smoke and if only there were upholstered chairs, this would be one of the most delightful places in the world."

Well, I don't smoke, but I found it to be "one of the most delightful places in the world," nonetheless. The Bodleian's Duke Humphreys' room contained ancient tomes. I, myself, ordered, held, and perused a more recent, modern volume, a book in its first edition, published in 1651.

Reading and Eating

My idea of a good time is to be seated in an isolated corner of a good—but not too good—restaurant, back to the wall so as to view the comings and goings before me, even from my private perch. From this vantage point, I can order an unsweetened iced tea, peruse a menu briefly for a simple meal, and then settle back for the real feast of the evening, a favored book, perhaps a memoir or a new work of fiction.

I would rather have a quiet meal with my family, a time to discuss the events of the day, or simply to delight in each other's company, but on the rare occasions when it is necessary for me to dine alone, I can find solace in the written word.

I have gone, book in hand, to the Eagle and the Child pub—the Bird and the Baby where C. S. Lewis and J. R. R. Tolkien read chapters from the *Narnia* tales or *The Lord of the Rings* aloud to each other in their Inklings meetings—to the Dinky Diner in Madisonville, Kentucky, and to a number of haunts here in Murray, my hometown. It doesn't matter. Any place will do, as long as there is a modicum of good food and adequate light to see the page.

It is a delight to drive to Mazzoni's Café in Louisville, the home of the "rolled oyster," or to Dudley's or Joe Bologna's in Lexington to participate in this time-honored ritual: reading and eating. In Lexington, for example, it is best to go for a meal after a two-hour splurge at Joseph-Beth bookstore. My favorite bookshop, I never fail to discover some new treasure at Joseph-Beth, and a visit there is a highlight of every trip from western Kentucky to Lexington.

So, I take my stash, still in the Joseph-Beth shopping bag, to a Lexington restaurant, and after being seated, I lovingly take out each new volume. I scan the blurbs on the book's dust jacket, I read the expressions of gratitude in the author's acknowledgements, and then I turn to the blank page at the very front of the book to inscribe the name of the book's new owner. I always write my full name, "James Duane Bolin," on the first line, followed by my home, "Murray, Kentucky," on the second line, and then the present date, the day that I purchased the book. This is my record of this important event.

By this time, my dinner has arrived, so I carefully place the books aside, just long enough to enjoy the meal. Then I pick up a volume again, ask for another iced tea, and begin reading in earnest. Our son, Wesley, reads like this even in our company, but I can only do it when alone out in public. For me, reading is at once solitary and communal; I read silently in delicious isolation, and then, only later, I dish out favorite passages aloud to my family and friends.

Perhaps there is a more profound connection between reading and eating. A Teddy Roosevelt biographer wrote that TR "devoured" his books. And John Steinbeck wrote about his suggestion to his publishers, a suggestion "which they have stupidly failed to follow." Steinbeck was convinced that weightier, thicker books sold better, and he suggested, "If the book were printed on rye bread it would be very much thicker."

"Further," he wrote, "your bread book would solve two problems. The reader would never lose his place since he would eat each page as he finished it; also the lost profit of the borrowed book would be eliminated." "And people do like to read while they eat," Steinbeck concluded. Jesus agreed. "Man shall not live by bread alone," he quoted from Deuteronomy to Satan. Bread is important, but there is also the Word. I must agree with John Steinbeck and Jesus. After all, there is something very filling and fulfilling about reading and eating.

An Odd Shelf of Books

The summer is all but over, and I am trying to think what we have accomplished during these hot, dry months of June, July, and August. Wesley and Cammie Jo have enjoyed a few weeks—fewer and fewer weeks each year it seems—off from school, and Evelyn and I have savored more time spent with them and with each other. Around the house, we have trimmed the ivy, consistently mowed the yard, and weed-eated the borders. We made a decision not to water the grass, and the drought has done its work. For the first time all summer, I waited two weeks to mow instead of one; there was just no need.

At the beginning of the summer, we accomplished something of lasting value. We unloaded a large painted bookshelf from the garage, laid it on its side, and sawed off the top four inches before re-nailing the top board back on. Several years ago we had gone through the same exercise with a twin shelf. These are large shelves: 7'8" tall (after the sawing operation) and 4' wide with seven shelves each. Each shelf will house almost 400 books. We needed to cut a few inches off the top in order for the shelves to fit in our family room. Stacks of books had multiplied around the house, and no space for them. So we had to haul in yet another shelf.

These are nice shelves. Dr. Ray Moore, a retired professor in Murray State's College of Education and a fine craftsman, had built the shelves for our church library. When a new library, complete with new shelving, was included in the plans for an addition to our church building, the old shelves were no longer needed. We bought two of the old shelves to supplement ten equally sturdy shelves that we had purchased soon after Evelyn and I married from the old public library in Dixon, Kentucky. Those ten old public library shelves, along with several built-in shelves and an odd assortment of smaller, movable shelves, no longer accommodated our ever-growing collection of books.

We needed help; the books threatened to take over hallways, bedroom corners, and almost every tabletop in the house. So we brought in Dr. Moore's shelf from the garage, positioned it next to its twin opposite the fireplace in the family room, and without moving a book from an already existing shelf, lovingly filled all but one row. We all worked to move the stray books from the floors and tabletops from rooms all over the house. This was a very fulfilling adventure.

I noticed, though, when repositioning the books, that several of them, rather than being novels or history books, were—now this is scary—books about books, books about the reading, writing, and collecting of books. One of these books was Anne Fadiman's *Ex Libris: Confessions of a Common Reader.* Fadiman, the daughter of Clifton Fadiman, the writer and intellectual who served as chief editor at Simon & Schuster and then as the book review editor of the *New Yorker*, confessed, "I have never been able to resist a book about books." I am afraid that I am suffering from the same condition, for I have a growing odd shelf of books about books.

Fadiman maintains that everyone should keep an odd shelf of books devoted to the quirks and unique fancy of the book owner. George Orwell, for example, held "a collection of bound sets of ladies' magazines from the 1860s." Vice Admiral James Stockdale "brought to Vietnam the complete works of Epictetus, whose Stoic philosophy was to sustain him through eight years as a prisoner of war." In addition to all of her own books about books, Anne Fadiman keeps an "odd shelf" of some sixty-four books about polar exploration.

Fadiman has books about Captain Lawrence Edward Grace Oates, a courageous explorer who brought with him on an expedition to Antarctica "all five volumes of Charles James Napier's *Peninsular War*, an epic study of the Napoleonic campaigns in Iberia." Oates was described by a fellow explorer as "a gentleman, quite a gentleman, and always a gentleman." According to Fadiman, when Oates arrived at the South Pole on March 17, 1912, and when he realized "that his frostbitten and gangrenous feet were handicapping the rest of the party, [he] uttered the most famous and gallant words in the history of polar exploration: 'I am just going outside and may be some time.' Then he stumbled out of the tent into a blizzard, never to be seen again. It was his thirty-second birthday."

I don't know what happened to Oates's "odd shelf of books" on the Napoleonic campaigns in Iberia, but I do know that I can find my own "odd shelf" of books about books on one of Dr. Moore's beautifully crafted bookshelves on the west wall of our family room.

On Books and the Housing of Them

Perhaps no one knew more about books and the housing of them than William Ewart Gladstone (1809-1898), the author of a book—well, it is really a tract, only twenty-nine pages long—titled *On Books and the Housing of Them*. The writer, Anne Fadiman, found a copy of Gladstone's book in a secondhand bookshop, and at first it didn't dawn on her that the author was *that* Gladstone, but, as Fadiman put it, "It *was* that Gladstone: four times British Prime Minister, grand old man of the Liberal Party, scholar, financier, theologian, orator, humanitarian, and thorn in the side of Benjamin Disraeli, who, when asked to define the difference between a misfortune and a calamity, replied, 'If Mr. Gladstone were to fall into the Thames, it would be a misfortune. But if someone dragged him out again, it would be a calamity.'"

Fadiman knew that Gladstone's little book is a jewel with many facets and "if you wish to understand the character of both W. E. Gladstone and Victorian England, everything you need to know is contained within the small compass of *On Books and the Housing of Them*." Gladstone deals with the old problem of "too many books, too little space," a problem certainly in the Bolin household.

Gladstone argued that this problem might be solved by some sort of sophisticated shelving system, a system that might "prevent the population of Great Britain from being extruded some centuries hence into the surrounding waters by the exorbitant dimensions of their own libraries."

On Books and the Housing of Them is almost impossible to find, unless one could fortuitously happen upon a copy in a used bookstore. I did, however, find a digitized copy on the Internet, but the printed copy of loose pages is just not the same as the real thing, some dusty, frayed, bound copy, published in New York by Dodd, Mead & Company in 1890. I noticed that in a "Note" at the beginning of the book, the publisher wrote, "It is well to remember concerning *Books and the Housing of Them* that the books themselves should be worthy the care the owner bestows on them." Surely, a more careful selection of books would cut down on any housing crisis.

But after the books have been meticulously selected, and after thousands of books have been deemed so meritorious that one just has to own them, what then? Gladstone suggested an elaborate shelving system around the walls of a room. Shelves would be built along the walls, but every few feet, shelves would also be built projecting at right angles into the room. I wish I could draw you a diagram, but I will just have to let Gladstone describe it for you. He calculated that a library room, twenty by forty feet, with projecting bookcases three feet long, twelve inches deep, and nine feet high, "so that the upper shelf can be reached by the aid of a wooden stool of two steps not more than twenty inches high," would accommodate between eighteen thousand and twenty thousand volumes. In addition to his idea of shelves projecting into a room, Gladstone also designed a system of rolling shelves, a system that is used today in the Radcliffe Camera room of Oxford's Bodleian Library and at *The New York Times Book Review*. I suppose Gladstone's system is the basis of the plan used as well in the basement stacks at Murray State's Waterfield Library.

Fadiman has seen a photograph of Gladstone sitting in his own library at Hawarden Castle, a room that he called the Temple of Peace. As Fadiman describes it, "He sits in a wooden armchair, surrounded by leather-bound volumes on shelves that are, of course, constructed according to the principles set forth in *On Books and the Housing of Them*." Gladstone spent many a happy hour in his Temple of Peace, reading books of course, but also caring for them. "The book must of necessity be put into a bookcase," he wrote. "And the bookcase must be housed. And the house must be kept. And the library must be dusted, must be arranged, must be catalogued. What a vista of toil, yet not unhappy toil."

When I retire from Murray State's Department of History, I will be faced with the task of moving all of those history books from my sixth floor Faculty Hall office to our home. Perhaps I will build shelves, or rather have them built, and fashion a room according to Gladstone's plan. And perhaps with Evelyn I can while away the days of my retirement in just such a room, reading, writing, and caring for books.

Picture in a Frame

My songwriting friend Daniel Martin Moore from Elizabethtown, Kentucky, performs Tom Waits's unbelievably poignant song titled "Picture in a Frame." Evelyn and I drove to Lexington to hear Daniel, and sitting there with Evelyn we almost fell out of our seats when we heard his crystal clear voice sing:

I come calling in my Sunday best
I come calling in my Sunday best
I come calling in my Sunday best
Ever since I put your picture
In a frame
I love you baby and I always will
I love you baby and I always will
I love you baby and I always will
Ever since I put your picture
In a frame.

We have framed pictures throughout our house—family members, the children at various ages, our parents and grandparents. There is indeed something about placing a picture in a frame that legitimizes the moment. The theologian, Frederick Buechner, wrote about this very thing. "What the frame does," Buechner writes, "is enable us to see not just something about the moment, but the moment itself in all its ineffable ordinariness and particularity." According to Buechner, "That is the nature and purpose of frames. The frame does not change the moment, but it changes our way of perceiving the moment. It makes us notice the moment."

The purpose of literature and painting and music is to make us notice the moment. "From the simplest lyric to the most complex novel and densest drama, literature is asking us to pay attention," Buechner writes. "Pay attention to the west wind. Pay attention to the boy on the raft, the lady in the tower, the old man on the train. In sum, pay attention to the world and all that dwells therein and thereby learn at last to pay attention to yourself and all that dwells therein."

For Buechner, "The painter does the same thing, of course. Rembrandt puts a frame around an old woman's face.... It is not a remarkable face. You would not look twice at the old woman if you found her sitting across the aisle from you on a bus. But it is a face so remarkably seen that it forces you to see it remarkably, just as Cezanne makes you see a bowl of apples or Andrew Wyeth a muslin curtain blowing in at an open window. It is a face unlike any other face in all the world. All the faces in the world are in this one old face."

And just as painters work with space, musicians such as Daniel Martin Moore work with time.

> "Listen! say Vivaldi, Brahms, Stravinsky. Listen to this time that I have framed between the first note and the last and to these sounds in time. Listen to the way the silence is broken into uneven lengths between the sounds and to the silences themselves. Listen to the scrape of bow against gut, the rap of stick against drumhead, the rush of breath through reed and wood. The sounds of the earth are like music, the old song goes, and the sounds of music are also like the sounds of the earth, which is of course where music comes from. Listen to the voices outside the window, the rumble of the furnace, the creak of your chair, the water running in the kitchen sink. Learn to listen to the music of your own lengths of time, your own silences."

Only Frederick Buechner writes like that. Only Daniel Martin Moore sings like he sings. According to Buechner, "Literature, painting, music—the most basic lesson that all art teaches us is to stop, look, and listen to life on this planet, including our own lives, as a vastly richer, deeper, more mysterious business than most of the time it ever occurs to us to suspect as we bumble along from day to day on automatic pilot."

And then, as you might expect from a theologian, Buechner takes art into the realm of the spiritual. "In a world that for the most part steers clear of the whole idea of holiness, art is one of the few places left where we can speak to each other of holy things," he writes. "Is it too much to say that to stop, look, and listen is also the most basic lesson that the Judeo-Christian tradition teaches us?" Buechner is convinced that "if we are to love our neighbors, before doing anything else we must see our neighbors. With our imagination as well as our eyes, that is to say like artists, we must see not just their faces, but the life behind and within their faces. Here it is love that is the frame we see them in."

Emily Dickinson wrote to a friend that "Consider the lilies of the field" was the only commandment she never broke. Buechner thought, "She could have done a lot worse." For to consider the lilies is the "sine qua non of art and religion both."

And when we put a picture in a frame, that person, that moment, must be special indeed.

Do Libraries Really Destroy Books?

As unfathomable as it might seem to me, apparently libraries do indeed destroy books. Now I understand the need for public librarians to conduct a weeding out of old, worn-out books. In fact, my family and I have bought many a volume at our library's book sales over the years. I am writing about something else entirely. I am referring to a university library's systematic destruction of perfectly good bound volumes filled with precious information or stories.

In an October 11, 2011, post on National Public Radio's "Monkey See" blog, Linda Holmes wrote in "Hard Choices: Do Libraries Really Destroy Books?" about another piece written by the Australian blogger, S. Peter Davis, for *Cracked* (the surprisingly interesting online offshoot of the old comedy print magazine) called "6 Reasons We're In Another 'Book-Burning' Period In History." "It's not about the destruction of books based on content or community objections," Holmes wrote, "it's about the destruction of books because libraries (and sometimes bookstores) don't know what to do with them, or don't know what to do with them that makes economic sense." Of course all decisions these days must come down to the almighty dollar.

Here is the situation according to S. Peter Davis: "Libraries have a certain amount of space and a certain amount of money. The careful culling of books is painstaking work." "Imagine you're the manager of a library," Davis wrote, "and some accountant tells you that you need to get rid of 100,000 books, and do it in a week. You really have two options. One, you can get a bunch of academics to scour your collection and painstakingly rate each book according to its value and importance. Then you can hire a bunch of people to take down the 100,000 least important books and painstakingly stamp and debug them, one by one."

"Your second option," according to Davis, "is to get the computer to spit out a list of the 100,000 least borrowed books, and hire a few people to walk down the aisles with their arms out, throwing those books in a shredding machine." For which option do you think many university library deans opt?

Oh, they might even go to the trouble to "find a paper recycling centre that will pay you for the pulp, so destroying the books leads to a net profit." "That's sobering stuff," Holmes wrote, and "it's obviously an oversimplification, but it's a stark choice."

Holmes spoke with Betsy Simpson, president of the American Library Association's Association for Library Collections and Technical Services. Simpson told Holmes that librarians do care. "Libraries really take seriously their mission to preserve the cultural record," she assured Holmes. There is the obvious problem of limited space and the thousands of new books published each year, but today, libraries serve new functions.

"We are not going to be a book warehouse," one library dean said crassly, as if libraries have ever been that. "The space issue is a concern," Simpson said, "because more and more, there's a realization that our users need space to interact and collaborate and space to contemplate." "When you need more space for group work," Holmes wrote, "you can't pack every inch of your library with more shelves just to avoid getting rid of books." After all, there absolutely must be room for the ever-present cafe; all of us readers and researchers must have our lattes and americanos.

According to Holmes, "There are ways other than destroying books to deal with space limitations," and some libraries try those first. Simpson pointed out "that libraries have book sales and, in some cases, permanent bookstores for books they don't want to keep (there's a bookstore just like that where she works, at the University of Florida)."

And then, books sometimes are destroyed. I'll admit that a historian might not shed a tear for television repair manuals or the like, but what about when scores of bound volumes of the *American Historical Review*, the *Journal of Southern History*, and the *Journal of American History* are summarily removed from the shelves of a university library without so much as a heads-up or an FYI to the history department chair or faculty. The volumes were undoubtedly shredded or burned, their ashes strewn over the Tennessee or Cumberland Rivers or wherever it is that fields of "progress" are fertilized.

The point is not that we can access each of these volumes online. Some of us still like to show our students how to get dirty in the stacks of a library, how to "do" history in an archive, how to experience the joy of a sleuth—Sherlock Holmes fashion—and detective-like, research historical information in multiple ways.

And then there is the argument that an antiquarian book collector might use, that "some of these books are their own important documents, because an out-of-date atlas, for instance, may not record the world as it is, but it records the world as it was, and isn't that a better source, in fact, than a perspective we have now on the way things were then?"

In conclusion, however, Linda Holmes delivered what was perhaps her most powerful point. "Let me tell you something," she wrote. "My grandfather died many years before I was born. I've seen pictures of him, and I know he had the same face as my father and uncles and one of my cousins and one of my nephews. I call it the 'Holmes face.'" "But my grandfather also wrote this book, *Air Conditioning in Summer and Winter*," Holmes continued. "It was published in 1938." According to Holmes, "there is absolutely no reason I could demand that it be kept with any degree of remove. It's a 74-year-old book about air conditioning. My father is not living off the royalties. My parents have a copy of it on their shelf at home, so it's not as if I've never seen it.... It's a thing.

It's in the world. Somewhere, nine copies of *Air Conditioning in Summer and Winter* still exist for sale. And I clicked around to the university libraries that still have it, too. (Holmes found it on WorldCat). I visited it. Someone is even selling it on eBay."

Holmes wrote, "You can try to separate the utility of the information in a printed book from its dearness to you as an object, but you can't entirely. And my guess is that nobody knows that better than people who spend their days working in libraries, which takes you back to Betsy Simpson's request that you not picture librarians throwing out books with their cold, cold hearts." True librarians—the real ones—found their callings because they love books. They love being around them, and they love helping folks find them. The new, young upstart technocrats are something else altogether. Can you imagine a dean of libraries who does not like books? They exist; believe me. How they came to that position is beyond me.

Holmes admitted that some of her concern "is sentiment, and sentiment is personal. Maybe finding a home for every library book would require a loving book detective to find the granddaughters of authors who know their grandpas from pictures. "It's too much to ask, I know," she wrote. But her name IS Holmes. And her final plea to American librarians is a simple one: "let me know if you're thinking about pulping a copy of *Air Conditioning in Summer and Winter.* I'm pretty sure I have the shelf space."

Comfort and Joy

It is not just for historians that December is the time of year for remembering. The end of the year causes all of us to take stock, to think about the failures and the victories of the past, and perhaps even to make preliminary plans for the new year. Christians and secular observers of Christmas alike also remember about this time in the middle of December the celebrations of Christmases past, those joyous times of families gathered around groaning tables laden with sumptuous food and then around decorated, lighted trees to open presents, to laugh, to share stories, and to bask in the glow of love and security and care.

We remember just such a Christmas. Perhaps we are anticipating another one just like it in a few days. Others, however, have burdens to bear, burdens that seem especially heavy this time of the year. My mother's dear mother, my grandmother, died on Christmas Day. I only came to understand my mother's bout of melancholy each Christmas once I had grown to manhood, finally able to take in exactly what having a loved one's death on Christmas Day must have meant. Christmas would have never been the same.

Of course, for thousands of others living far below the poverty line, Christmas only heightens the struggle for the basic necessities of life. Homeless men and women roaming city streets, taking in the Christmas decorations in store windows, realizing they will never be able to enjoy the riches within. Their only compensation, perhaps, might be the temporary spirit of good will that causes Christmas shoppers to hand out dollar bills instead of quarters and dimes to the sick and the dirty individuals they encounter as they duck in the downtown shoppes.

Think of the mothers and fathers, the brothers and sisters, the grandmothers and grandfathers, the rest of the extended families and friends, as they sit around living rooms on December 25 this year in entire communities where tragedy has struck. What comfort will they find? What solace will the Christmas story bring to them?

The heart of the matter is that if we read the Christmas story without the usual accouterments of traditions of tree and lights and wrapping paper and eggnog and all of the mass and crass commercialism that we have made synonymous with the yuletide season, the central characters in this most important story relate much more readily to the individuals I described above who live below the poverty line, to the homeless people unable to find a place to sleep at night, to the hungry, the tired, the dispossessed, the dirty, the distraught.

Back in Jerusalem, when Herod heard that the Christ was born, he decreed that all newborn baby boys be killed immediately upon their birth. Of course it is no comfort now, but the grieving of Newtown and Connecticut and all the parents of the United States and the world, if remembering Christmas at all, should remember that the Christ child was born in a holocaust under conditions of poverty.

It was for those of us who have been brought up in peace and comfort and security that the Christ child came. But He also came for those who were more like His earthly family, poor and dispossessed from a small town, having traveled a long way before that day, having come into Bethlehem tired, dirty, tattered, taking shelter in a stable or cave.

And so it was that the Christ child came into the world. It was Mary and Joseph who represented the underclass. That is why we all can take comfort at this time of year, whether we are celebrating a life of joy and peace, or suffering, devastation, and death in a world of woe. Whatever our condition, we can "go tell it on the mountain, that Jesus Christ is born."

More Than Words

With all of our Kindles and Nooks and iPads, we wonder at times if in a few years books—made of paper and boards—will be relegated to museums where they will be viewed as relics under glass along with the Rosetta Stone, papyrus scrolls, and stacks of cuneiform clay tablets. Wesley is taking a summer school class at Yale on the history of publishing, and he has handled the relics: portions of the first three chapters of Genesis thousands of years old, early writing on skins of animals, scrolls, a copy of the first Gutenberg Bible, Shakespeare folios, a first edition of *Paradise Lost*, the first book ever published in the English language, a volume by Erasmus, and other first editions of some of the world's classics.

Wesley said that he "reverently turn[s] the pages and touch[es] the covers with the delicacy and care with which I would caress a newly hatched hummingbird." He will have, Wesley said, "an old book smelling high for days." Evelyn and I made sure that Wesley and Cammie Jo grew up with books. They knew early on how to navigate their way around a library. But for Wesley, this class on the history of publishing is an academic experience that he will never forget.

Before an appreciative audience at Harvard University, Annie Dillard told about a recent visit to China. The author of *Pilgrim at Tinker Creek* revealed that "the room in which a Chinese reader lives may, or may not, have a single 25-watt bulb. China has little paper, for printing books or anything else. How many trees should they fell to print what, and why?" And books? What books are precious enough to print? What books are valuable enough to expend the scarce paper to print them, to make them available for the people to read? Dillard was asked these questions point blank by members of her Chinese audience: "Which are the best fiction writers in the United States? Whose fiction should we translate for China?" Dillard could not answer immediately. "We are struck dumb," she told the Harvard gathering. "Our six person delegation of US scholars, publishers, and writers cannot think of a blessed thing to say. One man suggests *Lolita*. He receives a light, surreptitious kick. We appear never to have heard of any American writers in our lives."

Dillard's story has been published in a thoughtful collection of essays, titled *More Than Words: Contemporary Writers on the Works that Shaped Them*. I was immediately drawn to this book because I myself have been shaped by the books I have read and continue to reread. From the characters of Dickens, to the memoirs of the blind Indian writer Ved Mehta, to the fantasy and apologetics of C. S. Lewis, to the biographies of Edmund Morris, to the travelogues of H. V. Morton, to the histories of Barbara Tuchman and Shelby Foote and William Leuchtenburg, and to the King James and New International versions of the Bible—I have surely been shaped by these books, in my thinking and in my feeling and in my living.

In the book *More Than Words,* editor Philip Yancey wrote, "In a nation that publishes over fifty thousand new titles a year, it is easy to lose sight of the almost sacred aura that once surrounded books. John Updike has written of the products…of the [underground] press in Eastern Europe in the 1970s: blue carbon typing on onionskin paper, bound in leather, their titles stamped in hand-punched silver letters. The sight of such fragile books, so lovingly assembled, restored for [Updike] the archetypal sense of what a book was, 'an elemental sheaf, bound together by love and daring, to be passed with excitement from hand to hand.'"

Across time and generations, Yancey wrote, "books carry the thoughts and feelings, the essence, of the human spirit." There is a African proverb that when an elderly person dies, it is as if a whole library is destroyed. Oh yes. Lifetimes of experience are buried each day in silent graves. And oh yes. Here in the United States, where books are so plentiful, when a volume is left unread, years of experience and research lie buried between two boards on a dusty shelf in some silent library.

My Life With Books: A Love Story

Wesley Seaton Bolin

(Our son, Wesley, wrote this essay for his application to Yale University. Wesley's love for books is a comfort for him and an inspiration to his parents. Wesley has passed on his love for books to his sister, Cammie Jo.)

I read. I read books. It is what I do. This is my identity. Thomas Jefferson said, “I cannot live without books.” Neither can I. I come from a bookish family. My parents are both teachers and readers, and their love of books has been instilled in me, whether through nature or nurture, I don’t know. I have many memories of them reading to me when I was very small, but my fondest memories come from the summer before I began kindergarten, when we spent five weeks in Virginia. We lived in a small house right off the grounds of the William Faulkner house, on the campus of the University of Virginia, and it was there, sitting on a bench, that my father read to me Lewis’s *Chronicles of Narnia* and books from the *Great Illustrated Classics. David Copperfield* was always my favorite. My mom read to me in a slightly different setting, seated on a log hidden inside the branches of a giant bush growing near our house. It was there that we devoured *The Boxcar Children* books. Another favorite reading memory came eleven years later. At 2:00 a.m. one summer morning, after reading *One Hundred Years of Solitude* to its pig-tailed finish, unable to sleep, I lay there staring at the ceiling trying to grasp the immensity of the Buendia family’s story. Though I was finished with the book, the book wasn’t yet finished with me.

For the past several years I’ve kept a reading list. This past year I’ve read over 140 books. I decided to concentrate on twentieth century American literature, and although dozens of books fell outside that category, I was able to cover many classic American writers and their books. I read the entire Vonnegut canon, some twenty-two volumes in total, and the major works of Steinbeck and Walker Percy. When reading such a volume of books, interesting juxtapositions emerge. *All the President’s Men* connected nicely with the Watergate coverage of two dozen collections of Garry Trudeau’s *Doonesbury*. Nabokov’s *Lolita* and Updike’s *Rabbit, Run*, dissimilar works, merge into a symbiotic portrayal of 1950s America. Incredible vignettes come to mind from all the books: the hurricane in *Their Eyes Were Watching God*, the death of Willie Stark in *All the King’s Men*, the village of Holcomb from *In Cold Blood*, James Thurber’s account of the night the ghost got in, Yossarian rowing to freedom in *Catch-22,* and even the perils of the passive voice in Strunk and White’s *Elements of Style*.

Vonnegut wrote that literature is the only art form that requires those who enjoy it to be performers. I read. I read books. It is what I do. This is my identity: a reader, and a performer.

Part Eight

Writing

"Well, everything in there's true. What they wrote in there was true."
Ellie Mae Burroughs

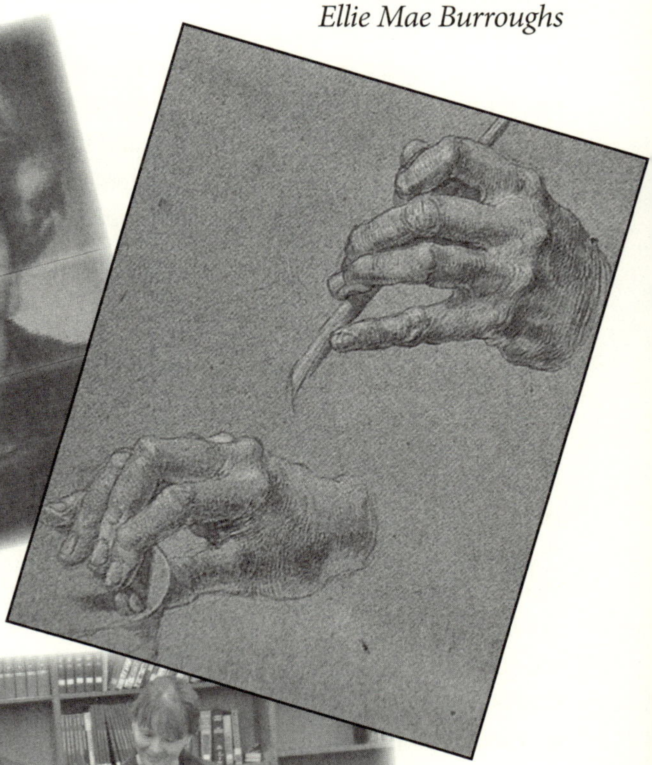

Top Left: Eudora Welty. Top Right: Dürer hands, Albrecht Dürer. Bottom: Cammie Jo Bolin, Signing Day for Centre College at the Murray High School Library, Murray, Kentucky. Bottom, L to R, Duane Bolin, Cammie Jo, Evelyn Seaton Belin; top, Coach Mark Boggess, Principal Teresa Speed.

Bird By Bird

The act of writing remains a mystery to me. Sometimes I may sit down—in a coffee shop, legal pad and pencil in hand, or in my study at home, in front of my computer screen—and the words flow. Now, whether the words make sense, or whether they tell the tale that I am trying to tell, is another matter altogether. At other times, I sit, staring off into space, and find that thirty minutes later the lined paper is still empty, or the computer screen is still blank. The sportswriter Red Smith said it best. "Writing is easy," he wrote. "You just sit down at a typewriter, open up a vein, and bleed it out drop by drop."

Why is it that some of the sweetest things, the most enjoyable of life's offerings, are so many times the hardest to endure, or the most gut-wrenching to complete. Writing, for me, is hard work. Yet, the process of writing, as difficult as it may be, is also fulfilling and satisfying work. Someone said that he really did not wish to be a writer; he wanted rather to be someone who had written. But it is in the act of writing itself, much like the act of living, that a writer may be fulfilled. We would not say that we would not wish to live, but only to have lived. Would we?

An editor encouraged me to forge ahead on an overdue manuscript. He put me on to a book by Anne Lamott titled *Bird By Bird: Some Instructions on Writing and Life*. I ordered the book immediately, and, putting off my writing, read it cover to cover. A prolific and inspirational writer of essays, novels, and memoirs, Lamott offers instruction on the art of writing, but more importantly for me, on the art of living. After lending another one of her books, *Traveling Mercies: Some Thoughts on Faith*, to a History Department colleague, she thanked me, and after reading the book remarked that Lamott was "quite a character." Quite a character indeed!

Lamott's salty language belies her commitment to a pilgrimage of religious faith and a determination to live a life of service. The title of her book, *Bird By Bird*, comes from a word of encouragement given by her father to her older brother. She writes:

> Thirty years ago, my older brother, who was ten years old at the time, was trying to get a report on birds written that he'd had three months to write. [It] was due the next day. We were out at our family cabin in Bolinas, and he was at the kitchen table close

to tears, surrounded by binder paper and pencils and unopened books on birds, immobilized by the hugeness of the task ahead. Then my father sat down beside him, put his arm around my brother's shoulder, and said, "Bird by bird, buddy. Just take it bird by bird."

The wise father's instruction gave solace to a son struggling with a project, the completion of which made seemingly impossible by the son's procrastination. The story gave encouragement to me because of my own penchant for procrastination and my own unwillingness to focus on the task at hand. When I am tempted to allow writing projects, essay examinations, and committee reports to pile up shoulder high on my desk, or when I allow thank-yous to go unwritten or unsaid, long walks and talks with those that I love to be put off, and common decencies and kindnesses to be neglected altogether, I can tell myself to at least start somewhere. At least do something. And let the enjoyment begin.

"Bird by bird, buddy. Just take it bird by bird."

"What They Wrote in There Was True"

My students are struggling to write book reviews in my American History classes. They are to pick a book of history on a topic of their choosing and then read the book critically. They must learn to read with a critical eye, because the paper they produce is much more than the sort of book report they might have written in elementary or middle school. Rather than a book report, they are to write a book review, a critical analysis of the book. I want them to pick the book apart.

The writer of a book review should go beyond a mere summary of content; the reviewer identifies the topic of the book and the thesis, or the main idea, the main point of the book. What arguments did the author put forth to prove the thesis? Did the author prove the thesis? On what sources, primary or secondary, did the author rely? What about the author's writing style? Was the book understandable to a general reader? Or was the book written for other experts in the discipline? After reading the book, would you recommend the work to other readers? Why or why not?

As you can see, students are asked to analyze the book, not just retell it. A close reading is required. We teach critical thinking skills, but a book review, properly written, requires critical reading and critical writing skills too.

The most remarkable book review that I have ever read was provided by a poor farm woman from Alabama. On assignment for *Fortune* magazine, writer James Agee and photographer Walker Evans traveled to rural Alabama in the depths of the Great Depression to live with three different tenant-farming families. Out of this experience, Agee wrote *Let Us Now Praise Famous Men*, and Evans contributed a series of extraordinary photographs, documenting the lives of these struggling folks. The eloquence of the photographs match the eloquence of the prose.

I would think this book would be most difficult to review. *Let Us Now Praise Famous Men* defies categorization. Part documentary, part memoir, and part biography, Agee and Evans transformed what was to be a magazine piece into a complex work of literature.

When Ellie Mae Burroughs, a wife and mother in one of the tenant families, read the book a decade after it was published, she did not consider thesis, sources, or any other component of a formal book review. Instead, she simply gave her honest assessment of the book. John Hersey included Ms. Burrough's assessment in his introduction to a new edition of the book, published in 1988:

"I don't guess it's been over ten years ago that I seen the book, if it's been that long," Ms. Burroughs said. "My daughter got one of 'em; I don't know where in the world she got it, but she got it and told me she had it, and she wanted me to look at it and give it to me. And I took it home and I read it plumb through. And when I read it plumb through I give it back to her and I said, 'Well everything in there's true.' What they wrote in there was true."

"Well everything in there's true." "What they wrote in there was true." I don't expect any of my students to write such a review. I doubt they would be able to give such unvarnished praise to their chosen volume of history. I have a feeling, though, that Ellie Mae Burroughs's analysis of *Let Us Now Praise Famous Men* is an accurate display of critical reading. Very few book reviews could be so positive.

Making Things

Observing members of my family create things is a dear blessing to me. Whether it is my children creating art, writing, and making music, or whether it is Evelyn making a home, the act of making beautiful things is surely one of the unique gifts that we enjoy as human beings. In fact, a characteristic of being human is the ability to make things.

My son is convinced that even reading is a performance art. The act of reading, according to Kurt Vonnegut, requires a creative performance on the part of not just the writer but the reader as well. And the easier the writer makes this collaboration for the reader, the better. What if a composer made a piece of music so difficult that a philharmonic orchestra could not perform it? Likewise, what if a writer made a poem or short story or novel or memoir so unintelligible that the reader was unable to perform the act of reading? It is, after all, the performance of the reader that gives the performance of the writer value and worth.

Anyway, a characteristic of being human is the ability to make things, whether that act of creation involves painting, music, writing, or even reading. Evelyn and I cherish the various creative performances of our children, even more so now that our children are all but grown. We have kept every scrap of their drawing and painting from their very earliest efforts. We hoard their writing pieces, their portfolios, and even their random scribblings. We have stashed their creations in drawers and file cabinets, stacking them in piles in chests in the attic.

At the same time, we have tried not to miss any of their musical offerings—the children's choir at church, a Christmas or spring band concert, the high school choir, or the series of marching band performances each fall. In fact, it seems that at times our lives revolve around these various performances, these creative acts of our children. These performances often move me to tears, and I remain grateful for the creative gifts of our children.

This is as it should be. This is as it is meant to be. The Genesis account of creation explains that we are made in the image of God. "So God created man in his own image, in the image of God he created him; male and female he created them." (Genesis 1:27) I think it is significant that the image of God portrayed in these first verses of Scripture is the image of a creator. So, if we are indeed made in the image of God, I suppose we are also made with the ability to create.

We live in close proximity to man-made things, but we also have close at hand here in western Kentucky the results of the creation of woods and waters, of natural and living things that we have not made ourselves, but over which we have been given the daunting responsibility of conserving and preserving.

But we are ourselves creators, not in the sense that we are able to create something out of nothing, but in the various degrees of our abilities and through various creative forms, we have been gifted with the ability to create. How could we live without experiencing in ourselves and in others the act of creating art and architecture, music and literature, film and dance. We came into being through a creative act, and we live and move and have our being in the acts of making things.

G. K. Chesterton said it best when he wrote in his book *The Everlasting Man,* "Art is the signature of man." He explained that our ability to make things sets us apart from the lower creatures. Art, the ability to create, makes us truly human.

So here's to all the acts of creation that will sustain us and enrich us in the coming days.

A Writer's Life

I have just completed a second reading of Ernest Hemingway's *A Moveable Feast*, his memoir published posthumously about his early years as a writer in Paris. Hemingway discussed the full range of joy and temptations leading to sorrow that he experienced in Paris during the 1920s when he himself was in his early twenties. Hemingway had given up his journalism, from which he made money, to concentrate on what he considered serious literature, stories, and novels.

In Paris with his wife Hadley and their young son, Bumby, or as they often called him, Mr. Bumby, Hemingway wrote in the cafes, while his wife and son stayed back in a spare apartment. Hemingway's lean prose mirrored his Spartan lifestyle, although he found a way to enjoy wine and aperitifs before cheap meals of oysters and snails and bread.

Still unpublished, Hemingway also experienced hunger before his first book, *Three Stories and Ten Poems*, came out in 1923, and before a collection of short stories, *In Our Time*, appeared in 1925. With the publication of *The Sun Also Rises*, in 1926, Hemingway could rest easy in the knowledge that he had become, according to the blurb at the back of *A Moveable Feast*, "the preeminent writer of his time," the leading voice of what Gertrude Stein dubbed "the lost generation."

Before all the fame, however, Hemingway knew what it felt like to miss a meal. "You got very hungry when you did not eat enough in Paris," he wrote, "because all the bakery shops had such good things in the windows and people ate outside at tables on the sidewalk so that you saw and smelled the food." "When you had given up journalism and were writing nothing that anyone in America would buy," he said, "the best place to go was the Luxembourg gardens where you saw and smelled nothing to eat." According to Hemingway, an artist—a writer or a painter—could learn from poverty and hunger. At the Luxembourg museum, "all the paintings were sharpened and clearer and more beautiful if you were belly-empty, hollow-hungry," he wrote. In such a state, Hemingway "learned to understand Cezanne much better and to see truly how he made landscapes when I was hungry. I used to wonder if he were hungry too when he painted; but I thought possibly it was only that he had forgotten to eat. It was one of those unsound but illuminating thoughts you have when you have been sleepless and hungry."

"Later I thought Cezanne was probably hungry in a different way," Hemingway wrote. Hemingway believed that "hunger is good discipline and you learn from it." He learned well. Hemingway went on to write such masterpieces as *The Old Man and the Sea* and *For Whom the Bell Tolls.*

But it was in those early, hungry years that Ernest Hemingway experienced joy. He was happiest then, when he was unpublished and unknown. In a conversation with his poet friend, Evan Shipman told Hemingway, "We need more true mystery in our lives, Hem." According to Shipman, "the completely unambitious writer and the really good unpublished poem are the things we lack most at this time." "There is, of course," Shipman noted, "the problem of sustenance."

Do Not Mourn Me Dead

Anyone who has seen the Ken Burns's Civil War documentary must have been touched by the reading of the Sullivan Ballou letter at the end of the first segment. My students react to the force of the letter as the haunting violin strains of "Ashokan Farewell" play in the background. For them, the reality of the letter sinks in at the end of the letter when the narrator announces, "Sullivan Ballou was killed a week later at the first Battle of Bull Run, July 21, 1861."

A Union soldier in the Civil War, Ballou was born on March 28, 1829, in Rhode Island, educated first at Phillips Academy in Andover, Massachusetts, and then at Brown University in Providence, Rhode Island. Following his graduation from Brown, he attended the National Law School in Ballston, New York, and was admitted to the Rhode Island Bar in 1853. He was elected to the Rhode Island House of Representatives and later served as speaker.

Ballou married Sarah Hart Shumway on October 15, 1855. Sullivan and Sarah had two sons together, Edgar and William. At the beginning of the Civil War in 1861, Ballou immediately joined the Union army at the age of 32. Sarah was 24.

His letter to Sarah is dated July the 14th, 1861, and written from Washington, DC. I will not quote to you the entire letter, although it is worthy to be quoted in full, but here are some poignant excerpts:

My very dear Sarah

> The indications are very strong that we shall move in a few days - perhaps tomorrow. Lest I should not be able to write you again, I feel impelled to write lines that may fall under your eye when I shall be no more.
>
> Our movement may be one of a few days duration and full of pleasure - and it may be one of severe conflict and death to me. Not my will, but thine o God, be done. If it is necessary that I should fall on the battlefield for my country, I am ready. I have no misgivings about, or lack of confidence in, the cause in which I am engaged, and my courage does not halt or falter. I know how strongly American Civilization now leans upon the triumph of the Government, and how great a debt we owe to those who went before us through the blood and suffering of the Revolution. And I am willing - perfectly willing - to lay down all my joys in this life, to help maintain this Government, and to pay that debt."...
>
> Sarah, my love for you is deathless, it seems to bind me to you with mighty cables that nothing but Omnipotence could break; and yet my love of Country comes over me like a strong wind and bears me irresistibly on with all these chains to the battlefield.
>
> The memories of the blissful moments I have spent with you come creeping over me, and I feel most gratified to God and to you that I have enjoyed them so long. And hard it is for me to give them up and burn to ashes the hopes of future years, when God willing, we might still have lived and loved together and

> seen our sons grow up to honorable manhood around us....my dear Sarah, never forget how much I love you, and when my last breath escapes me on the battlefield, it will whisper your name.
>
> Forgive my many faults, and the many pains I have caused you. How thoughtless and foolish I have oftentimes been! How gladly would I wash out with my tears every little spot upon your happiness, and struggle with all the misfortune of this world, to shield you and my children from harm."...
>
> But, O Sarah! If the dead can come back to this earth and flit unseen around those they loved, I shall always be near you; in the garish day and in the darkest night - amidst your happiest scenes and gloomiest hours - always, always; and if there be a soft breeze upon your cheek, it shall be my breath; or the cool air fans your throbbing temple, it shall be my spirit passing by.
>
> Sarah, do not mourn me dead; think I am gone and wait for thee, for we shall meet again.

After Sullivan Ballou's death at the first Battle of Bull Run, Sarah Ballou never married again. She died at 80 in 1927. Sarah and Sullivan Ballou are buried side by side at Swan Point Cemetery in Providence, Rhode Island.

Do Not Take the Press For Granted

In this computer age when print newspapers in major American cities struggle to survive, we can be thankful that small-town papers, both weeklies and dailies, fill a niche on which we depend. For small-town newspapers provide local news, news not covered in larger, regional, or metropolitan newspapers owned by huge faceless conglomerates.

I have not taken the time to tell my publishers and editors thank-you for giving me the opportunity to connect with Kentucky readers on a regular basis. My newspaper columns are rarely political, and only twice have readers taken issue with something I have written, but the rest of my readers have repeatedly offered encouragement and support. I am grateful for them.

A free press in Kentucky has a long and distinguished history. John Bradford published the first newspaper west of Pittsburgh in Lexington on August 11, 1787, five years before Kentucky became a state. Tom Eblen, a columnist for the *Lexington Herald-Leader,* gave an unpublished talk on the history and present state of the press in Kentucky at the Cardome Center in Georgetown several years ago. Eblen stated that Bradford, at that time a 38-year-old publisher, "had little or no training as a printer, reporter, writer or editor." He did understand deadlines, however, because he wrote in that first issue of the *Kentucky Gazette*, "My customers will excuse my first publication, as I am much hurried to get an impression by the time appointed."

Bradford's only assistant—his brother—had been ill for ten days "and was of no help whatsoever." But despite the rough start of Kentucky's first newspaper over 225 years ago, Eblen said that the *Gazette's* publication "began a long and illustrious newspaper tradition in Kentucky."

One simply cannot say enough about John Bradford. He was not just a publisher. He was an early Kentucky version of a Renaissance man. Eblen listed the wide range of Bradford's activities on the western frontier: "a land surveyor, Indian fighter, politician, moral philosopher, tavern owner, sheriff, civic host, community booster, postal service entrepreneur, real estate speculator, subdivision developer, mechanic, and mathematician."

Bradford did all that in addition to his primary calling: publishing newspapers and books. For it was also Bradford who published Kentucky's first books, organized its first public library, and ran one of the commonwealth's first bookstores. He also served as one of the first historians of Kentucky's pioneer period, as well as the chair of the trustees of Kentucky's first institution of higher learning—Transylvania University.

The 180 subscribers of Kentucky's first newspaper surely appreciated the role the press played in 1787, just as we still do today. According to Eblen, it cost "eighteen shillings per year for a subscription and three shillings for an advertisement of moderate length." If, however, a subscriber was not in possession of the hard specie so scarce on the frontier, payments could also be made with "corn, wheat, country-made linen, linsey, sugar, whiskey, ash flooring and cured bacon."

Among other things, Bradford, himself nicknamed "Old Wisdom," often published tidbits of "moral philosophy," such as the precepts of Benjamin Franklin. For example: "Narrow minds are like crooked bottles; the less they have in them, the more noise they make in pouring it out."

Today I am thankful to John Bradford and the great tradition of a free press that he began in Kentucky in 1787. I am also thankful for the readers of the *Murray Ledger & Times*, the *Providence Journal-Enterprise*, the *Sebree Banner*, the *Sturgis News*, the *Advocate-Messenger* in Danville, the *Winchester Sun,* and the present-day *Kentucky Gazette* for publishing my newspaper columns at various times since 2005. This collection of essays would not be possible without a free press.

Confluence

With our university's graduation and the all-too-fast approaching of our daughter's 2012 Murray High School graduation, I can't help but think of how so many streams seem to have converged at this exact time to make this celebratory moment such a watershed event in the lives of our students. Cammie Jo's classmates will be attending Murray State University, the University of Louisville, the University of Kentucky, Bellarmine University, and Centre College in Kentucky, and schools as far-flung as the University of Nevada at Las Vegas, West Point, Belmont University, and Holy Cross outside the state.

When I was a student at Belmont, majoring in history, my Western civilizations textbook was titled *The Mainstream of Civilization*, a thick tome that I marked up with underlinings and marginalia in an attempt to digest its contents. I still own the book, and just today I lifted it from an upper shelf in my History Department office to thumb through its pages. Only a brief perusal of the hefty volume brought back a confluence of memories about my undergraduate college days at Belmont: about lugging the book on the team bus, taking it along to study on away basketball trips; about taking the book across the campus to the library to find a quiet corner to prepare for a quiz or examination; and about the course itself, my favorite course at Belmont.

The course was called The Western World, and it counted as two course credits. We met each day of the week, Monday through Friday, and it was team taught by Professor Albert Wardin, a history professor, and Professor Virginia Chaney, a professor of literature. Dr. Wardin came in on Mondays and Tuesdays to teach a particular period of history—Mesopotamia, the Greeks, the Romans, etc.—and then Dr. Chaney met with us on Wednesdays and Thursdays to discuss the literature of whatever period of history we were considering that week. On Fridays, both Professors Wardin and Chaney came to the class together to lead a freewheeling discussion of the week's topic. It was all very invigorating, very intense, and very challenging. But we learned a great deal about the major civilizations of the world, and about the confluence of many of those civilizations.

I use the word *confluence* because of the image suggested by our textbook of "a mainstream of civilization," and because I just completed a rereading of Eudora Welty's *One Writer's Beginnings*, the great southern writer's memoir about her childhood and the beginnings of her calling to be a writer.

I picture myself standing in the middle of a stream with waters rushing by me. I am aware that upstream various tributaries have fed into the mainstream, and now there is a confluence of those streams into one mainstream. History is like that. All of these tributaries of the past—the Greeks, the Romans, Africa, China, India, the Reformation, the Renaissance, the Enlightenment—all of these tributaries have fed into the mainstream of civilization, and now we are the result; we represent the confluence of all of that.

At the end of *One Writer's Beginnings*, Eudora Welty wrote, "I'm prepared now to use the wonderful word *confluence*, which of itself exists as a reality and a symbol in one. It is the only kind of symbol that for me as a writer has any weight, testifying to the pattern, one of the chief patterns, of human experience." In her novel, *The Optimist's Daughter*, Ms. Welty describes the confluence of the Ohio and the Mississippi rivers, a confluence that my family and I have also experienced. "When they were climbing the long approach to a bridge after leaving Cairo, rising slowly higher until they rode above the tops of bare trees," she wrote, "she looked down and saw the pale light widening and the river bottoms opening out, and then the water appearing, reflecting the low, early sun. There were two rivers. Here was where they came together. This was the confluence of the waters, the Ohio and the Mississippi."

And then Ms. Welty likens that confluence of rivers to the confluence that is our history, our memory. "Of course," she wrote, "the greatest confluence of all is that which makes up the human memory—the individual human memory. My own is the treasure most dearly regarded by me, in my life and in my work as a writer." "Here time, also, is subject to confluence." And then she writes, so eloquently and so beautifully, "The memory is a living thing—it too is in transit. But during its moment, all that is remembered joins, and lives—the old and the young, the past and the present, the living and the dead." I am sure that I cannot fathom all the implications of Eudora Welty's statement, but I know that truth, as well as beauty, resides there.

Clio's Decalogue

George Brown Tindall is one of my favorite historians. He taught history for years at the University of North Carolina at Chapel Hill. He died several years ago. I use his textbook, *America: A Narrative History,* in my American History survey courses. The reason I like his textbook so much is that it is written so clearly.

I think about Dr. Tindall around this time of the semester when I am grading book reviews and research papers. With tongue in cheek, he gave ten rules for clear historical writing. He called these rules "Clio's Decalogue" or "The Commandments of the Muse." As you will see, Clio, the muse of history, followed closely the style of the King James Version of The Ten Commandments of the Old Testament:

1. Thou shalt smite the Philistines hip and thigh with thy first sentence. This is the First Commandment.
2. Thou shalt love the active verb with all thy heart, with all thy soul, and with all thy mind, and thou shalt have no passive verbs before me; the present tense, moreover, is an abomination unto the Muse.
3. Thou shalt not take the names of thy cast in vain, for the Muse will not hold him guiltless who faileth fully to denominate and clearly to identify in relation to his subject all persons or incidents, be they Thomas Woodrow Wilson, Lucius Quintus Cincinnatus Lamar, or the Scopes Trial in Dayton, Tennessee. Only after thou hast performed this ceremony of purification mayest thou employ familiar terms like unto Wilson, Lamar, or The Duel to the Death.
4. Remember the footnote, to keep it holy. In thy text shalt thou labor thy subject, but neither discuss thy documents nor yet thy methodology. Footnotes were made for scholars and not scholars for footnotes; yea, verily, the greatest is not he who citeth the most obscure document, not yet he who pileth Ossa upon Pelion.
5. Honor thy chronology, to keep it straight, and put thy time clause first, that thy days may be long upon the printed page.
6. Thou shalt not kill thy reader, neither with the dangling participle, not with the split infinitive, nor with strings of prepositional phrases, not yet with unceasing adjectives and adverbs.

7. Thou shalt not commit adulteration, neither with slang nor with jargon, yea though the words be favored of thine instructors.
8. Thou shalt not steal thy reader's attention by using this for the, nor the for a, neither shalt thou employ negations. Neither a no-er not a not-er be; but rather an accentuator of the positive; in this respect shalt thou do as these commandments say do and not as they, alas, do.
9. Thou shalt not bear false witness, not pass judgment upon humankind, not yet pardon anyone for anything; thou mayest seek the reason for one's error but neither the excuse not the blame. Vengeance is mine, saith the Muse.
10. Thou shalt not covet thy source's prose, nor his imagery, nor his purple passage, not anything that is thy source's, for lo, thou canst say it better thyself. Thou mayest quote only to season thy store, and that in fear and trembling.

George Brown Tindall heeded Clio's advice. He wrote clearly and well. Oh, that my students would do the same. Oh, that I would do the same.

Historical Evidence

Every semester I talk with my students about the sources used by historians to write history or to determine what happened in history. We discuss primary documents (eyewitness or firsthand accounts), such as letters and diaries and oral histories, and we discuss secondary works (secondhand accounts), such as textbooks and monographs. My students often tell me that they prefer primary sources, because there is a power, an authenticity, contained in a primary source, often missing in dry textbooks and secondary works of history. We also discuss, however, how secondary accounts provide context and perspective, qualities that primary sources cannot provide.

Historians sometimes argue whether history is the event itself or merely the recording of the event. We've all heard about the old dilemma, "If a tree falls in the woods, and nobody was there to hear it, did it make a sound?" Well, whacky historians ask the question, "If a tree falls in the woods, and nobody was there to record it, did it really fall, did it really happen?" You answer, "Yes." The historian then asks, "Well, how do you know?" "There is a tree on the ground," you respond. "Ah," returns the historian, "there is a recording of the fallen tree after all."

These records, these sources, this evidence, are the raw materials with which historians work. Students of history must consult the evidence, and the existing evidence is all we have to piece together the story of the past.

We also discuss how students of history only have access to a fraction of the story. Think of all the records that have not survived. That fallen tree for example, will eventually rot and turn to dust. During the Civil War, burning courthouses destroyed marriage licenses, deeds, and other valuable historical documents. Today, with the demise of the art of letter writing, unsaved e-mails mean the loss of millions of daily human communications.

With the unavailability of so much evidence, sometimes historians just throw up their empty hands, admitting that there is simply not enough extant evidence to make an educated guess as to what really happened. Let's face it: Sometimes historians just make things up.

G. K. Chesterton wrote about such a case in *The Everlasting Man*. "The other day," he wrote, "a scientific summary of the state of a prehistoric tribe began confidently with the words, 'They wore no clothes.'" "Not one reader in a hundred," Chesterton said, "probably stopped to ask himself how we should come to know whether clothes had once been worn by people of whom everything has perished except a few chips of bone and stone."

According to Chesterton, "it was doubtless hoped that we should find a stone hat as well as a stone hatchet. It was evidently anticipated that we might discover an everlasting pair of trousers.... But to persons of a less sanguine temperament it will be immediately apparent that people might wear simple garments, or even highly ornamental garments, without leaving any more traces of them than these people have left." Chesterton concluded that "it is not contended here that these primitive men did wear clothes any more than they did weave rushes; but merely that we have not enough evidence to know whether they did or not."

Sometimes, the honest historian must admit that there is just not enough evidence to know. We just don't know. For the great historian and writer, Barbara Tuchman, we must only rely on the evidence we have available to us. "I am content to define history," she wrote, "as the events of which we have knowledge and refrain from worrying about those of which we have none—until, that is, some archeologist digs them up."

How Important is a Word?

Whenever the Christmas season is upon us, I am reminded how much words matter. And I am not referring to that useless criticism that some Christians make when some folks, with open and joyful hearts, send cards or tell others, "happy holidays." What better way to refer to these holy days of Hanukkah and Christmas than with a word with the root of "holy"? I personally love it when one of my students or colleagues cheerfully wishes me "happy holidays."

How is it that we downgrade perfectly good words, make them second-class citizens, simply because we have heard some talk-radio lunatic or some talking head on television fill up the airwaves with nonsense. We then mimic what we have heard, much like a talking parrot. At such times we seem unable to think things through for ourselves. Words matter, dear reader. And I cherish those writers who can choose just the right word or place words together in just the right juxtaposition to create magic on a page.

Wendell Berry can do that. Jane Austen perfected the art. Charles Dickens, though long dead, still has the power to make me laugh while reading one page, or make my spirit soar while reading another. Trollope follows close behind. Still the best writer of history I know was the nonacademic, Barbara Tuchman. The best memoir I've ever read is *The Tender Bar* by J. R. Moehringer, but Thomas Merton's *The Seven Storey Mountain* follows close behind.

In Kentucky, no one was more eloquent or more convincing than Harry Caudill and James Still when writing about their beloved eastern Kentucky mountains. No one has brought Kentucky history to life better than the late Dr. Thomas D. Clark or the state historian, Dr. James C. Klotter. In Kentucky poetry, my pick is Davis McCombs, although he now writes out of Fayetteville, Arkansas.

In Murray, we have a treasure in Gary Garth, who has written the outdoors column for the *Louisville Courier-Journal* for some twenty years. Gary is that rare writer who has the ability to raise good journalism to the art of great literature.

Norman Maclean did not begin to publish words on a page until he reached his seventies, and even then he used words sparingly, writing essays or novellas, rather than long novels. His most famous piece ends with this: "Eventually, all things merge into one, and a river runs through it. The river was cut by the world's great flood and runs over rocks from the basement of time. On some of the rocks are timeless raindrops. Under the rocks are the words, and some of the words are theirs. I am haunted by waters." It is hard to find a more moving passage of literature.

Ernest Hemingway could move readers by using words sparingly. Someone asked Hemingway if he could write a novel using only six words. This was the great writer's offering: "For sale. Baby shoes. Never worn." This may be apocryphal, but it is Hemingway-esque, nonethe less.

Even a very few words, placed correctly on a page, can reveal a whole universe of love or care or longing. So that is why at Christmastime, I think of words. For even the Christ child was described as "the Word." St. John opens his Gospel with these poignant words about the Word: "In the beginning was the Word, and the Word was with God, and the Word was God." And then later in verse 14: "And the Word became flesh and dwelt among us, and we beheld His glory, the glory of the only begotten of the Father, full of grace and truth." And so, the apostle used words sparingly to present the Gospel story for which Christians all over the world celebrate Christmas. Only a few words about the Word. Full of grace and truth. Happy holidays.

In Awe of the Ordinary

So often we all get caught up in "the next big thing." I know I do. The danger for me is that while I am always on the lookout for whatever that "next big thing" might be, I often overlook the blessings and joy I have before me every day in the here and now. In fact, when I pause to think deeply about the life I have been given, waves of guilt wash over me in the face of the suffering of so many others all over the world. Although she herself suffered from debilitating depression before her untimely death at forty-seven in 1995, the New Hampshire poet Jane Kenyon recognized the gifts of the ordinary in her poem "Otherwise":

I got out of bed
on two strong legs.
It might have been
otherwise. I ate
cereal, sweet
milk, ripe, flawless
peach. It might

have been otherwise.
I took the dog uphill
to the birch wood.
All morning I did
the work I love.

At noon I lay down
with my mate. It might
have been otherwise.
We ate dinner together
at a table with silver
candlesticks. It might
have been otherwise.
I slept in a bed
in a room with paintings
on the walls, and
planned another day
just like this day.
But one day, I know,
it will be otherwise.

Yes, it might have been otherwise with each of us had we been born in Mogadishu or Khartoum or Basra. Carrie Newcomer, a Quaker singer-songwriter, believes that the everydayness of our lives, times that we often take for boredom, should be considered as holy experiences. In "Holy As a Day Is Spent," she wrote:

Holy is the dish and drain
The soap and sink, the cup and plate
And the warm wool socks, and the cold white tile
Showerheads and good dry towels
And frying eggs sound like psalms
With a bit of salt measured in my palm
It's all a part of a sacrament
As holy as a day is spent

Holy is a familiar room and the quiet moments in the afternoon
And folding sheets like folding hands

To pray as only laundry can
I'm letting go of all I fear
Like autumn leaves of earth and air
For summer came and summer went
As holy as a day is spent

Holy is the place I stand
To give whatever small good I can
The empty page, the open book
Redemption everywhere I look
Unknowingly we slow our pace
In the shade of unexpected grace
With grateful smiles and sad lament
As holy as a day is spent

And so, I live out my days, in the classroom teaching students, in my university office, chatting amiably with students and my colleagues, and in my home with my family, each moment of quiet and calm elevated to a holy experience, the everydayness of our lives, not taken for granted, but cherished and even sacred.

Last Words

One cannot read John Green's novel, *Looking for Alaska*, without becoming interested, along with the narrator Miles Halter, with individuals' last words. Miles has learned the last words of hundreds of famous people and upon first meeting him, Alaska Young, the novel's exotic, tragic figure, tests him.

"You want to quiz me," Miles asked her. "JFK," she said.

"That's obvious," I answered.

"Oh, is it now?" she asked. "No. Those were his last words. Someone said, 'Mr. President, you can't say Dallas doesn't love you,' and then he said, 'That's obvious,' and then he got shot."

Looking for Alaska swirls around the last words of Simon Bolivar and Francois Rabelais. For Green's protagonist, Miles Halter, Bolivar's last words are quoted in *The General in His Labyrinth*, by Gabriel Garcia Marquez. "How will I ever get out of this labyrinth?" Bolivar asked before he died. Although these words may or may not have been the last words of the famous South American liberator, we have all surely had the same sentiment at some point in our harried lives.

The last words of Francois Rabelais, the Renaissance scholar and writer, caused Miles to leave his public school in Florida to attend Culver Creek, a boarding school in Alabama. Just before he died, Rabelais said, "I go to seek the Great Perhaps." And so it was that Miles went off to boarding school "to seek the Great Perhaps." And so it is with us in the here and now. We get off the couch. We get out the front door. We travel abroad. We try something entirely new. We "go to seek the Great Perhaps."

In one of the great ironies of American history, Thomas Jefferson, the third president and the author of the Declaration, died within hours of John Adams, the second president of the United States and Jefferson's one-time political enemy. They both died on July 4, 1826, the fiftieth anniversary of the signing of the Declaration, the document penned by Jefferson and revised by Adams.

Upon learning of Jefferson's death, John Adams uttered on his own deathbed his last words: "Thomas Jefferson still survives." Adams was wrong in his facts, not realizing that Jefferson had already died a few hours earlier, but his last words were nonetheless prophetic in that Mr. Jefferson still lives through the words he penned in our nation's founding document.

To me it is hard to top the last words of Kentuckian Alben Barkley who, as a junior senator, gave a speech at a mock convention at Washington and Lee University in Lexington, Virginia, on April 30, 1956. The 78-year-old Barkley had been a member of the United States House of Representatives, the Senate majority leader, and vice president of the United States, but now he was back again as a junior senator.

The old war horse assured the Washington and Lee students that he did not mind sitting on the back row of the Senate chamber, and quoting from the 84th chapter of the Book of Psalms he declared, "I would rather be a servant in the house of the Lord than to sit in the seats of the mighty." With that, Barkley collapsed at the podium of a massive heart attack.

Upon first hearing Senator Barkley's final speech, I thought, how tragic. But the more I think about it, what better way out of the labyrinth.

Part Nine

Calling

"Our calling is the place where 'our deep gladness and the world's deep hunger meet.'"

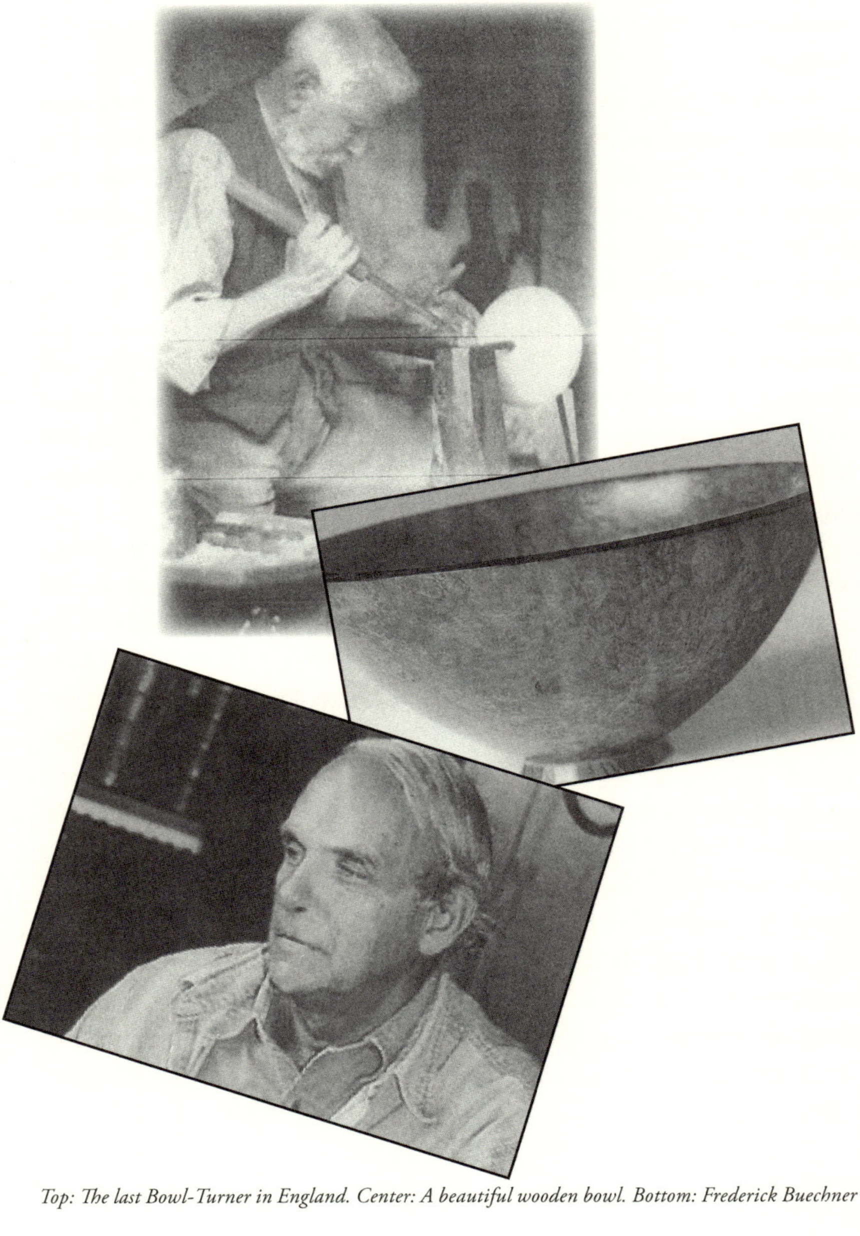

Top: The last Bowl-Turner in England. Center: A beautiful wooden bowl. Bottom: Frederick Buechner

Calling

I watch my students closely in their academic struggles and sometimes wonder about the values they take with them from their undergraduate years. Other than the grades on a transcript, what do they really gain from a university education? As the perceptive southern novelist and essayist Walker Percy claimed, "You can get all A's and still flunk life."

How will they make a living, but more importantly, how will they make a life? I am convinced that to make sense of our lives and to make our lives count, we must have a strong and sure calling. Not just a job. Not just an occupation. Not just a career. But a calling or a vocation, an English word derived from the Latin *vocare*, which means literally "to call."

Ministers speak of being called by God for a life of ministry, but I believe that individuals can be called to so-called secular vocations. For some, the call for a life's work comes as a sort of sudden epiphany. A school field trip to a hospital might convince a young girl or boy that medical school calls. An early morning visit to a barn might convince a teenager that life on a farm is the life for him or her. A student in a classroom or a player on a team might suddenly realize that they could be a teacher or coach. For the Murray poet Constance Alexander, the winning of a fourth-grade poetry contest at St. Francis School at once amazed her and convinced her that she could write poetry. Epiphanies do happen.

For others, like me, a calling has come in fits and starts, with a door cracked open here and another door closed there. We all would like to be sure that we live and work in our callings, whatever those callings may be.

According to Os Guinness in his book *The Call*, "The bricklayer with the trowel, the farmer behind the plow, the artist before the easel, the chef beside the oven, the magistrate presiding at the bench, the teacher in the classroom, the nurse by the bedside, the parent at the crib—each one is to live out his or her calling in joy and service."

The writer/theologian Frederick Buechner said that our calling is the place where "our deep gladness and the world's deep hunger meet." According to Buechner, a good rule for finding one's vocation is this: "This special mission in our life is usually (a) that which we need most to do or love to do; and (b) it is work that the world most needs to have done."

Buechner says "that if we really get a kick out of our work, we have probably met requirement (a), but if that work is writing TV deodorant commercials, chances are we haven't met requirement (b). If our work is being a doctor in a leper colony, we probably have requirement (b) covered, but if most of the time we are bored and depressed by doctoring, the chances are we have not only bypassed requirement (a), we probably aren't helping our patients much, either." Our calling is the place where "our deep gladness and the world's deep hunger meet."

The Danish theologian Soren Kierkegaard wrote in his journal, "The thing is to understand myself, to see what God really wants me to do; the thing is to find a truth which is true for me, to find the *idea for which I can live and die.*" Or as the poet Gerard Manley Hopkins put it, "What I do is me: for that I came."

Besides the getting of a degree, besides giving students a foundation for the next step in a graduate or professional school or in the workplace, if a college education is worth its salt, it should also guide students toward a sense of calling, what they are meant to do in their lives, and how they are meant to live.

Called Back

One of my favorite Old Testament passages is the last section of Isaiah 40. "Do you not know? Have you not heard?" Isaiah asks. "The Lord is the everlasting God, the Creator of the ends of the earth. He will not grow tired or weary, and his understanding no one can fathom." And then Isaiah promises, "He gives strength to the weary and increases the power of the weak. Even youths grow tired and weary, and young men stumble and fall; but those who hope in the Lord will renew their strength. They will soar on wings like eagles; they will run and not grow weary, they will walk and not be faint."

Emily Dickinson's epitaph reads simply: "Called Back." At the end of a life of poetry and devotion, Dickinson believed she was called back into eternity. But what does one make of being called back into this world, to live and breathe, or as Isaiah said, to "run and not grow weary," to "walk and not be faint"?

On the sunny Thursday afternoon of April 29, 2010, I drove Cammie Jo to track practice at Stewart Stadium. Wesley was still at school in New Haven, Connecticut and Evelyn had gone to Calvert City to visit her sisters. I had decided to finally do something about the shape of my physical condition, to begin an exercise program that had gone dormant for half a decade. As I drove home from the stadium, on a whim I turned the car around and headed back to Hibbet's sporting goods to buy a new pair of running shoes. Paid up, I drove home, changed into some running clothes, and headed out the front door onto Earl Court.

I had walked for 30 minutes the evening before, so my intent was to walk again, to gradually build up my endurance until I could one day resume a running schedule that I had abandoned in 2005. Ever impatient, I thought that I could at least start out in a slow jog, so coming out of Earl Court I turned right onto Fairlane. I didn't get very far. Feeling dizzy, I sat down on the side of the street. I tried to go again, got up, and made it across the street, only to sit down again in the grass on the corner of Fairlane and 11th Street. I remember lying back in the grass, and that is all I remember; I passed out. The next thing I remember was the face of a kindly paramedic who insisted that I be loaded into a waiting ambulance and taken to the emergency room.

It is that blank period—between passing out and coming to—that made all the difference. Alesia and Tony Knight, my next-door neighbors, didn't know why they came home that way that day. They always went home by another way. In fact, Tony turned to Alesia and asked, "Why are we going this way?" "I don't know," Alesia said. It was then that they saw me stretched out on the grass at the edge of the street.

Tony backed up and Alesia, a trained nurse, got out and ran to my side while Tony called for an ambulance. I had no pulse, I had stopped breathing, and I was already turning blue, but Alesia knew just what to do. She administered CPR. When I didn't respond, Alesia beat me on the chest. "Don't do this to me, Duane," she said. She continued with the CPR and finally, only because of God and Alesia, my heart started beating again, my breathing resumed, and I came to. Neighbors and friends gathered around, including Raymond and Susan Sims, and another registered nurse whom I still do not know by name.

The rest of the story is that a faulty aortic heart valve had shut down. I came out of the hospital fourteen days later with a new aortic valve and a pacemaker, along with a new appreciation for life and a list of questions that I must ponder.

Why did Tony and Alesia Knight go home by another way on that particular day? Why was my life spared? How does one thank someone who has saved your life? What is it, after all, that I still need to accomplish in this old world? Why was I called back?

The Last Bowl-Turner in England

I have an opportunity in my Freshman Transitions class and in my Teaching History class to talk with my students about how they envision their lives after graduating from Murray State University. In fact, I have focused on that very thing. That might seem odd for a class full of first-year students or for a class full of prospective teachers, to talk about life after college, but I think it is crucial for students to consider seriously during their college years how they plan to spend the rest of their lives. Is it possible for these bright and hopeful students to discover while here at Murray a life's work? How does one decide what to do when one "grows up?"

In the 1920s, H. V. Morton perfected the art of travel writing. Jan Morris, an admirer and present-day travel writer, described Morton as "the much-loved master of the genre, often imitated but never matched." Morton produced books such as *In Search of London, A Traveler in Spain, In the Steps of the Master, A Traveler in Italy*, and my favorite, *In Search of England*. I have a friend who reads Morton's *A Traveler in Rome* nonstop. No; I mean nonstop! When he finishes the book, he turns back to page one and begins again. I don't know how many times he has read the book. It's now beyond counting. He simply reads it perpetually.

That brings me to the point of this essay. Morton knew much about an idea that is usually reserved for religious folk, for ministers or priests or shamans (I mean those who follow a religious vocation as opposed to a secular job). I am referring to the idea of "calling." H. V. Morton demonstrated through his life and work that one can be called to a vocation without donning religious garb. If anyone was called to write sophisticated, eloquent travelogues, it was Morton. I know of individuals who have been called to be pharmacists, teachers of preschoolers, doctors, veterinarians, lawyers, coal miners, college presidents, farmers, and whether called by Clio or God, historians. The writer/theologian Frederick Buechner broadened the concept by simply stating that "calling" is the place where "our deep gladness and the world's deep hunger meet."

In his travels through England, Morton met up with a man on a country lane carrying, conspicuously, a wooden bowl. "Well," the man called out holding up the bowl. "What do you think of that?" Morton did not know how to respond, although he didn't fail to notice that the "bowl had a marvelous grain," and an unusually "fine smooth finish." "That," the man said, "is the work of the last bowl-turner in England. He lives over the hill at Bucklebury. A most interesting survival. Quite remarkable. You ought to look at his workshop, for you will never see another one like it!"

"Before people used pewter for plates and tankards," he explained, "wooden trenchers, drinking cups, and bowls…were used by everyone." "Well, in Elizabethan times pewter came in fashion and wooden things were used only by poorer people. Then came china and glass." Now, there was only one maker of wooden bowls left, and Morton was encouraged to meet him. He did as he was told. And when he found his way to the bowl-turner's workshop and peered inside, Morton wrote, "to say that eight hundred years seemed to have stopped at the door conveys nothing. The room was an Anglo-Saxon workshop!" After the craftsman demonstrated his art, Morton could not help but tell him: "You could make a lot of money if you wanted to."

"Money?" [the artist] said with a slow faun-like smile. "Money's only storing up trouble, I think. I like making bowls better that I like making money."

Astonished, Morton asked him, "Will you say that again?"

"He leaned against the door of the hut, his homely brown face shaded by his green floppy hat, and said it again, slightly puzzled." "I like making bowls better than I like making money."

"But you will have guessed that I wished to hear for the second time the voice of a craftsman," Morton concluded, "the lover of his job, the proud creator of beautiful, common things; a voice that is now smothered by the scream of machines." Morton had experienced the art of an artist who, unable and unwilling to do anything else, lived out his calling as the last bowl-turner in England. That is my wish for my students, that during their time at Murray State they will discover a calling, work that they simply cannot live without.

A Sense of Where You Are

There he stood. Under a basket at Princeton University's Dillon Gymnasium. In his basketball practice uniform. Still sweating from a demanding workout. Now he caught questions, not basketballs, passed to him by the acclaimed writer John McPhee. On assignment for *The New Yorker*, McPhee interviewed the Princeton All-American for a long piece centered on his senior year at Princeton, a year in which he led the nation in scoring and secured a Rhodes Scholarship to study history and political science for two years at Oxford University in England.

Bill Bradley fielded questions just as he played basketball, effortlessly and with grace. In those early 1960s, before Pistol Pete, before Dr. J, before Air Jordan, and before Lebron James, Bradley's style was decidedly straightforward and unexaggerated. "He dislikes flamboyance," McPhee wrote, "and, unlike some of basketball's greatest stars, has apparently never made a move merely to attract attention."

"Nonetheless," according to McPhee, "he does make something of a spectacle of himself when he moves in rapidly parallel to the baseline, glides through the air with his back to the basket, looks for a teammate he can pass to, and, finding none, tosses the ball into the basket over one shoulder, like a pinch of salt." McPhee concluded that the shot "has the essential characteristics of a wild accident, which is what many people stubbornly think they have witnessed until they see him do it for the third time in a row."

The unorthodox, over-the-shoulder shot had no name. Bradley said that "he had never heard a name for it, but that he had seen Oscar Robertson, of the Cincinnati Royals, and Jerry West, of the Los Angeles Lakers, do it, and had worked it out for himself." Yes, he had worked it out for himself.

On that day while answering the author's questions, Bradley insisted that the maneuver "is a much simpler shot than it appears to be, and, to illustrate, he tossed a ball over his shoulder and into the basket while he was talking and looking [McPhee] in the eye." McPhee retrieved the ball and handed it back to the Princeton star.

"When you have played basketball for a while, you don't need to look at the basket when you are in close like this," Bradley explained as he flipped the ball over his shoulder again cleanly through the hoop. Eventually, he said, "You develop a sense of where you are." *You develop a sense of where you are.*

Since my teenage years I have respected and admired Bill Bradley, first for his exploits on the hardwood and now for everything that he has done since he laced up his high-top Converses for the last time. After graduating from Princeton, he turned down a lucrative contract with the New York Knickerbockers to study at Oxford. He returned from England to play for the Knicks, winning an NBA championship and writing *Life on the Run*, a poignant memoir about the grueling, exotic life of an NBA star. Upon his retirement from professional basketball he ran successfully for a US Senate seat from New Jersey, and then in 2000, he ran unsuccessfully for the presidency of the United States. He has continued to write books about what it means to live a life in service to others.

As a teacher of history, what I admire most about Bradley is that he has insisted that the only way to develop "a sense of where we are" in the world, at "home and away," wherever we find ourselves in the world, is to study and understand the past. How can we make a difference? What is our niche? How can we make our lives count for something beyond ourselves? Only by understanding something about where we come from are we able to develop "a sense of where we are" in our communities, in our state, in our nation, in our world, in the whole scheme of things.

The Verger of Winchester Cathedral

"He was standing in the choir of Winchester Cathedral surrounded by the first tourists of the year. He was a clean-shaven man with the mobile face of an actor; shrewd, humorous eyes, and white hair brushed straight back over his head." Thus began H. V. Morton's description of the verger of Winchester Cathedral in his book *In Search of England.*

A verger is one who takes care of the interior of a church, but they often served as guides for tourists. This was no ordinary verger and this was no ordinary guide. One tourist nudged Morton and said, "This chap's good, isn't he? I expect he's pulling our legs a bit. He talks about the old days as if he had been there."

Indeed "as the man with the white hair talked in the silent choir of Winchester—before him the long sweep of that marvelous nave, on either side those lovely Norman transepts soaked in a pale gold light—he moved his hands in time to his words, and his eyes went over the group to each listener. There was not a shuffle. He had gripped them! They had come prepared to be bored; they stayed strangely thrilled by this man's enthusiasm and by the pictures he called up. That was it; he humanized the history book."

Morton wrote, "the old story, like all old stories told properly, took on a new importance, became dramatic and somehow near at hand. The crowd had heard it before at school; but they had never *seen* it before." Oh, that I could have that effect on my students. I know that they have heard it all before, but what if I could make them *see* history? Perhaps it must begin with a love of history on the part of the teacher. That was the case with the verger of Winchester Cathedral.

"'I love it,' said the verger. 'You ought to come up here on a moonlit night and look down. You can imagine things: you can see ghosts...'" Morton chatted with the verger at the conclusion of the tour. "You must have devoted your life to this," Morton said. The verger responded: "When I was appointed verger, the spirit of Winchester gripped me and I knew that I had found my right job. I love every stone of this cathedral."

At one point in the tour, the verger gave each of the tourists a bell, "delivered a lecture on bell-ringing, numbered us off from the right, and pointing to each one in turn as he wished him to ring, drew forth from the unpromising assembly 'Abide with Me.'" "We were delighted with ourselves," Morton said.

"Up we went again, and round and round, till we bent under a little stone doorway and came out on the roof of the cathedral.... We looked down on the tops of feathery lime trees, on the river and the distant hills, the little town lying pleasantly in a blue haze of smoke from its chimneys, Winchester!"

"Down we all trooped over those sheer corkscrew stairs and out into the lime avenue. We found that we all knew each other. We all shook hands before we parted. Such is the power of one man's enthusiasm."

There was really no doubt about it. The verger had been called to guide tourists around Winchester Cathedral. He would be happy doing nothing else.

The Master Painter

It was at the Camp Ridgecrest for Boys during the summer of 1976 that I heard a story that continues to intrigue and inspire me. I remember that Jamie Cotton, a senior counselor, came to our cabin one evening to give a short devotional. I have never forgotten the story he told that night to a group of twelve-year-old boys in a rustic cabin in the mountains of North Carolina.

Here's the story…the way I remember it. It seems that the king of a kingdom decided to honor his subjects in a unique way. The king planned to have a banquet to which he would invite all of the subjects of his kingdom. The banquet would be held in a large banquet hall. A sumptuous feast would be served. Jesters would provide entertainment. The king's subjects would be honored.

To honor his subjects adequately, however, the king decided to prepare the banquet hall in a particular way. He called in the kingdom's two great artists, one an elderly master painter who was recognized as the greatest artist in the kingdom, and the other, the old master's apprentice, a young, up-and-coming artist who had studied at the feet of the master. The king took the artists into the banquet hall, and he explained to the two painters his idea: They would be responsible for painting two adjacent walls in the room. The king would honor the subjects of his kingdom with these two commissioned works of art, to be unveiled the night of the banquet.

With his instructions given, the king put the two artists to work. The artists gathered their supplies, and came in the next morning to begin the work. Much preparation was required; preparation of the walls, I mean. Old paint had to be scraped away, the walls had to be smoothed and polished before the actual painting began.

From time to time the king stopped by to check on the painters' progress. After several weeks he noticed that the old master painter had outlined on his wall a landscape scene: mountains, valleys, a waterfall, a beautiful landscape scene. The king noticed, however, that the young apprentice had still not begun to paint. He continued to scrape and smooth and polish.

A week before the banquet the king stopped by once again to make sure everything was in order. That's when he began to worry. With the banquet only a few days away, the old master painter had all but finished his painting. He used a brush to put on the finishing touches of what the king could tell was a most beautiful landscape scene. To the king's horror, however, the young apprentice had yet to pick up a brush. He continued to scrape and smooth and polish, still preparing his wall for the first brushstrokes.

The king expressed his concern to the young artist in no uncertain terms. "Don't you know," he said, "that the banquet will be held only a few days from now?" "Don't you realize," he said, "that I want to honor the subjects of my kingdom with two beautiful paintings?" "After all," the king explained, "I have put my faith in you to complete this task. What can be done?"

The young apprentice tried his best to calm the king, explaining to him that his painting would indeed be completed by the night of the banquet. He would, he assured the king, fulfill his promise. His painting would be complete.

Well, the king reasoned that there was nothing else to be done. He must take the young artist at his word, and hope for the best. So the evening of the banquet came. The king's subjects came on foot, some on horseback, all gathering at the beautifully lit banquet hall. The banqueters enjoyed a sumptuous feast, along with humorous and captivating entertainment.

Then it came time for the highlight of the evening. Workers had covered the two adjacent walls with heavy veils. The king gave the signal, ropes were pulled, and simultaneously the veils fell to the floor. And then? And then, a gasp from the gathered subjects, followed by silence. The audience sat there in awe of two remarkable works of art. They looked at the old master's wall to see the most beautiful landscape painting they had ever seen. But when they cast their gaze at the painting of the young apprentice, they noticed that his painting was just as beautiful. In fact, every detail was exactly the same; every mountain, every valley, the waterfall, all the same.

Called by the king to the head table, the young artist gave his explanation. "When you commissioned me to do this work," he said, "I knew that it would not be possible for me to produce a painting as beautiful as my master, my mentor. My painting would pale in comparison. So what I decided to do was to scrape and smooth and polish my wall so that it would reflect the painting of the old master's wall. So that's what I did. My painting is a reflection of the painting of the master."

Well, for thirty-two years I have been retelling that story. I have told it to my history classes as a way to suggest to my students that in many ways we are reflections of our past. I have told the story at church to Sunday school classes and as devotionals to youth groups to suggest that we should polish our lives so that we reflect the Master. I have told the story with no point in mind, no lesson to be learned, just for the fun of telling the story. But after all of these years, I will never forget the gasps followed by a hushed silence in that rustic cabin when a dozen twelve-year-old boys realized that the young artist's painting was but a reflection of the painting of the old master.

Truly Happy

"We are only truly happy when we are doing what we are meant to do and being what we are meant to be." Thus concluded the late Peter Gomes, the Plummer Professor of Christian Morals at Harvard College. Novelist Louis Auchincloss said much the same thing—albeit more subtly—in his *East Side Story* when he recorded the funeral address of the Presbyterian minister for Auchincloss's fictional character David Carnochan. The minister stated, "Of any man it is sufficient eulogy to say that he so uses his powers as to be virtuously successful in his chosen calling."

In his book, *The Good Life*, Professor Gomes had been inspired to write on calling by his long friendship with the cellist, Yo-Yo Ma. When Ma was a student at Harvard, Gomes attended a Saturday morning class session that the young cellist had with the great Russian master Rostropovich. Each of seven undergraduate musicians played for Rostropovich, and then the master would give instruction.

When it was Ma's turn, Gomes said, "He began to play, and when Ma plays, his whole being becomes an extension of the music and of the instrument; rather than being solely an instrumentalist, he is instrumentalist, instrument, and, indeed, even conductor." According to Gomes, "Ma plays everything, is everything, and well before he had finished—in that particular Saturday morning session—the maestro jumped up, gesticulating wildly, and, in a torrent of Russian too fast for translation, forced the young player to stop. We were stunned. Was he pleased, impressed, angry, dismayed?"

Rostropovich did indeed instruct Ma, and, taking the bow from him, leaned over his shoulder, and then asked the young man to repeat a measure. Gomes wrote, "We could tell that Rostropovich was excited beyond words, and we thought he was about to throw a tantrum.... Only in the wake of the pandemonium did the translator have a chance to say that the maestro had said he had never before heard such playing in his life and that he, the maestro, was in the presence of genius."

In trying to describe the moment, Gomes quoted Aristotle's definition of happiness: "the exercise of vital powers along lines of excellence, in a life affording them scope." According to Gomes, "the good cellist is one who is good at playing the cello, just as the good person is one who is good at being a person, doing what is most good, most noble, and most pleasant. What the good person and the good musician do is perform virtuously, and the virtue of something is related to the notion of its ability to perform excellently its characteristic activity."

Gomes continued, "We do not do virtuous things in order to be happy; rather, we are happy because we do virtuous things." Anyone paying close attention to the life and calling of Yo-Yo Ma will realize that he loves what he does, and he does what he loves. And he does it so well.

What about the rest of us? Wouldn't it be wonderful to be able to say that we are doing what we are called to do, and that we are living as we are called to live? As Gomes would have it, "We are only truly happy when we are doing what we are meant to do and being what we are meant to be."

The Greatest Kentuckian

Ask any group of native Kentuckians this question and they will usually round up the usual suspects. Who is the greatest Kentuckian? I pose this question to students in my History of Kentucky class. I suppose one's response to the question depends on how you define the term "great." After all, the term has been attached to only a handful of individuals in world history—Alexander the Great, Peter the Great—and no Kentuckians that I know of, except, of course, Muhammad Ali, a native Louisvillian, who proclaimed of himself, "I am the greatest!" But I ask this question from time to time to my university students, as well as to fourth graders in public schools in western Kentucky.

When I ask fourth graders the question, Who is the greatest Kentuckian?, they invariably suggest...Daniel Boone, Abraham Lincoln, James Harrod, Isaac Shelby, George Rogers Clark, and maybe Alben Barkley (we are in western Kentucky, after all). My university students include these names as well, but sometimes add Henry Clay and Harland Sanders. Don't laugh. When I played on a basketball team in the Philippines the summer of 1978, Filipinos in Manila and Mindanao knew only two Kentucky names when they found out that I hailed from the Bluegrass State, Colonel Sanders and Muhammad Ali. Kentucky Fried Chicken had built restaurants in Manila, and Ali had just fought Joe Frasier in the Thrilla' in Manila. Somehow they knew that he had been born in Louisville.

A common trait of the lists generated by Kentucky fourth graders and university students is that they are composed of all males. No women! Only rarely does Laura Clay or Mary Todd Lincoln or Martha Layne Collins (or once, Ashley Judd!) break into my students' lists of greatest Kentuckians. Perhaps these male-dominated lists tell us more about our state and the written history of our state than about the students who suggested the names.

All I know is that the students have never heard of the individual that I might place at the top of the list. I write the name Linda Neville on a chalkboard, and the silence in the classroom is stunning. Fourth-grade faces scrunch up and in unison the students mouth the timeless question, "Huh?!?" And then I tell them about Linda Neville, someone whom I knew little about until my history professor friend, Dr. Thomas Appleton, told my son Wesley and me about her over dinner one evening.

Born in Lexington in 1873, the daughter of a University of Kentucky professor, Neville studied at home as a child and then graduated from Bryn Mawr College. After college, she learned of the dreaded eye disease, trachoma, which afflicted over 33,000 residents of eastern Kentucky. Neville learned that untreated trachoma caused blindness, so she devoted her considerable energies and resources to found the Kentucky Society to Prevent Blindness and to establish eleven clinics in mountain hollows in eastern Kentucky. A decade before her death in a Lexington nursing home in 1961, Neville saw the disease eradicated, and the last of Neville's clinics, no longer needed, closed.

One little boy, cured of the disease and his sight restored, wished to thank his benefactor. He had never learned her name, but he wrote her a letter anyway and addressed it to "The Lady Who Helps Blind Children See, Lexington, Kentucky." The postman apparently figured out that the letter was meant for Linda Neville because you can find it among her papers in the University of Kentucky's Special Collections today. Helping children see! Not a bad legacy for Linda Neville, a great Kentuckian by any measure.

The Clammy Grip of the Future

In the 1970s, William Zinsser, a teacher and musician and writer—and the author of *On Writing Well*, which has sold over a million copies—served as the master of Branford College at Yale. Zinsser later wrote in *Writing About Your Life: A Journey Into the Past*, "Being a college master was the perfect cure for the loneliness of the freelance writer." "Like any pastoral job," he wrote, "it consisted of small personal encounters from morning to night."

It was during those years at Yale that Zinsser wrote a much-anthologized essay titled "College Pressures," which described four different types of pressures that "were turning Yale undergraduates into workaholics obsessed with high grades." According to Zinsser, "One was parental pressure to succeed, often in subjects that would prepare them for careers in medicine or law that they really didn't want to enter. Another was financial pressure: the need to pay back all those student loans. The third was peer pressure—the belief that their fellow students were getting higher grades—and the fourth, worst of all, was self-imposed pressure."

Zinsser's advice to his students is sound counsel for all college students. He assured his students "that there is no one 'right' way to get ahead—that each of them is a different person, starting from a different point and bound for a different destination." Zinsser told his students that, despite the insistence of parents and friends, "change is a tonic and that all the slots are not codified or the frontiers closed."

Each Wednesday afternoon, Zinsser held a master's tea in the college, to which he invited men and women the students "might not otherwise meet," individuals "who have achieved success outside the academic world." These guests were "a mixed bag of achievers," the "heads of businesses and ad agencies, editors of magazines, politicians, public officials, television producers, Broadway producers, filmmakers, artists, writers, musicians, photographers, scientists, historians."

Zinsser asked these achievers to tell a little bit about how they got their start in their various callings. According to Zinsser, "the students assume that they started in their present field and knew all along that it was what they wanted to do." To the students' surprise, however, the guest speakers, more often than not, came to their present position of achievement by "a circuitous route," and only "after many detours." There were many bumps in the road along the way.

Zinsser wrote that upon learning this, "the students were startled." They could "hardly conceive of a career that was not preplanned." To Zinsser's own surprise and consternation, "they can hardly imagine allowing the hand of God or chance to nudge them down some unforeseen trail."

Zinsser is now concerned that his essay, "College Pressures," continues to be anthologized and reprinted. Although he regrets that the article is "as pertinent today as it was 25 years ago," he realizes that "in fact, it's more pertinent." Students still find themselves under enormous pressure to perform and succeed, and the ambition of students is often ambition manufactured by parents or friends, and not of their own choosing. Zinsser was a caring residential college master in the 1970s, and he continues to care about students today. Our Wesley has been the beneficiary of his personal as well as his literary care.

"What I want for all young people," Zinsser writes, "is a release from the clammy grip of the future. I'd like them to savor each step of their education as a rich experience in itself, not as a preparation for the next step." I wish this release for my students and for my son and daughter as well.

Devoted to a Work

The writer William Zinsser has written that "change is a tonic," and certainly a fresh start in a new work (even for those of us in our middle years) is often just the thing that is needed. For Zinsser's father, however, and for my own, an unswerving life's work proved to be another way to live a life. For an individual to be devoted to a life's work is an awe-inspiring thing, requiring a drive and a focus and a patience that very few people have.

I know of a friend who has literally given his life over to a small liberal arts college. He could have gone to any number of colleges or universities, "bettering" himself and his financial lot, but he has instead chosen to remain at his post, quietly molding his college into an institution of note and worth. I admire his devotion, his focus, his patience, manifested in his life of service to a cause.

I heard about Donald Grey Barnhouse, a Presbyterian minister in Philadelphia, who wanted to study and understand St. Paul's Epistle to the Romans. He decided to preach his way through that New Testament book. He became so entranced by the book and devoted to its exposition that he found himself preaching from Romans Sunday after Sunday. It took him thirteen years, and his congregation came to mark the weeks sermon by sermon by how many verses he covered each Sunday morning.

Will and Ariel Durant spent twenty years of their married lives working together on their magnum opus, an eleven-volume *Story of Civilization*, almost ten thousand pages in length. Can you imagine being married to a historian who committed over one-fourth of a life to write a *Story of Civilization*? Can you imagine being married to a historian? Can you imagine being a historian who devotes so much time and energy to a study of the past? Can you imagine devoting your life to a particular work?

The great Kentucky novelist, poet, and essayist Wendell Berry has devoted his life to writing about the farmers of Port William, Kentucky, and to farming himself. Story after story, and year after year, tilling the mind with a pen and the soil with a trusty team of mules. Devoting his life to the farm, in his writing and in his being.

I heard about scribes in Oxford, England, who, before Gutenberg's invention of movable type, meticulously copied out manuscripts by hand. Sometimes one scribe took a whole lifetime to copy out one book. Think of the commitment! Think of the drudgery! But think of the accomplishment, the worth of spending a lifetime saving a significant manuscript from being swept into the dustbin of history.

My mother and father and Evelyn's mother and father devoted their married lives to their family. They nurtured my brother and me, and Evelyn and her three sisters, and then our children, their grandchildren and great-grandchildren, always putting our lives ahead of their own. They literally devoted their lives to the lives of others.

How do we spend our lives? What will be left to show for it? A college, a work of history, a farm, a recovered manuscript, another life perhaps? To what or to whom are we devoted? What matters, after all, in the end?

In Search of Dietrich Bonhoeffer

For a trip to Regensburg, Germany, I prepared a two-hour presentation required of each faculty member in Murray State's Europe in Transition Program. My presentation explored the enduring significance of Dietrich Bonhoeffer, the theologian whose resistance to Hitler resulted in his execution less than a month before Hitler's suicide and the end of World War II.

We discussed important ethical questions, important to Bonhoeffer then and just as important to each one of us today: For whom would you die? For what would you die? What good am I? I paired the music of Bob Dylan with Bonhoeffer's life and theology. Dylan performed in Regensburg in 2000, had 18 concerts in Berlin, 13 performances in Munich, and a memorable gig in Dresden.

Bonhoeffer himself was an accomplished musician, and indeed his family had hoped that he would pursue music as a career. I am guessing, of course, but I think that Bonhoeffer would have felt a real affinity with Dylan and his social commentary on war and faith.

Bonhoeffer visited the United States twice, in 1930-1931 and again in 1939, both times to study and teach at Union Theological Seminary in New York City. There Bonhoeffer studied with Reinhold Niebuhr and met A. Franklin Fisher, a fellow seminarian, an African American, who introduced him to the rich culture of the Harlem Renaissance and took him across the way to worship each Sunday at the Abyssinian Baptist Church.

At this historic church, Bonhoeffer sat under the preaching of Adam Clayton Powell Sr. and was moved by the inspirational singing of the Abyssinian Baptist Church Choir, hearing such historic black hymns as "Go Down, Moses" and "We are Climbing Jacob's Ladder."

Bonhoeffer found no Gospel teaching at Union. He was even less impressed with the preaching of Harry Emerson Fosdick at the nearby Riverside Church. Only at the Abyssinian Baptist Church and the preaching of Powell Sr. and the singing of that magnificent choir did he find what his soul yearned for.

During one semester break, Fisher took Bonhoeffer to Washington, DC, where he had studied at Howard College, one of the great historically black institutions in America. This was Bonhoeffer's first foray into the American South. Later he would tour the South, traveling through Mississippi, Alabama, Louisiana, Texas, into Mexico, and back through Georgia, Tennessee, and Virginia.

Bonhoeffer witnessed firsthand the Jim Crow South of the 1930s—the segregation, lynchings, abuse, and racism—an "American Problem" he called it, that appalled him. It was this "American Problem" that he compared to what came to be referred to as "the Jewish Question" back in Germany. Bonhoeffer's twin sister, Sabine, had married a Jewish man, and when Bonhoeffer returned to Germany to find Adolph Hitler and the Nazis rising to control the country, it was his American experience that convinced him to put his theoretical theological concepts into practice.

And this he did. Bonhoeffer witnessed Hitler's plan to systematically annihilate the Jews. He became a leader in the resistance movement against Hitler, a leader in the Confessing Church against the Nazi-approved state church, and was eventually imprisoned and hanged on April 9, 1945, at Flossenburg, just an hour or so north of Regensburg, where I lived during my German sojourn. We visited Nuremburg, Prague in the Czech Republic, and other wonderful sites during our trip, but I learned more about Bonhoeffer too. He has been a great hero of our son, Wesley, for a long time, and through Wesley, I have learned to love and respect what Bonhoeffer stood for and died for as well.

Epitaphs

Perhaps we can tell a great deal about the callings of individuals from their epitaphs. What about our epitaphs? At the end of a life of calling, what assessment will we make of it all? How will your epitaph read? What will my epitaph say?

Will it read with comic cynicism like the epitaph of W. C. Fields? "Better here than Philadelphia." Or will it reek of fatalism or resignation or insignificance?

Danville, Kentucky's Thomas Johnson published his poetry in *The Kentucky Miscellany* in 1789, making him one of Kentucky's earliest poets. His nicknames—"Drunken Tom" and "The drunken poet of Danville"—tell us something about where he received his inspiration. His poem, "The Author's Hatred of Kentucky in General," shows us why he was never chosen as Kentucky's Poet Laureate:

I hate Kentucky, curse the place,
And all her vile and miscreant race!
Who make religion's sacred tie,
A mash through which they cheat and lie;

I hate all judges here of late,
And every lawyer in the state.
Each quack that is call'd physician,
And all blockheads in commission

Worse than the Baptist roaring rant,
I hate the Presbyterian cant.

Their parsons, elders, nay the whole,
And wish them gone with all my soul.

Far worse than these, I yet do hate,
All those who pimp or speculate.
All rogues and villains, men in trade,
(If a distinction may be made.
Glad would I be: 'twas quickly done,
For my own part I know of none).

It shouldn't surprise us that Drunken Tom's epitaph, written by the poet himself, was as unedifying as his published poetry:

Underneath this marble tomb,
In endless shades lies drunken Tom;
Here safely moor'd, dead as a log
Who got his death by drinking grog,
By whiskey grog he lost his breath,
Who would not die so sweet a death.

Other grave markers are just as flippant (or profound?) as Drunken Tom's. One read:

Once I wasn't
Then I was
Now I ain't again.
Or:

Rest in peace, dear Cousin Hewitt. We all know you didn't do it.

Or:

Here lies the father of 29
There would have been more
But he ran out of time.

Other epitaphs express more serious—although just as fatalistic—sentiments. Os Guinness includes some of these epitaphs in his book,

The Call. A sense of failure permeates the epitaph of Cecil Rhodes at his grave in Zimbabwe: "So much to do, so little done." Or consider the epitaph written by the young journalist Malcolm Muggeridge: "Here lieth one whose soul sometimes burned with great longings. To whom sometimes the curtain of the Infinite was opened just a little, but who lacked the guts to make any use of it."

In contrast, some epitaphs are infused with a sense of calling like that of Emily Dickinson after her life of poetic accomplishment. Dickinson's epitaph reads simply, "Called Back."

What about our epitaphs? At the end of a life of calling, what assessment will we make of it all? How will your epitaph read? What will my epitaph say?

Part Ten

Life

"With all my road before me."

C.S. Lewis

Top: C. S. Lewis. Center: Cammie Jo Bolin, Kentucky High School Kentucky State Class A long jump champion, 2012. Bottom: Wesley and Cammie Jo in Fall Leaves, c. 1999.

Here's a State of Things

The beginning of any new year is a time for taking stock, a time to remember the past, to assess the present state of things, and then to make plans for the future. So, here we are in 2015, a brand new year full of hope and opportunity. Where do we stand? What did we accomplish this past year? And what do we hope to accomplish this next year? What, after all, in this first week of a new year, is the state of things?

In 1992, my father asked me if I would be interested in going through papers stored in an old safe in the back of Bolin's Drugstore in Dixon, Kentucky. I jumped at the chance. Dad was preparing to sell our family-owned, western Kentucky, county-seat business, yet another casualty of the big chain stores. He didn't want to leave anything of real value to be heaped into a dumpster in the back alley when the new managers took over. I carefully went through the papers and old ledgers, a treasure trove for an aspiring historian. Among the yellowed scraps and clippings I found several gems. One was handwritten in pencil, a list of "Isms," terms ending in "ism." This 1940s scrap of whimsy indicates the humorous cynicism of the writer, a cynicism penciled in terms that a western Kentucky small-town school girl or boy could understand:

> **"Isms"**
>
> *Socialism*: If you have two cows, you give your neighbor one.
>
> *Communism*: If you have two cows, you give them to the government and the government gives you some milk.
>
> *Fascism*: If you have two cows, you keep the cows, and give the milk to the government and the government then sells you some milk.
>
> *New Dealism*: If you have two cows, you shoot one and milk the other and pour the milk down the drain.
>
> *Nazism*: If you have two cows, the government shoots you and keeps the cows.
>
> *Capitalism*: If you have two cows, you sell one and buy a bull.

I found, stashed nearby the "Isms" scrap, a small newspaper clipping tucked among other clippings from 1892 newspapers. Apparently an editorial, the clipping is titled, "Here's a State of Things." The writer declared, "Science…has diminished hope, knowledge has destroyed our illusions, and experience has deprived us of interest.

Here, then, is the authorized dictionary of discontent." Because I found the clipping in 1992, it interested me that I held in my hand a writer's opinion of the "State of Things" from exactly a century before. The editorialist posed a series of questions followed by his own answers to the questions. The writer reveals his nineteenth century chauvinism, and again, the writer's answers reveal a prevailing cynicism, indeed a fatalism, not unlike, perhaps, the attitudes of many Americans in this new year of 2015:

What is creation? A failure.
What is life? A bore.
What is man? A fraud.
What is woman? Both a fraud and a bore.
What is beauty? A deception.
What is love? A disease.
What is marriage? A mistake.
What is a wife? A trial.
What is a child? A nuisance.
What is the devil? A fable.
What is good? Hypocrisy.
What is evil? Detection.
What is wisdom? Selfishness.
What is happiness? A delusion.
What is friendship? A humbug.
What is generosity? Imbecility.
What is money? Everything.
What is everything? Nothing.

This is not a happy thought, but the heart of the matter is that, still today, a prevailing materialism only results in a meaningless existence devoid of faith, hope, and love. How will we prioritize our lives in this new year? What will the new year bring? And what will we bring to this new year?

All My Road Before Me

My students at Murray State University are all in the process of figuring out who they are and how they will spend the rest of their days. Now in their youth, they have, stretched out before them, the rest of their lives. They have decisions to make, both academic and personal.

Where will their roads take them? And how will they find the way?

C. S. Lewis, the Oxford scholar, Christian apologist, and writer of children's stories and science fiction novels, found what was for him the "narrow road that leads to life," a "road less traveled," but only after he had journeyed along for some time. He documents his own experience in a conversion autobiography, *Surprised by Joy*. Long before he wrote *Surprised by Joy*, he began a long narrative poem in 1922 that he titled "Dymer." The poem, published in 1926, over four years after it was begun, "had many favorable reviews, but few readers." A line from the poem, however, came to serve as the title for a published collection of Lewis's diary entries from the mid-1920s: *All My Road Before Me: The Diary of C. S. Lewis, 1922-1927*. The collection's title is taken from these lines found early on in the poem:

> You stranger, long before your glance can light
> Upon these words, time will have washed away
> The moment when I first took pen to write,
> With all my road before me—yet to-day,
> Here, if at all, we meet…

These were heady days for the young Lewis, and he did indeed have all the road before him. In two years he would take a "First" (at Oxford University, a rare A+) in Classical Moderations (the Greek and Classical writers) and he was then, in 1922, studying for another examination in "Greats" (or Greek and Latin historians and philosophers). He yearned for an Oxford fellowship to teach and write. These were Lewis's pre-Christian days, and as he wrote in his diary on that "beautiful spring" April Sunday, sitting in his "bedroom by an open window in bright sunshine" struggling to begin his poem, how could he have known what twists and turns his road would take?

Robert Frost, a more accomplished poet, wrote familiar lines about a "road not taken":

> Two roads diverged in a yellow wood,
> And sorry I could not travel both
> And be one traveler, long I stood
> And looked down one as far as I could
> To where it bent in the undergrowth;

Then took the other, as just as fair,
And having perhaps the better claim,
Because it was grassy and wanted wear;
Though as for that, the passing there
Had worn them really about the same,

And both that morning equally lay
In leaves no step had trodden black.
Oh, I kept the first for another day!
Yet knowing how way leads on to way,
I doubted if I should ever come back.

I shall be telling this with a sigh
Somewhere ages and ages hence:
Two roads diverged in a wood, and I—
I took the one less traveled by,
And that has made all the difference.

Along with Frost, C. S. Lewis himself chose a road less traveled, and what a difference that choice made for the thousands of us, later readers of *The Chronicles of Narnia, The Screwtape Letters, The Weight of Glory*, and all the rest! Just like my students, we too have all our roads before us. What choices will we make? Where will our roads take us?

Melancholia

I have before me the image of Albrecht Durer's "Melencolia I," completed in 1514 as perhaps the finest of his copperplate engravings. According to the *Britannica*, Durer (1471-1528), born and died in Nurnberg, Germany, painter and printmaker, "generally regarded as the greatest German Renaissance artist." Durer has interested me for some time, ever since I saw his Christlike self-portrait, an oil on wood that he painted in 1500.

It is the subject of his 1514 copper engraving that is of interest to me, however, largely because I sometimes suffer from melancholia, a state of depression that sometimes leaves one helpless in its grip. I wonder if Durer suffered from the same ailment? After all, he chose it as the subject for his engraving, and a glance at his somber self-portrait perhaps gives a further clue. Melancholia. Winston Churchill called it "the black dog." In

Durer's engraving, a robed scholar, surrounded by symbols of alchemy, holding a pen in one hand and leaning on the other, looks off into the middle distance contemplating the depths of his despair.

The writer, Paul Laurence Dunbar, wrote knowingly about the condition in his poem, "Melancholia":

Silently without my window,
Tapping gently at the pane,
Falls the rain.
Through the trees sighs the breeze
Like a soul in pain.
Here alone I sit and weep;
Thought hath banished sleep.

Wearily I sit and listen
To the water's ceaseless drip.
To my lip
Fate turns up the bitter cup,
Forcing me to sip;
'T is a bitter, bitter drink,
Thus I sit and think...

Eyes that look into the future,—
Peeping forth from out my mind,
They will find
Some new weight, soon or late,
On my soul to bind,
Crushing all its courage out,—
Heavier than doubt.

Now that's depressing. Perhaps it hit me today, when Evelyn and Cammie Jo left this morning for church camp in Panama City, Florida, leaving Wesley and me at home to fend for ourselves. Wesley and I drove with them to the church parking lot to see them off.

It will be a wonderful week for them with worship and Bible study mixed in with relaxation on the beach. Thanks to cellphones, we can call them any time we want. And they will be home before we know it. Still, we already miss them.

Back home, Wesley and I spent the morning reading. I rearranged books, an activity to which I often resort for soothing relief. At lunchtime, Wesley and I sat down at the kitchen table, just the two of us, sharing pitiful frozen pot pies that we prepared in the microwave oven. Just two pot pies and a father and son, sitting quietly together at a table with two empty places, missing a mother and wife, a sister and daughter.

We looked down at the pot pies. Pitiful. Then, we looked at each other. Pitiful. And then, unable to help ourselves, we broke up laughing; laughing, not out of joy, but laughing because we were indeed quite a pitiful sight. Two men, one young, one aging, both longing for loved ones that we love beyond measure.

Sports and Life

I have the pleasure of teaching HIS 330, Sports in America, an upper-level history elective. I love to teach this course, because each time I teach it I learn so much more about American history.

Murray State's Sports in America course, offered every now and again by our Department of History, is a rigorous, reading-and-writing intensive course. The course includes demanding reading assignments of primary and secondary sources, oral and written student presentations, and midterm and final essay examinations. Students are required to read and write a book review, as well as produce a research paper on a topic of sports history. The course demands intensive study of the rise of sports in America from Native American Indian games, to the age of folk games in the colonial period, to the age of televised sports in the modern era. The course requires critical thinking and analysis of the cultural, social, economic, and political aspects of the sporting scene, and extensive study and thought on sports and race issues and sports and gender issues.

OK sports fans. Have I ruined it for you? I hope not, because the course is a celebration of sports in America. The course is also a celebration of the life of the mind and the world of ideas. We are simply concentrating on a topic of extreme interest and relevance and fun for a large number of Americans (and especially Kentuckians). Sports!

I developed an interest in sports history out of osmosis, I think. As a boy I spent hours studying and discussing and trading baseball cards on my front porch in Dixon, Kentucky with my friend Duane Clark.

Memorization of the batting averages, RBIs, home runs, strikeouts, and earned run averages of my favorite New York Yankees taught me the connections between sports and ideas and facts.

My father took my brother and me to see Mickey Mantle as he signed autographs at a Montgomery Ward store in Fort Worth, Texas, where we lived at the time. I promptly took the signed baseball home and ruined it with grass stains playing pitch in my back yard. I wish I still had that baseball today, minus the grass stains.

Playing basketball back in Kentucky, often alone on the concrete court behind the old Dixon Grade School, I tried to imitate the picture-perfect jump-shot form of my hero, Rick Mount, the sharpshooter of the Purdue Boilermakers, the first high school player whose picture graced the cover of *Sports Illustrated*. I idolized the Blond Bomber, and I tried to learn everything I could about his background. I am embarrassed to admit that I carried a magazine photograph of Mount in my wallet. Anyway, Mantle and Mount taught me the connection between sports and biography.

In the summers in between semesters at Belmont University, where I played basketball and majored in history, I went with Alan Vaughn and Jay Cobb and Charlie Hust and Bob Mantooth to old Bosse Field in Evansville, Indiana, to watch the Evansville Triplets, the Detroit Tigers triple-A affiliate. There, in that historic old ballpark, the location for the shooting of the film, *A League of Their Own*, about the All American Girls Professional Baseball League during World War II, we sat along the third-base line, harassing the umpires. We saw future big league stars Mark "the Bird" Fidrych and Kirk Gibson just before they were called up to the Tigers. After the game, we bought hot tamales from a vendor, relishing what we knew to be a "historic experience." Those games at old Bosse Field taught me the connection between sports and history.

Once, on a weekend, during an autumn semester at Belmont, I went with my east Tennessee teammate, Mitch Keebler, to a home football game at Neyland Stadium at the University of Tennessee. There, we watched the Volunteers play the LSU Tigers before over eighty thousand screaming fans. This was more than a mere game; it was a pageant, a social extravaganza, and from that game I learned the connection between sports and society.

After learning the game of basketball from the masters, having played for Eddie Ford in high school and coached as the assistant of Phil Gibson, two of the very best coaches in the business, I went to graduate school in Lexington. There I attended all of the University of Kentucky Wildcats home basketball games at Rupp Arena and the women's games at Memorial Coliseum. I also sat in Dr. Bert Nelli's sports history class and his History of UK Basketball course. I learned from those classroom experiences the value of sports as an academic exercise.

I tell you all of that to try to relate how I came to teach a class in sports history at Murray State. I hope to teach it again and again, because it is such a rewarding experience, rewarding for me at least, and I hope for the students too.

Painting by Numbers

As I write this, I have before me a painting. The painting tells a story. It unmistakably shows a barn-red barn, a sky-blue sky, forest-green evergreen trees behind the barn, and snow in various shades of white and gray. A brown-barked tree with snow-laden branches, otherwise bare, dominates the right side of the painting, and ruined fence posts lean drunkenly in front and beside the barn. Only a hint of blue water, suggesting a farm pond, is visible in the bottom left corner, and for years I thought that the red and brown tones at water's edge represented a Georgia red clay bank (My aunt and uncle lived in a red cabin of that very same color down a gravel road in central Georgia). Now, upon closer inspection, I see that the earth-tone red is a reflection of the barn in the pond. I never saw it that way before. Only now is it clear to me.

Perhaps my misapprehension was the result of the crudity of the painting. After all, the painting came out of a box, a present given to me by my parents, perhaps for a birthday or Christmas gift; I have forgotten which. The box contained an entire paint-by-numbers set. I also have a paint-by-numbers palomino horse that reminds me still today of Trigger on the lid of my Roy Rogers lunchbox. That lunchbox also told a story. I extracted school lunches of peanut butter and jelly sandwiches and pieces of fruit regularly from it in the lunchroom of Oak Lawn Elementary School in Fort Worth, Texas. Not just Roy and Trigger, but Dale Evans and her Buttermilk graced the box's top cover. The lunchbox is long gone, discarded after the vinyl corner tear spread completely across the edge. From then on, it was school chili for me.

The *Antiques Road Show* people now tell me that such lunchboxes are coveted items for collectors. And, to my surprise, so are the paint-by-numbers paintings. Real painters and artists surely shudder at the things, although I suspect that even they might see in these primitive renderings art of a kind. Perhaps they tell us about a search for order in the America of the 1950s and 1960s. Along with Woodstock and pot came paint-by-numbers. My brother had a van and played in a rock band; his youthful years were altogether balanced and well rounded. I worked at my numbered paintings, and before that, wooden puzzles (if they didn't take too long to complete). Those wooden puzzles also held stories. There I am in a photograph during playtime at my seminary kindergarten, hunkered down in deep concentration over a wooden puzzle of seven or eight pieces.

Perhaps my own search for order—made clear early on in my formula painting and piecing together of simple puzzles—foreshadowed my life's work, my calling, to teach and do history. The teaching of history involves the telling of stories. Now, in my history classroom at Murray State, I have a responsibility to teach my sometimes uninterested students why history is important. How can the study of history make our lives more fulfilling? Can the study of history lead to a more "wholesome" life?

Peter Gomes, the late minister of Harvard's Memorial Church, reminded us in his book, *The Good Life*, that history, or collective and individual remembering, suggests the piecing together of a story. In his boyhood at his tiny Baptist church in Plymouth, Massachusetts, the few partakers of the Lord's Supper were instructed to pass the time (as well as the cup and bread) remembering: "We knew," Gomes wrote, "we were remembering, or, as our pastor always reminded us, 'putting back together,' for that is what it means to remember." Re-membering, as opposed to dis-membering, does indeed suggest "putting back together," or making something or someone whole again, whether that something is a crude paint-by-numbers picture, or a simple wooden puzzle, or that someone is a man or woman living in the disarray of a complicated, complex world.

Abou Ben Adhem

I remember Gail Magruder only vaguely. He was an insurance man with an office just a few doors down from my father's pharmacy in Arlington, Kentucky. I can't see the man in my mind's eye, but I remember the respect that my father had for him. In Arlington, along with the Hocker family, my father held Mr. Magruder in high esteem.

My mother and father always remembered the five years that we spent in Arlington as sort of the Golden Age of the Bolin family. My brother and I came into the family there, and that close-knit community served as the perfect, nurturing place for a young family, with all of the possibilities of life stretched out before us.

Friends such as Robert and Mary Helen Hocker, and their children, Robert Peck and Melinda, made us feel right at home. A loving church family greeted us into the congregation, and the small but thriving business community initiated my father into the intricacies of operating a family-run drugstore. We lived in a small rental house, just down from the church.

Life was not always easy. Another brother and sister, Timothy and Cathy, both died after living only a day, so my mother and father struggled and suffered especially. Yet, years later, after much of her life had already been lived, my mother remembered those Arlington years with gratitude and even joy.

So did my father. Eventually, he was called to preach, ordained in the Arlington church, and we moved away for my father to attend the seminary. The folks back in Arlington followed our family's progress and my father's ministry, despite the lapse of years. I know this because I have seen some of the cards from the Hockers, along with some of the letters that Mr. Magruder sent to my father after we left Arlington.

Mr. Magruder wrote letters the way letters were meant to be written. In those years before e-mail, his letters were filled with wit and charm. We rarely see letters today, written in that wonderful, some would call it quaint, style. Even as I read those letters secondhand, years after they were written, I can see in his words the goodness of Gail Magruder.

Mr. Magruder often filled his letters with poetry, some of the lines his own, others from his favorite poets copied down from memory. In one letter, Mr. Magruder copied out a poem that my father remembered to be one of his favorites, a James Henry Leigh poem, titled "Abou Ben Adhem":

Abou Ben Adhem (may his tribe increase!)
Awoke one night from a deep dream of peace,
And saw, within the moonlight of his room,
Making it rich, and like a lily in bloom,
An angel, writing in a book of gold.

Exceeding peace had made Ben Adhem bold,
And to the Presence in the room he said:
"What writest thou?" The vision raised its head,
And, with a look made of all sweet accord,
Answered, "The names of those who love the Lord."
"And is mine one?" said Abou, "Nay, not so,"
Replied the angel. Abou spoke more low,
But cheerily still, and said, "I pray then,
Write me as one who loves his fellow men."
The angel wrote, and vanished. The next night
It came again, with a great awakening light,
And showed the names whom love of God had blest,
And lo! Ben Adhem's name led all the rest.

I've always thought that the poem applied to Gail Magruder, although I think he included it in his letter as a tribute to my father and mother, as a way to describe the way James Wesley and Cammie Bolin lived their lives. For them and for their friends, the Hockers and the Magruders of the world, to love is to live, and to live is to love. The poem "Abou Ben Adhem" is about a Sufi saint, but the poem also summarizes the greatest two commandments of Christianity: "Love the Lord your God with all your heart and with all your soul and with all your mind" and the second is like unto it: "Love your neighbor as yourself.""

Perspective

Perspective is something that we try to teach our history students at Murray State. We talk about point of view or the "climate of opinion" in which historians write a book or article of history. Sometimes in our everyday lives we take for granted our own perspective, our own point of view. Or we make the mistake of believing that we are always right, that we always have a clear view of things. What if we were able to look through the eyes of others, or as the old Native American adage would have it, "walk a mile in his moccasins?" Perhaps it would make us less self-centered, less parochial, less set in our ways.

Samuel Woodworth wrote nostalgically about his childhood, and particularly about his memories of an old oaken bucket from which he would quench his thirst:

How dear to my heart are the scenes of my childhood,
When fond recollections presents them to view!
The orchard, the meadow, the deep tangled wildwood,
And every loved spot which my infancy knew,
The wide-spreading pond and the mill that stood by it,
The bridge and the rock where the cataract fell.
The cot of my father, the dairy house nigh it,
And e'en the rude bucket that hung in the well.

That moss-covered bucket I hailed as a treasure,
For often at noon, when returned from the field,
I found it the source of an exquisite pleasure,
The purest and sweetest that nature can yield.
How ardent I seized it, with hands that were glowing,
And quick to the white-pebbled bottom it fell.
Then soon, with the emblem of truth overflowing,
And dripping with coolness, it rose from the well.

Well, you get the idea. This poet is remembering back to his childhood to an article of delight, an old oaken bucket, that came to represent for him the innocence and joy of the simple pleasures of youth.

There always has to be some crank with a different perspective, a different point of view. And, sure enough, some "Unknown" poet rewrote the poem, "The Old Oaken Bucket," with a different slant, an angle the poet said, "as censored by the Board of Health." Here, then, is a different version of the poem:

With what anguish of mind I remember my childhood,
Recalled in the light of knowledge since gained,
The malarious farm, the wet, fungous-grown wildwood,
The chills then contracted that since have remained;
The scum-covered duck-pond, the pigsty close by it,
The ditch where the sour-smelling house drainage fell,
The damp, shaded dwelling, the foul barnyard nigh it—
But worse than all else was that terrible well,
And the old oaken bucket, the mold-crusted bucket,
The moss-covered bucket that hung in the well.

Well now. The unknown parodist clearly has a different perspective. And as much as we sometimes dislike challenges to our own points of view, points of view often clouded over with nostalgia, by taking seriously the perspectives of others, as hard and inconvenient as that might be, we can learn much about the truth of our lives, the reality of our world.

Taste and Scent

Sitting on our back deck in the cool of a recent evening, sipping an iced tea, brought to me memories of the past. I'm not sure if it was the taste of the cool tea or the scent of that languid moment, an evening scent of early summer, that caused me to remember, but I understood again the power of the sense of taste and the sense of smell, the two senses that perhaps more than any other can bring on the remembrance of things past.

It caused me to remember the sweet sensation of taking a break from a baseball game to drink from a tin cup in a neighbor's back yard. It caused me to remember the crunch of garden fresh cucumber on a summer visit to my aunt and uncle's farm just north of Memphis. It caused me to remember our own back yard in Arkansas where a fence was laden with honeysuckle vine. Our daughter Cammie Jo, though just a baby then, still recalls that wonderful summer scent of honeysuckle.

I often go to the front of our house here in Murray to run my hands through a boxwood, just to recall through that musky smell the head-high boxwood mazes that we walked through one summer in Virginia, in Lexington and Williamsburg, when Wesley was just a small boy. Wesley still remembers that smell from the times that summer when Evelyn would read to him *The Boxcar Children* beneath a boxwood arbor in Charlottesville. I encouraged Wesley to take the time to run his fingers through our boxwood, just for no other reason than to recapture that magical summer in Virginia.

I remember the scent of the sourdough bread, freshly baked, that filled my mother's home. That scent represented to me the care that went into the preparation of the starter and then the kneading of the dough. I remember an indefinable smell that greeted customers walking into my father's drugstore, what must have been a potent mixture of salves and ointments and elixirs mingled with the scent of boxes of King Edward cigars.

Years ago, my pastor, Dr. Terry Ellis, preached a sermon that I will never forget. He told us about the scent of a charcoal fire around which Peter denied Christ three times just before the crucifixion. And then, after the resurrection, Peter encountered the risen Lord, this time cooking breakfast on a charcoal fire. Dr. Ellis reminded us of the powerful sense of smell and suggested that Peter must have remembered that first charcoal fire when he denied knowing Jesus, even as he was given the opportunity around this second charcoal fire to state—three times—his unequivocal love of the Lord. For Peter, the scent of charcoal became the scent of grace.

Marcel Proust knew the power of taste and smell in remembering his childhood in the first volume of his *In Search of Lost Time*. "But when from a long-distant past nothing subsists," Proust wrote, "after the people are dead, after the things are broken and scattered, taste and smell alone, more fragile but more enduring, more immaterial, more persistent, more faithful, remain poised a long time, like souls, remembering, waiting, hoping, amid the ruins of all the rest; and bear unflinchingly, in the tiny and almost impalpable drop of their essence, the vast structure of recollection."

Saint Peter knew. Marcel Proust knew. And we know too. The power of the sense of taste and smell to conjure up the remembrance of things past.

Catching Our Breaths

I often think about—in between going somewhere or hurrying off to somewhere else—the hurried pace of our lives. At certain times of the year, the pace quickens considerably. The swirl of end-of-the-school-year activities is upon us. We wonder if we will survive, if we will finally find an opportunity to catch our breaths. This is one of those times when there is simply too much to do, too many deadlines to meet, too many tests to take, too many papers to complete, too many banquets and ceremonies and practices and concerts and track meets and programs to attend. Too many and too much. Just too much.

I am not questioning the worth of each of these activities. There is, of course, a reason, a necessity, for each of these end-of-term responsibilities. Of course, we understand that teachers must assess the cumulative learning of content and skills. Teachers too have endured course evaluations and principal observations.

It is worthwhile and only right to honor students for intellectual and artistic and athletic accomplishments. Of course, it is necessary to observe graduation ceremonies, commencement exercises, to mark the significant transitions in the lives of talented students, all full of promise and hope. Of course, there is a need to be involved in a wide range of activities, to be devoted to worthy causes, to lead active, purposeful lives.

It just seems that at certain times of the year—and this is surely one of those times—the accumulation, the sheer volume of these activities overwhelm us, inviting us to go from event to event, from venue to venue, in a daze. Like zombies, we stumble from one program to the next, then we rush from home to school to church to stadium to park in mad dashes, checking our watches and calendars and datebooks all the while, fearful that we will forget or neglect or overbook ourselves, causing us to—perish the thought—miss some significant observance, our absence threatening to scar us or our loved ones for life.

In our haste, I fear we are missing the restorative pleasures of the front-porch swing, the park bench, the wooded trail. We are missing out on the healing value of reflective neighborhood walks, of quiet afternoons in a television-free parlor, or of leisurely suppers around a family table. We, as parents, surely miss these delights, but what's worse is the fact that we are teaching our children to disregard the necessity of slowing down, of simply catching our collective breaths.

We teach, after all, by example, rather than by breathless words, forced out between gulps—not sips—of coffee or coke. We want our children to know how to relax, how to reflect, how to experience peace. Still, we continue to rush headlong like mice on a treadmill as if our happiness depended on it. Forget about our sanity. Forget about our emotional and physical and spiritual well-being. We want to be happy, and happy now!

We want contentment now. We want peace immediately. We want to relax right this second. "Hurry up and slow down," we say by example. "Wake up and go to sleep," we kid each other. Hurry up and catch your breath, before it escapes altogether. I would love to write another line or two about the benefits of slowing down, of the need to catch our breaths, but, sorry (checking my watch), I have to run.

Elvis is Dead and I Don't Feel So Good Myself

"Elvis is dead, and I don't feel so good myself." Dr. Bill Ellis, professor of history, writer, and *Kentucky Monthly* columnist, reminded me of the Lewis Grizzard quotation as we chatted in Poor Richard's Bookshop in downtown Frankfort one Friday night. Bill and his wife Charlotte had just come in the shop for a gathering of *Kentucky Monthly* writers, a stop on Frankfort's Candlelight Tour. Charlotte, herself a wonderful lady, is the niece of Murray's own Lorraine Adams, a wonderful, remarkable, thoughtful lady who befriended my mother after my mother moved to Murray. Bill has made the acquaintance of Murray's Gary Garth, another *Kentucky Monthly* writer, whose outdoors column has been a popular addition to the magazine. Gary has taken Bill fishing twice, once on the Cumberland and once on Kentucky Lake.

A prolific writer, Dr. Ellis has published books on the Kentucky River, Robert Worth Bingham—the owner of the *Louisville Courier-Journal*—the history of Eastern Kentucky University. His latest book, published by the University Press of Kentucky, is *A History of Education in Kentucky*. Now he is at work on a book about humor. So, we talked about Irvin Cobb and Will Rogers and Garrison Keillor, all humorists who could make you laugh without ever really telling a joke. Lewis Grizzard was the same way in his syndicated humor column.

I guess, though, that "Elvis is dead, and I don't feel so good myself" is Grizzard's most famous quotation. After all, it became the title for one of Grizzard's twenty-five books. Like me, Grizzard struggled with heart-valve trouble. According to Grizzard, "There are three little leaflets that control the flow of blood to the heart. I was born with only two of those leaflets. It was just after the Great War, so there may have been a shortage. Either that or my daddy didn't get a good toe-hold." Grizzard had three heart-valve-replacement surgeries back when the procedure was far less advanced than it is now. After his last surgery in 1993, over fifty thousand letters poured in from well-wishers. "He later attributed his miraculous recovery to the prayers of his fans."

Dr. Ellis told me that the public Grizzard was considerably different from the private Grizzard. The humorist went through three divorces and married four times. At the *Atlanta Journal-Constitution*, the base where he worked, he was apparently a terror. He drank heavily, and he once got an editor fired. On his many book tours, publishers never knew what would happen. Bill wondered if some of his meanness could have been attributed to his heart troubles.

After the Frankfort event at Poor Richard's, I drove to Lexington the next day to do some research at the University of Kentucky's Young Library. As I came down the stairs out of the stacks, my feet slipped out from under me, I fell, and to prove the fall to the world I now sport a black eye where my new glasses (now broken) hit my eye. My knee is bummed up a little, my shoulder aches, and to tell you the truth, in the words of Lewis Grizzard, "I don't feel so good myself."

I don't like the fact that I now have a pacemaker or that I have a piece of a cow inside me (moo, moo) or that I don't seem to have the energy that I once had either. I yearn for physical, mental, emotional, and spiritual health. I am astonished at folks in their 90s who are my mentors and exemplars. I am amazed at Evelyn and Wesley and Cammie Jo who remain constant in their love and support.

Nevertheless, I understand the rage of Lewis Grizzard, and I too realize that Elvis is indeed dead (may he rest in peace), and I have made peace with the fact that the reason I don't feel so good myself is simply because I am not 16 anymore.

Politics and Life

Sometimes my emotions get the better of me, and it is at those times that my words fail me the most. And my emotions get the better of me especially when I write about my family. Regarding politics, my mother's family were diehard Democrats, converted to that party by Franklin Delano Roosevelt and his New Deal. My mother's father, John Mann, my grandfather or Pa Pa, owned a meat shop, and he was a fine butcher. My Pa Pa signed up immediately under the Blue Eagle, the NRA, not the National Rifle Association, but the National Recovery Administration. He proudly displayed a poster of the NRA Blue Eagle in the plate glass window at the front of his shop. He appreciated Roosevelt's concern for the unemployed and the poor, of which Pa Pa was one, and he believed that FDR's New Deal at least made an effort to lift the country out of despair.

After Pearl Harbor, Roosevelt's leadership during World War II cemented my grandfather's regard for the president, and he voted for him in four straight elections. Pa Pa sent his only son to fight and at D-Day, my Uncle J. C. landed behind enemy lines as a paratrooper. Missing in action for four-and-a-half months, my mother remembered the heartbreaking days of waiting and waiting until they finally heard that he was safe again.

Mom remembered the national mourning when FDR died in 1945. After all, he was the only president that she remembered clearly, having been only seven when Hoover was elected in 1928.

Now, on my father's side of the family, a different political story unfolded, again galvanized by the Great Depression. My father's father, Daddy Bolin as we knew him, suffered from tuberculosis and spent his waning years at the TB sanitarium in Dawson Springs, to no avail, as it turned out. Daddy Bolin was a kind man who passed on that trait to his twin boys, my father Wesley and his brother Eugene, as well as their sisters, Mary, Irene, and Elsie. In his politics, he was pragmatic and conservative and, unlike my mother's father, that innate conservatism caused him to distrust FDR from his first campaign in 1932.

A man of the soil in Van Dyke, out from Paris in Henry County, Tennessee, I think it was the Agricultural Adjustment Administration that was the last straw for Daddy Bolin as far as FDR and the New Deal were concerned. How, after all, can one justify keeping fields out of cultivation and killing thousands of piglets while Americans in the nation's cities starved? Indeed, in at least one American city, zoo animals were killed and the meat distributed to the poor. For a Republican such as my grandfather, Wesley Lafayette Bolin, the work of the AAA made no sense, no sense at all.

My father and his brother both volunteered during World War II before Pearl Harbor, my father in the navy and his twin in the air force. I am not so sure they had their father's blessing, but I am quite sure he was proud of his sons' service. My father took a train to New Orleans and then was stationed at St. Petersburg in Florida when he heard the terrible news of Pearl Harbor on December 7, 1941, after coming out of a darkened theater from a double-feature Sunday matinee. He had joined up just one month before. Within another month, Dad was on the West Coast at Bremerton, Washington, preparing to board a troop transport ship on which he would spend the next two-and-a-half years.

I'm sure, when my mother and father married after the war, a melding of the disparate politics with which they grew up took place, along with a sharing of everything else. My parents loved each other deeply, and I am not aware that they ever argued over politics. So, I imagine they both brought to the marriage their own moderated version of their parents' strong political opinions. By the time my father explained to his own two sons the meaning of the two maps of the United States behind Walter Cronkite's desk on our black-and-white television screen the night of the 1964 election, my parents practiced such a moderate brand of politics that we were not even aware of who they voted for—Johnson or Goldwater.

I do know this. Both my mother and father would have been more than proud that our son Wesley Seaton Bolin—named after both his grandfathers—went to Yale and ran for the United States Congress as a 25-year-old. And they would have been proud that our daughter Cammie Jo—named after both of her grandmothers—is finishing a double major in history and political science at Centre College in Danville, Kentucky. They would be proud of their commitment to their faith and for the love of their country they exhibit through their activism. Yes, they would be so proud.

Last Times

In these waning days of the year, my thoughts are drawn to last things and last times. The past year has been a year of triumphs and tragedies, of gains and losses, of joy and sadness. Now, with only a few days left before a brand new year, we remember these things. There will be time enough in a few days to celebrate a new year, but how can we remember the old, both good and bad, and still gain inspiration for the coming year?

The problem and the challenge is to live with the sense of urgency and hope that is demanded if an individual manages to rise above meaninglessness and despair. How can we make the minutes and seconds of our lives count for something more than the tick-tock inevitability of decline and death?

We are after all looking at the last, dying days of the year. Oh, I am not trying to be morbid, but there is something that unites us all, that we all hold in common. We all will die. When we say of an ailing old-timer, "He or she is not long for this world," we are uttering a truth for ourselves as well. We all are not long for this world. So how can we get the most out of our brief sojourns on this planet? What will we leave behind that will really matter, that will last?

David Thomson left behind a remarkable remembrance of his own experience in Ireland. His book, *Woodbrook*, is part history, part memoir, and part love story. I discovered the book when the Harvard historian, Bernard Bailyn, praised it in his own book, *On the Teaching and Writing of History*. And then the Irish writer, Seamus Heaney, the winner of a Nobel Prize for Literature in 1995, wrote that Thomson's *Woodbrook* "is simply one of the most enchanting books I've read in a long time…it begins in delight before it ends in wisdom." Heaney's review, this remarkable assessment, should serve as a guide for the well-lived life, a life that "begins in delight and ends in wisdom."

In *Woodbrook*, the author left behind his history readings at Oxford to serve as a private tutor for an Anglo-Irish family in County Roscommon in Ireland. There he taught and fell in love with Phoebe, a precocious pupil who became a striking woman before dying too soon. After Phoebe's family was forced to sell their estate and move to Dublin, David had to leave too. He decided reluctantly to return to England, to London, but before taking his leave, he made the rounds of friends and neighbors to express his thanks and to say goodbye.

He went to the cottage of the mother of a friend who had asked to see him one more time. Thomson remembered that he was touched by the old woman's thoughtfulness, and as he "walked up the path" to the house, he wrote that "the 'last time' thought was poignant." And then he wrote a line that I marked in my copy of this beautiful book, a line that I have been thinking about ever since reading it. He said, "There are so many 'last times' in everybody's lives that they don't know of while they happen." There *are* so many "last times" in everybody's lives that we don't know of while they happen.

Thomson admitted that the thought of last times "made the morning sadder than it need have been," and it makes me sad to think of it now. But maybe, just maybe, this melancholy thought will cause me to live more wisely, to think more deeply and with more appreciation about these times that I might just experience one last time.

A collection of pressed leaves and flowers that grew on the farm of the author's great-grandfather in Hickman County, Kentucky.

Epilogue

Throwing the Torch

One Labor Day we drove to an old family farm in Hickman County in far western Kentucky. We wanted our one-year-old son to meet his elderly relatives, two sisters, our distant cousins who lived together in a log cabin built by my great-grandfather in 1867. John Wesley Bolin had moved from North Carolina to Tennessee before heading north into Kentucky. His son, my grandfather, Wesley Lafayette Bolin, had been born in the cabin. My father, James Wesley Bolin, had visited the place often. We named our son, Wesley Seaton Bolin, after his forebears. Four generations of Wesleys. And we're not even Methodists!

The logs of the old house had since been covered on the outside with planed boards, but the log smokehouse, raised in 1870, still stood intact behind the main structure. We drove up the angled drive, parked by an ancient gingko tree with its fan-shaped leaves still two months away from turning a brilliant yellow gold before falling to carpet the ground around the house.

We knocked on the front door and waited a long time (both sisters were almost deaf) before Ms. Glenn came to the door with the aid of a walker. The tiny, stooped woman ushered us into the central room of the house, a room with a fireplace and with logs still exposed except where book-lined shelves covered two walls. Ms. Geneva, who was the perfect picture of Mayberry's Aunt Bea, had died a few years before. On this day, Ms. Patti soon joined Ms. Glenn in the room, and we presented our son Wesley—Cammie Jo was yet to be born—to them and visited for the better part of two hours. Evelyn and I sat on the edge of a rope bed on which my grandfather was born. Wesley had the run of the floor.

We finally got up to take our leave, but before we made it to the front door, Ms. Glenn instructed us to wait as she guided her walker to a back room. She returned with a stack of framed works of art. In retirement, the sisters had collected flowers and leaves from the grounds that made up the farm, pressed them, and arranged them on black velvet before placing them in frames. Ms. Glenn gave us four of the art pieces, one for my brother and his family, one for my mother and father, and two for us, one to keep at home and one for my college office. I cherish these works of art, and I show them off to my students each term.

On the back of one of them, the one I show to my students, Ms. Glenn had typed:

> To Duane and Evelyn and Wes:
>
> Plant material in this picture grew on a farm and along the roadside by the farm in Hickman County, Kentucky where we now live.
>
> The farm was bought by our grandfather [my great grandfather] in 1867. He built a house on it and moved into it with his wife and children, in November of that year. It has been home to his descendants, one or several at a time, in unbroken succession since that time.

Ms. Glenn then listed the line of our ancestors who had lived on the farm since 1867. Among the names are my great-grandfather and great-grandmother, and my grandfather, my father's father. When Ms. Glenn handed us the frames (you can imagine the scene) the small frail woman, hair up in a bun, balanced one hand on her walker and then handed me the works of art with her stronger, yet trembling, hand. As she handed them to me, she repeated the lines from John McCrae's World War I poem, "In Flanders Fields," lines that she had typed on the back along with the names of our ancestors: "To you from failing hands, we throw the torch, be yours to hold it high." I have yet to find a better reason to study history, or a more powerful injunction to share our knowledge of the past with the next generation. So, to the next generation of children and students: "To you from failing hands, we throw the torch, be yours to hold it high."

Selected Reading List

What follows is a very short list of books that have helped me in my quest to learn how to write, either by instruction or emulation. What may surprise readers is the lack of historians in the list. This is not to say that there are no historians who write well. On the contrary, my colleagues in Murray State University's Department of History write extremely well, and other than the usual suspects on the best-seller lists—David McCullough, Doris Kearns Goodwin, and Stephen Ambrose, for example, who all write or wrote beautifully, of course, but have or had a great deal of research assistance to help them along—I favor historians such as my department colleagues, and such as Dr. James C. Klotter, and Dr. Melissa McEuen and Dr. Thomas H Appleton, Jr. in Kentucky; or historians such as Hugh Ridenour, my high school history teacher, Dr. Albert W. Wardin Jr., Dr. Roy Z. Chamlee, and Dr. Gladys "Hap" Bryant, my mentors at Belmont University; and Dr. James Leo Garrett, Jr. at Baylor University; and Dr. Bert Nelli, Dr. Lance Banning, Dr. Carl Cone, Dr. George Herring, Dr. Nancy Dye, Dr. Dan Smith, Dr. Robert Ireland, Dr. Eric Christianson, Dr. Robert Seager, Dr. James Albisetti, Dr. John M. Carland, and Professor Harry Caudill, all my graduate school professors at the University of Kentucky. Each of these historians are or were working/teaching historians. And how they managed to publish their books, articles, book reviews, and essays while putting their families first and teaching classes full of high schoolers, undergraduates, and graduate students is beyond me.

The list that follows, however, includes authors and books that inspired me, not so much in my calling to do history, but in my writing vocation. I read some of these titles as a boy and many of them as a young man. All of these books made a deep impression on me at one time or another in my life. I commend them to you now and hope that they inspire and encourage you as much as they have me.

Axtell, James. *The Pleasures of Academe: A Celebration & Defense of Higher Education.* Lincoln, Nebraska: University of Nebraska Press, 1998.

Bailyn, Bernard. *On the Teaching and Writing of History.* Hanover, New Hampshire: University Press of New England, 1994.

Banner, James M. and Harold C. Cannon. *The Elements of Teaching.* New Haven, Connecticut: Yale University Press, 1999.

Berry, Wendell. *A Place in Time: Twenty Stories of the Port William Membership.* Washington, D. C.: Counterpoint, 2013.

Berry, Wendell. *A Place on Earth: A Novel.* Washington, D. C.: Counterpoint, 2001.

Berry, Wendell. *A World Lost: A Novel.* Washington, D. C.: Counterpoint, 2008.

Berry, Wendell. *Andy Catlett: Early Travels.* Washington, D. C.: Counterpoint, 2007.

Berry, Wendell. *Hannah Coulter.* Washington, D. C.: Counterpoint, 2005.

Berry, Wendell. *Jayber Crow.* Washington, D. C.: Counterpoint, 2001.

Berry, Wendell. *Life is a Miracle: An Essay Against Modern Superstition.* Washington, D. C.: Counterpoint, 2000.

Berry, Wendell. *Nathan Coulter: A Novel.* Washington, D. C.: Counterpoint, 2008.

Berry, Wendell. *Remembering: A Novel.* Washington, D. C.: Counterpoint, 2008.

Berry, Wendell. *That Distant Land: The Collected Stories.* Washington, D. C.: Counterpoint, 2005.

Berry, Wendell. *The Memory of Old Jack.* Washington, D. C.: Counterpoint, 1999.

Bonhoeffer, Dietrich. *Letters and Papers from Prison.* New York: Touchstone, 1997.

Bonhoeffer, Dietrich. *Life Together: The Classic Exploration of Faith in Community.* New York: HarperOne, 2009.

Bonhoeffer, Dietrich. *The Cost of Discipleship.* New York: Touchstone, 1995.

Buechner, Frederick. *A Room Called Remember: Uncollected Pieces.* New York: HarperOne, 1992.

Buechner, Frederick. *Now and Then: A Memoir of Vocation.* New York: HarperOne, 1991.

Buechner, Frederick. *Telling Secrets*. New York, HarperOne, 2000.

Buechner, Frederick. *The Eyes of the Heart: A Memoir of the Lost and Found*. New York: HarperOne, 2000.

Buechner, Frederick. *The Alphabet of Grace*. New York: HarperOne, 2009.

Buechner, Frederick. *The Hungering Dark*. New York: HarperOne, 1985.

Buechner, Frederick. *The Sacred Journey: A Memoir of Early Days*. New York: HarperOne, 1991.

Buechner, Frederick. *Whistling in the Dark: A Doubter's Dictionary*. New York: HarperOne, 1993.

Dickens, Charles. *David Copperfield*. New York: Penguin Classics, 2004.

Egerton, John. *Generations: An American Family*. Lexington, Kentucky: University Press of Kentucky, 1983.

Fadiman, Anne. *At Large and At Small: Familiar Essays*. New York: Farrar, Straus and Giroux, 2008.

Fadiman, Anne. *Ex Libris: Confessions of a Common Reader*. New York: Farrar, Straus and Giroux, 2000.

Fadiman, Anne. *Rereadings: Seventeen Writers Revisit Books They Love*. New York: Farrar, Straus and Giroux, 2006.

Feiler, Bruce. *The Council of Dads: My Daughters, My Illness, and the Men Who Could Be Me*. New York: William Morrow, 2010.

Feiler, Bruce. *Learning to Bow: Inside the Heart of Japan*. New York: Perennial, 2004.

Feiler, Bruce. *Looking for Class: Days and Nights at Oxford and Cambridge*. New York: Harper Perennial, 2003.

Feiler, Bruce. *The Secrets of Happy Families: Improve Your Mornings, Tell Your Family History, Fight Smarter, Go Out and Play, and Much More*. New York: William Morrow Paperbacks, 2013.

Gomes, Peter. *The Good Book: Reading the Bible With Mind and Heart*. San Francisco: Harper San Francisco, 1996.

Gomes, Peter. *The Good Life: Truths That Last in Times of Need*. San Francisco: Harper San Francisco, 2002.

Kluge, P. F. *Alma Mater: A College Homecoming*. Reading, Massachusetts: Addison-Wesley Publishing Company, 1993.

Lamott, Anne. *Bird by Bird: Some Instructions on Writing and Life*. New York: Anchor, 1995.

Lamott, Anne. *Grace (Eventually): Thoughts on Faith*. New York: Riverhead Trade, 2008.

Lamott, Anne. *Plan B: Further Thoughts on Faith*. New York: Riverhead Trade, 2006.

Lamott, Anne. *Traveling Mercies: Some Thoughts on Faith*. New York: Anchor, 2000.

L'Engle, Madeleine. *A Circle of Quiet*. New York: HarperOne, 1984.

L'Engle, Madeleine. *The Irrational Season* (The Crosswicks Journal, Book 3). New York: HarperOne, 1984.

L'Engle, Madeleine. *Two-Part Invention: The Story of a Marriage* (The Crosswicks Journal, Book 4). New York: HarperOne, 1989.

L'Engle, Madeleine. *The Summer of the Great-Grandmother* (Crosswicks Journal, Book 2). New York: HarperOne, 1984.

L'Engle, Madeleine. *Walking on Water: Reflections on Faith and Art*. Colorado Springs: Waterbrook Press, 2001.

Lewis, C. S. *Chronicles of Narnia Box Set*. New York: Harper Collins, 2010.

Lewis, C. S. *Mere Christianity*. San Francisco: Harper San Francisco, 2009.

Lewis, C. S. *Surprised by Joy: The Shape of My Early Life*. New York: Harcourt, Brace, Jovanovich; 1st Edition, 1955.

Lewis, C. S. *The Abolition of Man*. New York: HarperOne, 2009.

Lewis, C. S. *The Four Loves*. New York: Mariner Books, 1971.

Lewis, C. S. *The Weight of Glory*. New York: HarperOne, 2009.

Maclean, Norman. *A River Runs Through It and Other Stories*. New York: Pocket Books, 1976.

McPhee, John. *A Sense of Where You Are*. New York: Farrar, Straus and Giroux, 1978.

Mehta, Ved. *Face to Face: An Autobiography*. New York: Penguin, 2013.

Mehta, Ved. *Remembering Mr. Shawn's New Yorker: The Invisible Art of Editing*. New York: Overlook, 1999.

Mehta, Ved. *Up at Oxford*. New York: W. W. Norton, 1993.

Merton, Thomas. *The Seven Storey Mountain*. New York: Mariner Books, 1999.

Moehringer, J. R. *The Tender Bar*. New York: Hyperion, 2005.

Morton, H. V. *In Search of England*. Cambridge, Massachusetts: De Capo Press, 2002.

Taylor, Barbara Brown. *An Alter in the World: A Geography of Faith.* New York: HarperOne, 2010.

Taylor, Barbara Brown. *Home By Another Way.* Lanham, Maryland: Cowley Publications, 1999.

Taylor, Barbara Brown. *Learning to Walk in the Dark.* New York: HarperOne, 2014.

Taylor, Barbara Brown. *Leaving Church: A Memoir of Faith.* New York: HarperOne, 2007.

Zinnser, William. *American Places: A Writer's Pilgrimage to 16 of This Country's Most Visited and Cherished Sites.* Philadelphia: Paul Dry Books, 2007.

Zinnser, William. *Going on Faith: Writing as a Spiritual Quest.* New York: Wipf & Stock Publishers, 2011.

Zinnser, William. *Inventing the Truth: The Art and Craft of Memoir.* New York: Mariner Books, 1998.

Zinnser, William. *On Writing Well: The Classic Guide to Writing Non-Fiction.* New York: Harper Perennial, 2006.

Zinnser, William. *The Writer Who Stayed.* Philadelphia: Paul Dry Books, 2012.

Zinnser, William. *Writing About Your Life: A Journey Into the Past.* Cambridge, Massachusetts: De Capo Press, 2004.

Zinnser, William. *Writing Places: The Life Journey of a Writer and Teacher.* New York: Harper Perennial, 2010.

Zinnser, William. *Writing to Learn.* New York: Harper Perennial, 1993.

Acknowledgments

In October, 2005, publisher Alice Rouse accepted my proposal to write a weekly "Home and Away" column for my hometown newspaper, the *Murray Ledger & Times*. The *Ledger & Times* already published Constance Alexander's long-running, award-winning "Main Street" column, so I know that Alice took a chance on a university historian, when she already had a proven winner. I will always be grateful to Alice for allowing me this privilege. I wanted to see if I had the discipline to write a weekly column of some 600 to 700 words and if I might be capable of meeting deadlines. I wanted to see if a wellspring of ideas might always be available to me or if after a few months I would indeed run out of ideas to write about.

To my delight, finding ideas has never been a problem. In the ten categories of this book, and in many other topics I might have included, an inexhaustible store and range of stories from my own experience, my hometown, my reading, my travels, my family, my university, my teaching, my life in general have presented themselves to me week after week. Sometimes, a news item will trigger a remembrance of times past; sometimes some nugget of wisdom uttered by Evelyn, Wesley, or Cammie Jo is all I need to craft an essay; and sometimes something one of my students said or wrote made me think of a historical event in a new and different way. No, as many times as I have told readers, "One of these days I will run out of ideas," thankfully that has not happened.

At the *Ledger & Times*, Eric Walker, Tom Berry, Greg Travis, and Hawkins Teague have been so helpful to me in so many ways. They always answered my emails or telephone calls, and they spared me from embarrassing mistakes.

After publishing the "Home and Away" column in the *Ledger & Times* for several years, I have been able to branch out to other newspapers around the commonwealth. At the *Providence Journal-Enterprise*, publisher Charlie Hust and editors Kris Dunbar and Matt Hughes allowed me to reconnect with the folks in Webster County where I grew up. Tony Catlett and Regina Catlett, the publisher and editor of the *Sebree Banner* and the *Sturgis News* published my column in Webster County's oldest newspaper and in Union County right next door. I must admit that the pressure was on because both Tony and Regina—ahem, Mr. Catlett and Ms. Catlett—were my high school English teachers. So, I try my best to free my prose of grammatical errors, even though I do not always succeed.

John Nelson, recently awarded the Al Smith Award for his journalistic excellence, gave me a chance to publish my column in the *Danville Advocate Messenger* and from time to time in the *Winchester Sun*. Working with Jennifer Johnson at the *Advocate Messenger* has been a joy, and my column has appeared in that fine newspaper not only in the Opinion section, but also on the Religion pages and on the "Looking Back" page of the Sunday newspaper. Likewise Laura Glasscock decided to publish some of my politically-slanted pieces in the *Kentucky Gazette* in Frankfort. That historic newspaper goes to every member of congress in Kentucky's General Assembly, so I am thankful for that important audience. At Murray State University, Devin Griggs picked up my column at *The Murray State News* as "The Professor's Journal." I appreciated the opportunity to write a column for a time geared specifically for university students.

Doug Sikes at Acclaim Press seemed interested in this project from the beginning. Working with Doug and my editor, Randy Baumgardner, has been an enjoyable experience. I appreciate their professionalism and kindness.

Each week as I sit down in my writing cabin to put down my thoughts for the "Home and Away" column, my ritual is to take a deep breath and call to mind my friend and former member of my Sunday school class. There has been no greater encourager to me in my efforts to write the column each week. Indeed, for weeks and weeks, he called me on the telephone or stopped me in church to tell me how much he appreciated that week's column. Sometimes, he made copies of a column to give to members of his wonderful, devoted family.

After serving in World War II and receiving an undergraduate degree from Murray State University and a PhD in Biology from The

Ohio State University, Dr. W. J. Pitman taught Biology and chaired the Department of Biology at Murray State University, his alma mater. He married a beautiful, gracious Virginia girl, and together, W. J. and Martha Pitman raised their family and nurtured their grandchildren from their elegant home on Olive Street in Murray.

So, Dr. Pitman's constant encouragement will always mean the world to me and I shall never forget it. And when I sit down in my cabin to write my column each week, I think of Dr. Pitman in his chair in his cozy front parlor. He is reading the newspaper. And before I strike a key on my laptop, I think, "Just how can I write this column so that W. J. Pitman will really enjoy it."

The members of the Department of History at Murray State University where I teach are sometimes burdened with emails from me containing a column that I think might be edifying. O, the patience of my colleagues. How do they put up with me? I appreciate Dr. Ted Brown, the Dean of the College of Humanities and Fine Arts, whose timely emails and in-person acknowledgements of a particular column is always appreciated. The thoughtful comments of Dr. Robert Davies, the president of Murray State University, mean a great deal to me. Dr. Don Robertson, Dr. Bob Jackson, Dr. Bonnie Higginson and Dr. Ted Brown have also given frequent encouragement from the University. I have a thick file folder of copies of my column, along with thoughtful notes, from Kate Reeves, the former director of the Wrather Museum, that I appreciate so much. And how many emails and conversations have I had with Judge Sid Easley and David Parker concerning a book or poem mentioned in one of my columns? Dr. Martin Booth Tracy is also a valuable and trusted reader of the "Home and Away" column and I enjoy his emails and talking with Dr. Tracy and his wife Patsy at Murray State Racer basketball games. I also appreciate Kay Hays in the Department of History for her support.

Three readers of my columns deserve special mention. Dr. Kenneth Moore Startup, the vice president for academic affairs at Williams Baptist College in Walnut Ridge, Arkansas, reads everything that I write. He is a trusted friend and mentor. The same can be said for Dr. Thomas H. Appleton, Jr., professor of history at Eastern Kentucky University, who keeps a file folder of my offerings. When Tom was the editor of *The Register of the Kentucky Historical Society* he led me through the process of publishing my first historical article all those years ago. Gary Garth, long-time outdoors columnist for the *Louisville Courier-Journal*, and contributing editor for *Field and Stream*, *Kentucky Monthly*, and other publications, is a friend extraordinaire and another person who reads everything that I write. Gary often gives me ideas for columns and he has never steered me wrong. I especially thank him for writing the foreword to this book. Each of these three individuals are accomplished, published writers with a style that I admire so much.

Although the essays in this collection began as "Home and Away" newspaper columns, each essay has been carefully revised for this book. I want to thank our son, Wesley Seaton Bolin, for permission to publish his essay, "My Life With Books: A Love Story," in this collection. To say that I am proud of Wesley and our daughter, Cammie Jo, is a colossal understatement. Evelyn and I love them unconditionally, of course, but we stand amazed every day of what they are able to accomplish. We are thankful for their faith and for their seriousness about living lives that matter.

And then there is Evelyn. She is the very center of so many of these essays. And that is as it should be. Evelyn holds our family together. She holds me together. I love her. And I know she loves me. For obvious reasons, this book is dedicated to Evelyn, Wesley, and Cammie Jo. And to Dr. W. J. Pitman.

About the Author

Photo courtesy of Sherry McClain, Murray State University

James Duane Bolin is a professor of history at Murray State University, where he teaches courses in American History, Kentucky History, and Sports History.

Bolin is the author of: *Bossism and Reform in a Southern City: Lexington, Kentucky, 1880-1940* and *Kentucky Baptists, 1925-2000: A Story of Cooperation*. He is a Presidential Research Fellow at Murray State University (2003) and served as a Consulting Editor and Contributor for *Banner Years: Murray State Basketball, 1925-2013* (Acclaim Press, 2013).

His weekly column "Home and Away" is featured in several regional Kentucky newspapers including the *Danville Advocate-Messenger*, *Murray Ledger & Times*, *Providence Journal-Enterprise*, *Sebree Banner*, and *Kentucky Gazette*.

Bolin lives in Murray, Kentucky with his wife, Evelyn. Their daughter, Cammie Jo, is a senior at Centre College in Danville, Kentucky. Their son, Wesley, is an employee of Murray State University's Pogue Library.

Cover Photographer

Robyn Pizzo and her husband Dr. David Pizzo are educators, world travelers, parents, and photographers. They reside in Murray, KY. Find them on Instagram at @robynpizzo and @therealpizzo.

Index

A

Abyssinian Baptist Church 195
Adams, John 126, 177
Adams, Lorraine 216
Advocate-Messenger 167
Agee, James 161
A History of Education in Kentucky 216
Alamo 63
Albisetti, James 224
A League of Their Own 207
Alexander, Constance 50, 179, 229
Alexander, F. King 17
Ali, Muhammad 190
All My Road Before Me: The Diary of C. S. Lewis, 1922-1927 203
All the King's Men 157
All the President's Men 157
Alma Mater 82
Ambrose, Stephen 129, 224
America: A Narrative History 170
American Scholar, The 70
A Moveable Feast 163
Anguished English 105
Appleton, Jr., Thomas H. 191, 224, 231
A River Runs Through It 102
Arlington, Kentucky 67, 209
Arnold, Matthew 59
Asheville, North Carolina 55
Atlanta, Georgia 20
Atlanta Journal-Constitution 216
A Traveler in Italy 182
A Traveler in Rome 182
A Traveler in Spain 182
Auchincloss, Louis 189
Auden, W. H. 141
Austen, Jane 173
Axtell, James 71, 137

B

Bailyn, Bernard 220
Ballou, Edgar 165
Ballou, Sarah 165, 166
Ballou, Sullivan 164, 165, 166
Ballou, William 165
Banner, Jr., James M. 101
Banning, Lance 224
Baptist Seminary of Kentucky 120
Barkley, Alben 177, 190
Barnhouse, Donald Grey 193
Baxter, Jessica 14
Baylor University 67, 117
Beahan, Charlotte 88
Bear Bryant Inn 25
Beijing, China 69
Bellevue High School 84
Belmont University 55, 67, 108, 117, 207
Belue, Ted Franklin 88
Berry, Tom 229
Berry, Wendell 173, 194
Bethel College 56
Betjeman, John 59
Bingham, Robert Worth 216
Bird By Bird: Some Instructions on Writing and Life 159
Bodleian Library 6, 142, 147
Bodley, Thomas 142
Boggess, Mark 158
Bolin, Cammie Jo 7, 11, 14, 27, 28, 32, 34, 35, 36, 45, 49, 50, 51, 54, 61, 62, 65, 66, 67, 96, 103, 120, 137, 144, 155, 156, 158, 168, 180, 200, 205, 213, 217, 219, 222, 229, 232, 233
Bolin, Cammie Mann 14, 19, 50, 211
Bolin, Chris 25
Bolin, Elsie 218
Bolin, Eugene 90, 218
Bolin, Evelyn Seaton 7, 9, 11, 15, 23, 28, 29, 31, 32, 33, 35, 36, 38, 39, 49, 51, 62, 64, 65, 66, 67, 96, 120, 137, 140, 144, 145, 148, 155, 158, 162, 180, 205, 213, 217, 222, 229, 232, 233

Bolin, Ms. Glenn 222, 223
Bolin, Irene 218
Bolin, James Duane 6, 7, 14, 34, 74, 96, 106, 116, 144, 158, 233
Bolin, James Wesley 14, 54, 116, 134, 211, 218, 222
Bolin, John Wesley 222
Bolin, Mary 218
Bolin's Drugstore 20, 91, 201
Bolin, Sharon 25
Bolin, Stephen (Steve) 14, 24, 25, 134
Bolin, Wesley Lafayette 89, 218, 222
Bolin, Wesley Seaton 7, 11, 14, 27, 28, 32, 34, 35, 36, 45, 47, 48, 49, 50, 51, 62, 66, 67, 96, 104, 107, 112, 116, 120, 136, 137, 138, 144, 155, 156, 180, 191, 193, 200, 205, 206, 213, 217, 219, 222, 229, 232, 233
Bolivar, Simon 176
Bonhoeffer, Dietrich 194, 195, 196
Bonhoeffer, Sabine 195
Boone, Daniel 37, 52, 190
Bowie, James 63
Bowling Green, Kentucky 60
Boxcar Children, The 157, 213
Bradford, John 166, 167
Bradford, Mrs. 82
Bradley, Bill 184
Broadway Elementary School 32
Brown, Jerome 31
Brown, Ted 231
Bruno, Leonardo 119
Bryant, Gladys 123, 224
Bryn Mawr College 191
Buechner, Frederick 99, 149, 150, 178, 179, 182
Burgess-Carpenter Library 140
Burns, Ken 164
Burroughs, Ellie Mae 158, 161

C

Callahan, Kathy 88
Calloway County Courthouse 34
Call, The 179, 198
Calvert City, Kentucky 22, 24, 67, 180
Calvert City Library 23
Campbell, Dick 82
Camp Ridgecrest for Boys 54
Cannon, Harold C. 101
Carland, John M. 224
Carrey, Jim 68
Carter, Jimmy 116, 120
Carter, Rosalyn 120
Casey Creek 102
Catch-22 157
Catlett, Regina 230
Catlett, Tony 230
Caudill, Harry 173, 224
Centre College 158, 219, 233
Chamlee, Dr. Roy Z. 82, 224
Chandler, Raymond 59
Chaney, Virginia 108, 109, 168
Charlotte's Web 30
Cherokee, North Carolina 19
Chesterton, G. K. 48, 59, 163, 172
Christianson, Eric 224
Chronicles of Narnia, The 30, 57, 157, 204
Churchill, Winston 59, 121, 141, 204
Clardy, Brian 88
Clark, C. B. 107
Clark, Duane 106, 206
Clark, George Rogers 190
Clark, Kenneth 119
Clark, Thomas D. 123, 173
Clay, Henry 190
Clay, Laura 191
Clinton College 89, 90
Cobb, Irvin 216
Cobb, Jay 207
Coleridge, Taylor 65
College Grove, Tennessee 67
Collins, Martha Layne 191
Columbia University 140
Columbus, Christopher 123
Concord, New Hampshire 105
Cone, Carl 224
Conroy, Pat 65
Copperfield, David 157
Cracked 150
Crockett, Davy 63
Crowe, Russell 81

D

Danowski, Raymond 140, 141
Danville Advocate Messenger 230, 233
Danville, Kentucky 219, 233
Davies, Richard O. 96
Davies, Robert 231
Davis, Hugh 117, 118
Davis, S. Peter 150, 151
Delderfield, R. F. 108
Destin, Florida 61, 62, 63, 64, 66, 67, 68
Dexter, Colin 59
Dickens, Charles 156, 173
Dickinson, Emily 141, 150, 180, 198

Dillard, Annie 155
Disraeli, Benjamin 146
Dixon Grade School 207
Dixon, Kentucky 6, 8, 18, 20, 32, 37, 41, 67, 91, 106, 201, 206
Drake, Francis 106
Dreyfuss, Richard 81
Dunbar, Kris 230
Dunbar, Paul Laurence 205
Durant, Ariel 132, 194
Durant, Will 132, 194
Dürer, Albrecht 158, 204
Dye, Nancy 224
Dylan, Bob 195

E

Easley, Sid 231
Eblen, Tom 166
Edmundson, Mark 80, 110
Egerton, John 16, 17, 32
Elements of Style 157
Elements of Teaching, The 101
Eliot, T. S. 54, 64, 72, 141
Elizabethtown, Kentucky 148
Ellis, Bill 216
Ellis, Charlotte 216
Ellis, Terry 214
Emory University 140
Erasmus, Desiderius 137
Eubanks, Mrs. 82
European Discovery of America, The 123
Evansville, Indiana 207
Evans, Walker 161
Everlasting Man, The 163, 172
Ex Libris: Confessions of a Common Reader 145
Ezra Stiles College 35

F

Fadiman, Anne 145, 146, 147, 148
Fadiman, Clifton 145
Fanning, Ms. 84
Faulkner, William 157
Fidrych, Mark 207
Field and Stream 232
First Baptist Church, Calvert City 31
Fisher, A. Franklin 195
Foote, Shelby 156
For Whom the Bell Tolls 164
Ford, Eddie 82, 207
Fort Worth, Texas 18, 24, 42, 45, 63, 67, 207, 208
Fortner, Lexi 14
Fosdick, Harry Emerson 195
Franklin, Benjamin 167
Frasier, Joe 190
Frazier, Eddie 92
Frazier, Mr. 92
Frost, Robert 10, 52, 203, 204
Fulton, Kentucky 20

G

Galveston, Texas 63
Gardiner, John Rolfe 70
Garrard County, Kentucky 17
Garrett, Jr., Dr. James Leo 82, 224
Garth, Gary 7, 102, 173, 216, 232
Gass, William H. 48
General in His Labyrinth, The 176
Generations: An American Family 16, 32
Georgetown College 120
Gibson, Kirk 207
Gibson, Phil 207
Gladstone, William Ewart 146, 147, 148
Glasscock, Laura 230
Glendale Place 20
Go-Between, The 129
Gomes, Peter 189, 190, 209
Good Life, The 189, 209
Goodwin, Doris Kearns 224
Graham, Kenneth 30
Green, John 176
Griggs, Devin 230
Grizzard, Lewis 216, 217
Guinness, Os 48, 179, 197

H

Halter, Miles 176
Harding, Roy 82, 92, 107
Hardy, Thomas 59, 142
Harlan County, Kentucky 17
Harrod, James 190
Hartley, L. P. 129
Hays, Kay 231
Heaney, Seamus 220
Heern, Zack 88
Hemingway, Bumby 163
Hemingway, Ernest 163, 164, 174
Hemingway, Hadley 163
Henderson, Kentucky 32, 36
Henry County, Tennessee 18, 218
Henry, O. 59
Herring, George 224
Hersey, John 161
Heschel, Abraham 112

Hickman County, Kentucky 15, 89, 221, 222, 223
Hicks, Amanda Melvina 90
Higginson, Bonnie 231
Hilton, Marjorie 88
History of Kentucky 16, 21
Hitler, Adolph 194, 195, 196
Hocker, Mary Helen 210
Hocker, Melinda 210
Hocker, Robert 210
Hocker, Robert Peck 210
Holland, Glenn 81
Holmes, Linda 150, 151, 152
Hopkins County, Kentucky 121
Hopkins, Gerard Manley 180
Houston, Sam 63
Hughes, Matt 230
Humphreys, James 88
Hu, Mr. 70
Hussein, Saddam 125
Hust, Charlie 207, 230

I

In Cold Blood 157
In Our Time 163
In Search of England 87, 182, 185
In Search of London 182
In Search of Lost Time 214
In the Steps of the Master 182
Ireland, Robert 107, 224
Irvin, Aaron 88

J

Jackson, Bob 231
James, William 78, 79
Jefferson City, Tennessee 67
Jefferson, Thomas 25, 126, 136, 137, 157, 177
Jerrell, Carrie 50
John Adams 113
Johnson, Jennifer 230
Johnson, Robert 93
Johnson, Thomas 196
Jonesboro, Arkansas 32
Judd, Ashley 191
Jude the Obscure 142

K

Kajdacsi, Brittney 136
Keating, John 81
Keebler, Mitch 207
Keillor, Garrison 100, 137, 138, 216
Kennedy, John F. 25, 42
Kentucky Gazette 167, 168, 230, 233
Kentucky Miscellany, The 196
Kentucky Monthly 216, 232
Kenyon College 82
Kenyon, Jane 174
Kerr, Charles 21
Kierkegaard, Soren 180
King, B. B. 93
Kipling, Rudyard 59, 70
Klotter, James C. 173, 224
Kluge, P. F. 82
Knight, Alesia 181
Knight, Tony 181

L

Lamott, Anne 159
Lears, Frank 80
Leaves of Grass 141
Lederer, Richard 105
Ledford, Addie 17, 32, 33
Ledford, Burnam 17, 18, 32, 33
Leigh, James Henry 210
Lentz, Perry 74
Lessons of History, The 133
Let Us Now Praise Famous Men 161
Leuchtenburg, William 156
Lewis, C. S. 6, 30, 57, 142, 143, 156, 200, 203, 204
Lewis, Sinclair 45
Lewis, Warren 58
Lexington Herald-Leader 166
Lexington, Kentucky 32, 116, 131, 143
Life on the Run 185
Lincoln, Abraham 90, 190
Lincoln, Mary Todd 191
Little Kingdoms 107
Lolita 157
Long Journey Home 48
Looking for Alaska 176
Louisville Courier-Journal 102, 173, 216, 232
Louisville, Kentucky 143
Lowenthal, David 129

M

MacDonald, George 104
Maclean, Norman 102, 173
Madisonville Community College 67
Madisonville, Kentucky 97, 143
Magruder, Gail 209, 210, 211
Mainstream of Civilization, The 168
Main Street 45
Mann, J. C. 217
Mann, John 217
Mantle, Mickey 207

Mantooth, Bob 207
Maranatha Baptist Church (Plains, GA) 120
Marquez, Gabriel Garcia 176
Martin, Tennessee 20
Mathis, Gil 62
Ma, Yo-Yo 189, 190
McClain, Sherry 233
McCombs, Davis 173
McConaughey, Matthew 25
McCrae, John 223
McCullough, Jr., David 113
McCullough Sr., David 113, 129, 224
McEuen, Melissa 138, 224
McGillicuddy Sr., Cornelius 120
McMillan, Tom 97
McPhee, John 183, 184
McPherson, Jen 112
Medford High School 80
Mehta, Ved 156
Merrill, James 141
Merton, Thomas 173
Moehringer, J. R. 173
Montreat-Anderson College 55
Moore, Daniel Martin 148, 149, 150
Moore, Ray 145
More Than Words 156
Morison, Samuel Eliot 123, 124
Mornings on Horseback 113
Morrell, Emily 54
Morris, Edmund 156
Morris, Jan 142, 182
Morris, Willie 67
Morton, H. V. 52, 87, 156, 182, 185
Mount, Rick 207
Muggeridge, Malcolm 48, 198
Mulligan, Bill 88
Murray High School 168
Murray High School Library 158
Murray, Kentucky 32, 34, 39, 47, 48, 49, 60, 67, 143, 144, 158, 173, 213, 233
Murray Ledger & Times 167, 229, 233
Murray State News, The 230
Murray State University 6, 32, 60, 69, 71, 72, 74, 75, 85, 86, 93, 96, 101, 104, 118, 119, 121, 136, 141, 182, 202, 208, 209, 211, 230, 231, 233

N

Napier, Charles James 146
Nash, John 81
Neelon, Ann 50
Nelli, Humbert (Bert) 82, 107, 208, 224
Nelson, John 230
Neville, Linda 116, 191
Newcomer, Carrie 175
New Haven, Connecticut 6, 35, 67, 180
Newman, Bill 107
New Yorker, The 184
New York Times 128, 140
Niebuhr, Reinhold 195
Noyes, Alfred 18, 116, 134

O

Oak Grove Cemetery 8
Oaklawn Elementary School 42, 43, 82
Oates, Lawrence Edward Grace 146
Ohio State University 231
Old Man and the Sea, The 164
On Books and the Housing of Them 146, 147
One Hundred Years of Solitude 157
One Writer's Beginnings 169
On the Teaching and Writing of History 220
On Writing Well 191
Optimist's Daughter, The 169
Oregon City, Oregon 67
Orwell, George 146
Oshinsky, David 128
Oxford, England 6, 40, 58, 142, 194

P

Panama City, Florida 205
Parker, David 231
Parsons, Tennessee 67
Parton, James 25
Past is a Foreign Country, The 129
Peden, Harlan 82
Peninsular War 146
People's Education Press 71
Percy, Walker 28, 157, 179
Philadelphia Athletics 120
Pilgrim at Tinker Creek 155
Pitman, Martha 231
Pitman, W. J. 11, 231, 232
Pizzo, David 88, 233
Pizzo, Robyn 233
Plains, Georgia 120
Plymouth, Massachusetts 209
Pogue Library 74, 142
Poor Richard's Bookshop 6, 216
Port William, Kentucky 194
Powell Sr., Adam Clayton 195
Proust, Marcel 214

Providence Journal-Enterprise 167, 230, 233
Providence, Kentucky 32, 67
Pullam, Roy 82
Purcell, Lynda 52
Purdue Boilermakers 207

R

Rabbit, Run 157
Rabelais, Francois 176, 177
Rashid, Taufiq 88
Reasoner, Paul 56, 57
Reeves, Kate 231
Regensburg, Germany 194
Regent's Park College 54, 56, 58
Register of the Kentucky Historical Society, The 232
Rhodes, Cecil 198
Ridenour, Hugh 74, 79, 80, 81, 82, 107, 109, 224
Ridgecrest Camp for Boys 55, 56
Rime of the Ancient Mariner, The 65
Riverside Church 195
Robertson, Don 231
Robertson, Oscar 184
Rogers, Roy 22
Rogers, Will 216
Roosevelt, Franklin Delano 217
Roosevelt, Theodore 113, 144
Rostropovich, Mstislav 189
Rouse, Alice 229
Rupp, Adolph 21, 116

S

Sanders, Harland 190
Santayana, George 48
Schell, Bill 88
Screwtape Letters, The 204
Seager, Robert 224
Seaton, Evelyn 14, 21
Seaton, Jossie Wallace 14, 21, 22, 23, 24, 49
Seaton, June 21, 23
Seaton, Marilyn 21, 23
Seaton, Marlin 14, 21, 22, 23, 24, 62
Seaton, Rebecca 21, 23
Sebree Banner 167, 230, 233
Selected Verse of Alfred Noyes 134
Seven Storey Mountain, The 173
Shelby, Isaac 190
Sheldonian Theatre 142
Shipman, Evan 164
Shoulta, Jeremy 120
Shoulta, Josh 120
Shumway, Sarah Hart 165
Simon, Paul 45, 46
Simpson, Betsy 151, 153
Sims, Raymond 181
Sims, Susan 181
Sinatra, Frank 48
Smith, Bessie 93
Smith, Dan 224
Smith, Red 159
Spalding, Harry 112
Speed, Teresa 158
Sports Illustrated 207
Startup, Kenneth M. 134, 231
Steinbeck, John 144, 157
Stein, Gertrude 163
Still, James 173
Stockdale, James 146
Story of Civilization, The 132, 133, 194
St. Paul, Therese 69
Strieter, Terry 88
Sturgis News 167, 230
Sun Also Rises, The 163
Surprised by Joy 57, 203
Sydney, Australia 134

T

Tales of a Kentucky Town 112
Talks to Teachers on Psychology: And to Students on Some of Life's Ideals 78
Taylor, Dr. C. Pat 82
Taylor, James 47, 93, 94
Teacher: The One Who Made the Difference 80
Teague, Hawkins 229
Tender Bar, The 173
Thatcher, Margaret 17
Their Eyes Were Watching God 157
Thomas, Dylan 59
Thomson, David 220
Thoreau, Henry David 65
Three Stories and Ten Poems 163
Timmons, Kathy 69
Timmons, Tom 69
Tindall, George Brown 170, 171
Tolkien, J. R. R. 58, 143
To Serve Them All My Days 108
Townsend, Jim 107
Tracy, Martin Booth 231
Tracy, Patsy 231
Transylvania University 138, 167
Traveling Mercies: Some Thoughts on Faith 159
Travis, Greg 229
Travis, William Barret 63

Trigg County, Kentucky 6, 16, 102
Truman 113
Tuchman, Barbara 129, 156, 172, 173
Turner, Dicky 69
Tuscaloosa, Alabama 25

U

University of Florida 152
University of Kentucky 21, 32, 67, 107
University of Maryland 97
University of North Carolina 170
University of Oxford 56
University of Tennessee 207
University of Virginia 25, 80, 110, 157
Updike, John 71, 113, 156

V

Varieties of Religious Experience, The 78
Vaughn, Alan 207
Velveteen Rabbit, The 30
Vonnegut, Kurt 162

W

Wadham College Chapel 59
Waits, Tom 148
Walker, Cass 91, 92
Walker, Eric 229
Walnut Ridge, Arkansas 41, 67, 96
Wardin Jr., Dr. Albert W. 82, 108, 109, 168, 224
Washington and Lee University 177
Washington, Booker T. 132
Washington, George 17
Waterfield Library 141, 147
Waters, Muddy 93
Watson, Ron 121
We Are Still Married 137
Webster County High School 75, 79, 82
Webster County, Kentucky 18, 20, 26, 44, 106
Weight of Glory, The 204
Weil, Simone 48
Wellesley High School 113
Wellington, New Zealand 134
Welty, Eudora 158, 169
West, Jerry 74, 184
White, Beth 62
White, E. B. 30
White, Steve 41
Whitman, Walt 141
Wilcox, Ella Wheeler 97
Williams, Margery 30
Williams, Robin 80, 81
Williams, William Carlos 141
Winchester Sun 168, 230
Wind in the Willows, The 30
Wolfe, Thomas 48
Woodbrook 220
Woodward, C. Vann 103
Woodworth, Samuel 211
Writing About Your Life: A Journey Into the Past 191
Wyeth, Andrew 149

X

Xi'an, China 69

Y

Yale University 35, 36, 67, 136, 155, 156, 191, 192, 219, 233
Yancey, Philip 156
Yeats, William Butler 141
Young, Alaska 176
Young Library 217

Z

Zinsser, William 52, 191, 192, 193